NEALE DANIHER

with Warwick Green

WHEN ALL IS SAID & DONE

MACMILLAN

Pan Macmillan Australia

First published 2019 in Macmillan by Pan Macmillan Australia Pty Ltd
1 Market Street, Sydney, New South Wales, Australia, 2000

 A catalogue record for this
book is available from the
National Library of Australia

Typeset in 12.5/17.6 pt Bembo by Midland Typesetters
Printed by McPherson's Printing Group

The author and the publisher have made every effort to contact copyright holders
for material used in this book. Any person or organisation that may have been
overlooked should contact the publisher.

 The paper in this book is FSC® certified.
FSC® promotes environmentally responsible,
socially beneficial and economically viable
management of the world's forests.

WHEN ALL IS SAID & DONE

For my family:
those who have gone before,
those who are beside me now,
and those to follow.

Contents

CONTENTS

Foreword

Neale was taller than expected when our paths first crossed in early 2010. I knew of him as the former Essendon player. The Demons coach. One of 'the Daniher brothers'.

Those with a public profile have this challenge – what they do is often mistaken for who they are.

Neale and I ran into each other periodically over a few years through our respective roles in football – I was in football operations with the AFL. Our interaction was infrequent and seasonal but we always had a good working relationship.

Late on a Friday afternoon in 2012, my wife Ange and I went to see a neurologist who had offered to investigate her slurred speech. Ange walked into his consulting room as a fit and healthy 39-year-old. She walked out with MND. From 4.20 pm onwards on Friday the 29th of June, nothing would ever be the same. It was beyond our worst case scenario.

But even the darkest cloud has a silver lining. That diagnosis meant Neale would become a significant part of our lives and, in time, we would learn just who Neale Daniher is. And what a privilege that has been.

Neale was diagnosed with MND in 2013. On hearing the news, I sent him a text. To my surprise, he called immediately. The condolences were brief. 'No time for crap red wine anymore, Paddy!' he said. We chatted a little more, and agreed to meet up when he was next in Melbourne.

In the months that passed, with huge support from Ange's friends and family, we raised over $250,000 for MND research under the banner of Laugh to Cure MND. We also became aware of the great work of Dr Ian Davis, another MND sufferer, advocate and fundraiser. In mid-2014, Ange, Ian, Neale and I got together to discuss consolidating our efforts.

FightMND was launched in late 2014. We were yet another fundraising start-up with our hands out, and one of some 55,000 Australian charities. But we had a point of difference. We had Neale Daniher.

It became obvious to us all very quickly that Neale had the ability to move the needle significantly around MND awareness. He was a potent cocktail. Neale had a public profile *and* he had the bastard of a disease. He had the energy and inclination to fight it, and he was prepared to spend his precious time speaking about that fight. And finally, he could entertain and inspire people like no one else.

We launched the first Big Freeze campaign in 2015. We were optimistic and nervous. Optimistic that we could raise $250,000, and nervous because we didn't really know how the public would respond. Did they care?

The first Big Freeze raised $2.8 million. It has since become FightMND's centrepiece, and has given hope to those who are touched by the hideous disease. We quickly realised that Neale was the key to unlocking broad support for the cause.

So, what can I tell you about Neale that can't be googled or found in the chapters that follow? You will no doubt learn what Neale has done. But let me try and tell you, in my view, *how* he has done it. Because I think that's the man's genius. That is what separates him from everyone else – and that's what makes it all possible. *How* he does things is what makes Neale *who he is*.

Over the past six years I've seen Neale get things done, and I've noticed three things.

Firstly, Neale has an ability to see the challenge and the possibility quickly and clearly, and then prioritises and invests his time to gain the maximum impact.

Secondly, he has an extraordinary ability to anticipate any impediments that might limit progress, or minimise impact.

And finally, I've never known anyone who can use humour and honesty to put people at ease like Neale can. He can create an emotional connection and build rapport and trust like few people can. And I've never seen anyone hold an audience quite like Neale.

Neale's life has been filled with great moments. As a son, brother, father, husband. As a friend. Footballer, teammate, coach. But his work in fighting 'The Beast' will be remembered forever.

He has allowed his own private battle and physical decline to be the confronting public reality of an MND journey. His selflessness will help many people. And while he has committed considerable time and energy as the frontman of the fight, he has committed even more behind closed doors to ensure the fight will be as strong without him when the time comes.

Neale – thanks for showing and teaching us all so much. We are indebted to you for who you are.

Patrick Cunningham
Co-Founder and Vice Chair of FightMND

'Society grows great when old men plant trees whose shade they know they shall never sit in.'
—anonymous Greek proverb

Hold your beliefs to the Bunsen burner

Is this it? Is this how it ends? Slumped in a nondescript chair in the emergency ward of a Canberra public hospital, watching the thin red hand on the clock face ticking down the seconds to 6 am?

I can't breathe. For the thousandth time tonight I feel like I'm choking for air, like I can't draw any oxygen into my lungs. It feels like those panicky moments after someone crashes into your ribs on a football field, and you curl up on the turf, winded, your mind scrambling to make sense of what's happening to you.

But this is different to a few harrowing seconds in the hands of the trainers – I've been stranded like this for hours, propped up here on this chair throughout the night.

The sun is starting to creep above the horizon. I can't remember the last time I was up until dawn – it was probably back in my university days, playing cards on a table cluttered with little piles of $1 bills and longnecks of Melbourne Bitter.

But now I'm plunked here in the emergency ward with tubes up my nostrils, staring at a flimsy blue plastic curtain and a toilet that's tantalisingly out of reach. Whenever the percentage of oxygen in my lungs drops below a certain level, the machine I'm hooked up to begins beeping like it's telling the nurse in a TV drama that the patient is in real trouble.

I'd tried to clamber onto the bed next to me to lie down, but it had only made matters worse. I can't sleep. Now all I can do is sit here, helpless, watching the clock, hoping that life will get better, when I know it's inevitably going to get worse. This whole experience feels like a trailer for an upcoming feature film and I don't even want to play my role in the show when my time comes. I could definitely do without this dress rehearsal.

The seconds keep loudly ticking away and my mind is working overtime. I'm thinking about my family, about my wife, Jan, and my beautiful children, Lauren, Luke, Rebecca and Ben, and all of the gleaming memories they have given me. I'm thinking about their futures, and about how there will be grandkids I will never get to know.

How will those kids picture their grandpa in their imaginations? Will I be more than their grandfather who died of a cruel incurable disease? Will my grandkids wonder what kind of man their grandfather was? Will they wonder what he believed in?

I'm not fussed about what they will make of my time as a footballer or an AFL coach or even as a campaigner for Motor Neurone Disease. I don't care about a legacy, but I do care about what kind of people they'll grow up to become. I wish I could be there to help them make their way in the world, but I won't have the chance.

I would have given anything to wrap an arm around those grandkids as they sat on my knee. There are things I'd love to pass on to them, life learnings I would have enjoyed sharing. There are stories I'd like to tell them about growing up on a remote farm, about going away to boarding school, about life lessons to be gained from team sport, on and off the field.

I would love to explain to those kids that I believe there are a million ways to live a good life. Buddha lived this way, Gandhi lived that way, my parents lived their way and there are millions of great people on this earth right now, each with their own unique philosophy on life, living meaningful lives, whether they're the nurse in your local hospital or they work the canteen at your local footy club.

I would tell my grandkids to live life to the fullest, regardless of the difficulties that are thrown their way. Don't make excuses, I'd say. Never play the victim.

★

Anyway, there I was in a Canberra hospital emergency department at dawn. I hadn't seen that particular hospital stint coming my way. Motor Neurone Disease (or MND for short) had already conspired to slur my speech and had left me with wiry arms and palsied fingers that didn't work too well, but it hadn't got hold of my legs yet and I still felt strong.

The day before, I'd been for a bracing afternoon walk in the surrounds of Lake Burley Griffin while Jan was back in the hotel room, aching all over, laid low by the effects of a nasty flu that she'd no doubt picked up while working as a relief teacher.

Jan was too crook to join me at the evening function, the Parliamentary Friends of the AFL reception on 14 August 2017. But she helped me get dressed and whacked on my tie. I was starting to feel a bit tight in the chest and could hear a slight rasp in my breathing.

'I hope I haven't picked up your bug,' I growled at Jan.

She mustered a weak smile and a shake of her head. I'd often joke about how she was too impatient to wait for MND to do me in and was bringing home all manner of germs from school in an effort to knock me off quickly.

I decided to grab one of those asthma inhalers from the hotel pharmacy on my way to board the mini-bus that was ferrying us all to the Mural Hall at Parliament House for the big event.

The hall was full of bigwigs, including then Prime Minister Malcolm Turnbull, Opposition Leader Bill Shorten and AFL Chief Executive Gillon McLachlan. I'd probably landed an invitation because I ticked a few boxes: former player for Essendon Football Club and then senior coach of Melbourne Football Club, but more pertinently because the foundation for which I had become an enthusiastic advocate, FightMND, had secured significant federal government backing at our annual Queen's Birthday weekend fundraiser, the Big Freeze at the MCG.

After shaking more hands than a politician on the hustings, I started to feel my chest getting tighter; the virus was kicking in.

About halfway through the Prime Minister's speech, it felt like my body was beginning to shut down. I was thinking, *Geez, I'm in a bit of trouble here.* I made my way towards the back of the room and found a quiet corner where I could have a spell on a couch. Every now and again someone would edge over to ask for a selfie, and behind every thumbs up I was smiling through gritted teeth.

The AFL's Head of Government and Stakeholder Relations, Jude Donnelly – normally as bubbly a personality as you would ever meet – wandered over with a look of concern on her face.

'Are you OK, Neale?' she asked. 'You're not looking great.'

Before long I had Jude, Gillon and the Prime Minister's senior health adviser, Cindy Barry – a former emergency nurse – fussing over me, with Cindy suggesting my evening was done. I proposed sending me in a taxi back to the hotel, but Cindy kindly dashed off to get her car and drove me.

Back in the hotel room, Jan dragged herself out of bed and guided me to the couch. What a pair we made. I sat there for a while in a cold sweat, feeling faint, with no sign of improvement, until Jan piped up, 'This is crazy, we have to get you to hospital.'

We shuffled into a crowded emergency department, with the waiting area a menagerie of whimpering toddlers, and people with sporting injuries, bandaged heads and incessant coughing. When we got to the triage window I was praying that they would not send me over to wait in the rows of vinyl seats. *I'm dying here*, I kept thinking. *Please don't put me in the queue behind a sprained ankle.*

Fortunately one of the hospital staff came over to Jan and told her that he knew I had MND.

'Don't worry, leave it with me,' he confided, and somehow managed to rush me through to the acute care section.

After being attended by a doctor I sat there next to my trolley, hooked up to the beeping machine, oxygen pumped straight into my nose, wondering if I was going to make it through the night. At about 1 am, Jan – who was crook as a dog – reluctantly bowed to exhaustion and caught a taxi back to the hotel, reminding me that I had a tendency to be an awful patient and asking me to try to avoid being awfully impatient.

When she returned the next morning she found me in the same state, in the same chair. Knowing that I couldn't eat the sandwiches and diced fruit, she asked the nursing staff if there was any possibility of putting some food in a blender and feeding me through a straw. That wouldn't be possible until they could get me into a ward, she was told. Fortunately Jan noticed that the canteen downstairs sold smoothies. By that evening she was asking whether we should consider moving me to another hospital, but they advised her that would mean being admitted through the emergency department again and starting from square one.

In the end, despite the high number of severe flu patients, the hospital managed to find me a bed in their overburdened respiratory ward. Over the next three days I recuperated, firing off text messages, rescheduling meetings and trying my hardest not to be an awful patient. On the Thursday morning my doctor broached the subject of being discharged.

'How will you get back to Melbourne?' he asked. When I mentioned that there were seats available on several flights out of Canberra Airport, he expressed his concerns about reduced oxygen in the pressurised atmosphere of an airplane.

'You'd be better advised driving back,' he said.

Perhaps reading my look of exasperation at the prospect of an eight-hour drive back home, he relented.

'I know, I get it. Look, if you can guarantee me that if I give you the all clear you will promise to drive back then we can look at getting you out of here ASAP.' Now he had me smiling.

As he left the ward I phoned Jan, and a couple of hours later she arrived to collect me in a hire car. We dropped off the keys at the airport terminal ahead of our flight back to Melbourne.

I told him I'd drive. Well, I did drive . . . to the airport. I didn't have time to muck around.

★

I always wanted to make something of my time on this earth, to have my hands on the wheel of life, not just be a car crash waiting to happen. The thing about life is it's short and precious and there's nothing like a terminal illness to reinforce that.

I've lived a bloody good life and I'm grateful for all the people who have supported me along the way – those who have given me the faith to believe that tomorrow always has something to offer. Knowing that my time will run out sooner rather than later, I've turned to distilling my philosophy on life, examining my beliefs and attitudes, challenging my own thinking.

I know a lot of things that aren't important. I also know there are many things that are important, but alas I know far too few of them. The ones that I do know are in this book. I know I might not get to wrap that arm around my grandkids, so I am writing my thoughts down in these pages.

Maybe these thoughts will provide cause for others to pause and reflect as well. I'm not interested in preaching or telling people how to suck eggs; I don't want to come across as being holier than thou. Believe me, I'm not interested in setting up a cult and saying come and join me! I just want my grandkids to have a think about where they're at and where they're going. I would say, 'Now, upon reflection and drawing on my own varied experiences, this is where I've got to in my thinking. This is what I've learned up to this point and what I think is worth sharing.'

Thinking about what makes a good life is the hardest work there is, which is probably why most of us prefer to just keep muddling along. It sometimes requires an intellectual rigour and reflection that we all find hard to pursue in our busy lives.

Now, maybe you'll think I'm full of crap, and I wouldn't argue with you: all that would tell me is that you believe in something different. So what do *you* believe in? And why? And how much are you prepared to accept that your beliefs and values fundamentally influence the way you live your life? If so, to what extent? And, further, that they influence what you do when life throws any manner of circumstances your way?

See, I've got you thinking. Challenge your own beliefs. Challenge mine.

I know this much. If you can hold your beliefs and values to the Bunsen burner and they stand up to that heat, then you know you're backing the right ones.

Life doesn't promise to be fair

I've always accepted that you can't control everything in life, even though I'm a bit of a control freak. Farmers can work their guts out and take all of the appropriate precautions, but they still can't control the rain or a severe frost or a drought.

Footballers can't control popping a knee; business executives can't control disruptive technology or a global financial crisis.

The way I see it, life continually deals us hands of cards: sometimes we get a look at four aces, other times we pick up the two and three of spades and the four and six of clubs. But here's the thing: once we pick up our hand, it's up to us how we then choose to play those cards.

We have our beliefs, and we also have our plans and dreams, but when life throws us challenges, the only thing we can really control is how we react (attitude), and then think through what we are going to do about it (actions).

It's one thing to believe that we can control our attitude, and another thing altogether to test that belief when a grim situation demands it. And in 2013, I was dealt a hand of cards that pretty much tested everything I believed.

★

Cam Taylor narrowed his eyes and shot me a quizzical sideways glance.

'Whaddya call that?' he demanded as we shook hands. 'You've lost a bit of grunt in the old grip there, Nealo.'

'Mate, that's the best I've got,' I shot back.

Having a mate accuse you of a wet-fish handshake is mildly embarrassing, but hardly a moment you expect will change your life.

Jan and I had just pulled up at a picnic spot at Peppermint Grove on the north bank of Perth's Swan River. It was Christmas Eve 2012, and we settled in for a few cold drinks with Cam and Sarah, along with Phil and Ingrid Anderson, both farming couples from the wheatbelt town of Tambellup, 300-odd kilometres south-east of Perth. Also joining us were Paul and Mary Lim, all of them families we had grown to know through our sons attending the same school in Perth.

Cam's quip lingered. I'd taken to putting a heat pack on my right hand when playing golf on a crisp morning. The hand had also been giving me some grief with simple tasks, sometimes causing me to fumble a bit when trying to put the car key in the ignition or trying to peg washing on the clothesline.

But I put it out of my mind for now. It could wait till I was back at work.

When I clocked on in the new year at the West Coast Eagles, where I had been general manager of football operations for the past four years, I sounded out the medical staff about my hand. Maybe it was a nerve block, an old footy war wound. They felt it would be best to run some tests.

As the tests extended into weeks and months, the outlook became more mystifyingly grim. It was a matter of ruling out possible explanations – multiple sclerosis, Lyme disease, a tumour on the spine. At one point I overheard a doctor confiding to a colleague: 'We hope this is something we can sort out, a condition we can manage and treat. Hopefully it's not MND.'

MND? I didn't know a hell of a lot about Motor Neurone Disease at that point, other than that you didn't want to get it.

Unbeknown to me, others had started to express private concerns about my health. I'd headed back to the family farm in Ungarie, in the central west of New South Wales, for a gathering with Mum and Dad and my 10 siblings.

One morning a few of my seven sisters quietly spoke among themselves, wondering about the soft slur in my speech the night before. It didn't seem to them like I'd had all that many red wines. My older sister, Estelle, was nagged by the similarities to a friend of hers from Wagga Wagga, who had MND. *There seems to be a lot of it in this region*, she thought to herself. *People in Griffith, Lake Cargelligo, Ariah Park. But nah, not Neale, it couldn't be.*

It was a similar story at a golf reunion with my old school-mates from Assumption College. Apparently there was a bit of private chatter afterwards about me tripping over a few words in the clubhouse bar, and how I must have got the day off to a flying start with a few cold ones before arriving at the first tee.

Meanwhile, the medical tests continued: more bloods and infusions, then some nerve conduction studies, which involve taping electrodes over nerves and recording muscle activity when nerves are stimulated by electrical impulses.

The doctors were ruling out possibilities, until there was nothing else to rule out. In mid–May 2013, my neurologist in Perth laid out his conclusions in a written report, arriving at the judgement that all indicators pointed to MND.

I phoned Jan, who was in the middle of a 10-day stint in New Zealand in her role as operations manager with the West Coast Fever netball team. In the background I could hear the netballers' runners squeaking on the court as I broke the news.

'But what does that mean for you?' Jan asked, her voice beginning to tremble with emotion. Without saying it, she was probably processing the reality that MND is a terminal illness. How much longer did her husband have to live? What would this mean to *us*?

After training wound up, Jan headed back to her Wellington hotel room and googled MND, and what she read sent a wave of disbelief through her body: the average life expectancy for a person diagnosed with MND is 27 months; patients progressively lose the ability to walk, talk, feed themselves, swallow and eventually breathe; at least two Australians die every day as a result of the disease; there is no cure.

She was devastated.

Back in Perth, the meticulous, control-freak aspect of my personality kicked in. All indicators pointed to MND? I wasn't going to cop that. I needed to know definitively, and began the process of seeking a second opinion that could provide that certainty. An appointment with a leading neurologist was booked in Melbourne, to coincide with the Eagles' next AFL match in Victoria.

At St Vincent's Hospital in Fitzroy I would undergo more blood tests, brain scans and MRI (magnetic resonance imaging) scans to determine once and for all what was going on. They would have the results back later in the month.

For a man who struggles with patience at the best of times, that wait was purgatory. But being impatient wasn't going to help my cause this time.

★

The bleak overcast sky of a grey Melbourne winter was the first thing that hit me as I walked out of the St Vincent's Department of Neurosciences a couple of weeks later.

I felt surprisingly calm for a man who had just been handed a folder and told: 'Unfortunately these results confirm that it is definitely MND.' The neurologist across the desk had then almost remorsefully begun to talk about the need to get my affairs in order. What else could she say?

It was only once I was sitting in the taxi to Melbourne Airport that the weight of reality came down on me like a ton of bricks.

I muttered under my breath, 'Bugger! It's not something else, it is MND.' The cab driver looked over at me, wondering if he'd missed a direction.

I was straight into what psychologists describe as the five stages in the cycle of grief for people who have been diagnosed with a terminal illness: denial, anger, bargaining, depression and acceptance.

Why me? I thought, but the inclination towards denial didn't last long this time. Nor did the bargaining, where I searched in vain for a way out. *Have they've mucked up the diagnosis? I hope they have.* But I knew they hadn't and that futile hope faded quickly.

Soon there was only anger and anxiety. I sat there staring at this folder I'd been given, with my test results and some literature about MND and a letter from the Melbourne specialist for my neurologist back in Perth. I didn't open that folder, I just glared at it. And I thought, *Fuck, I'll be dead in two years.* I didn't know how it would play out, just that on average MND played out rapidly. My mind wouldn't go anywhere else other than: *You are about to die.*

Suddenly nothing else seemed important. It was a lonely cab ride along the Tullamarine Freeway.

The four-hour flight to Perth provided ample time for some soul-searching. I was riled as I boarded the plane, looking for a cat to kick. If the passenger in front of me had reclined his seat, I probably would have given him an almighty spray.

By the time the Airbus rose above western Victoria, I had a little man on each shoulder, each with a voice in my ear: Mr Positive and Mr Negative.

For the first half of the flight, Mr Negative was nagging away in my left ear: 'This is the dismal reality, mate. You can't sugar-coat this one, you're gone.' And he was going his hardest to push me towards doom and gloom.

But about halfway across the Nullarbor Plain, Mr Positive started to pipe up. 'How's that conversation going with your mate?' he asked, and I replied, 'Not too good.'

He said, 'Are you going to put up with him hanging around, chipping away with all of his fatalism? How's that going to work for Jan, for your kids?'

'Probably not that well. I'm not going to be much fun to be around, am I?' I said.

Mr Positive replied, 'No, to be honest with you, you're going to be a real pain in the arse if you listen to Mr Negative.'

By the time the plane was descending into Perth, I reckon I was about halfway through that grief cycle. The overriding resolution was that if I descended into a negative 'victim' attitude, it was only going to make things worse for my wife, my kids, my mates . . . and infinitely worse for me.

★

Realistically, deciding how to tackle my new reality was not so much a revelation, but was more a buttressing of what I have always understood about the importance of the attitude we choose to adopt.

Trying hard and doing the right thing might improve our prospects in life, but there are no guarantees, and sometimes problems and complications arise that are beyond our control. That's why it's often important to reframe our perspective. Faced with adversity, once we have had time to absorb the setback and accept 'it is what it is', we need to eventually ask ourselves, 'Where is the opportunity?'

We're better off gravitating towards and learning from people who have this sort of healthy attitude, rather than hanging around people who are eternally cynical or pessimistic. Cynics will give us the various reasons why something can't be done and if we listen too long, they'll probably make us feel as though nothing can be done.

Don't get me wrong: pessimists do have a place in this world, but it's probably in risk management – if you're going to embark on a risky endeavour it's good to have a pessimist on board. So I suggest generally steering clear of cynics and consulting in a pessimist!

Life is all about perspective. If we are born in Australia, in reality we've already won the lottery. A billion people would be rapt to take our position at the starting blocks. And yet so many of us want to adopt a woe-is-me attitude. People can't believe their misfortune when their internet goes down for 24 hours, or can't imagine how they will overcome the obstacles that turn up in front of them – yet we were not born in a little shanty in a village with no clean water and parents who earn $2 a week.

Life doesn't promise to be fair. We will all encounter setbacks and heartbreaks, and we need to put our energy into finding a way to overcome adversity, to try to find a way to deal with it. To try to find the opportunity. It's when we face impediments and challenges that our attitude is most crucial, because without a positive attitude you miss the great learning and growth opportunity that adversity presents you with.

When we are confronted with real adversity, Mr Negative will get in your ear and say, 'Opportunity? There is no opportunity.' That's what he whispered in my ear on that flight across Australia. 'Forget opportunity,' he sneered, 'you're about to die, you silly bastard.'

But I'm with Mr Positive: our world is a better place when we tell that voice to shut up.

I'm not saying it's easy. Wallowing, playing the victim, is easier in the first instance. But it doesn't get you far. Practise telling Mr Negative to piss off – it's habit forming.

⋆

By the time the plane's wheels touched down on the runway, I was determined not to let my diagnosis beat me into despair. I knew this malicious disease would gradually rob me of my health, my mobility, my breathing and eventually my life, but I wasn't going to let it take my dignity. I wouldn't let it kill my spirit.

To my mind this was a contemptible swine of a disease, hiding in a dark cave, quietly dragging people in and killing them in the most horrendous way. It helped me to personalise the disease – MND sounded too innocuous, too clinical. So I called it The Beast. An ugly piece of gear, hairy and dark, like a huge hybrid of a blowfly and a moth. I wasn't sure how, but I was going to take the fight right up to it.

I had confidence that a healthy attitude would help me deal with the tempestuous passage that lay ahead, and that it would help ease the anxiety and distress for my wife and children.

But for now, there were family members who needed to hear the news, with no more vague references to an unidentified nerve condition. For Luke and Ben, who were living with us in Perth, it was not just a matter of revealing that I had this disease, it was also a matter of explaining what it was: a progressive, terminal condition in which the nerve cells (neurones) that control the body's muscles undergo degeneration and die, while the mind and senses would probably remain intact. As an emergency nurse who had worked with MND patients in the respiratory ward, Lauren knew full well the gravity of the diagnosis.

The phone call back home to my parents on the family farm was heart-wrenching. My mother, wonderfully caring soul that she is, became emotional and promised to pray for me. And with 10 siblings and a fairly extensive bush telegraph network in place, there were many conversations with my broader family.

In virtually every discussion I had to explain The Beast – that it would try to strip away everything. How would I deal with such a wretched prospect?

Over the years I'd read numerous books about psychology and self-improvement, and one man whose story really reso-nated with me was an inspirational Austrian called Viktor Frankl. He was a leading neurologist and psychiatrist, but because of his Jewish faith the Nazis sent him to a concentration camp in 1942. He was later forced into months of slave labour and was helpless to prevent the deaths of his wife, parents and brother during the

Holocaust. Liberated by American soldiers in 1945, Frankl lived to the ripe old age of 92, writing numerous books and inspiring generations of humanistic psychologists. Reflecting on his ordeals in the camps, Frankl wrote: 'Everything can be taken from a man but one thing: the last of the human freedoms – to choose one's attitude in any given set of circumstances, to choose one's own way.'

The freedom to choose my attitude was never more relevant than after that MND diagnosis. I knew that no matter what the disease would take away from me, it would never take from me the freedom to control my attitude, to choose my own way. That conviction was in my DNA.

My attitude grew from my inherent beliefs . . . and those beliefs were sown with care in the baking red dirt of our family farm. Not long after the diagnosis, I had written down one of my mother's favourite sayings: 'Count your blessings.' In doing that, I began to think, *Well, maybe I have had a pretty charmed life.*

Know where you come from

There is considerable philosophical debate about whether we are shaped by our inherited genes or the environment we reside in – nature versus nurture. These days it's commonly agreed that both play crucial roles, but I would add that how we respond to the genetic and environmental hands we're dealt, and how we take responsibility for the choices we make, are equally important parts of the discussion.

Unquestionably, our formative beliefs are somewhat forced upon us, planted by our parents and then sculpted by our peer groups in ways that most of us don't notice, let alone comprehend. They are also shaped by the cultural setting of the time.

Much of who we are is strongly influenced by nature – height and shoe size, temperament, personality, IQ – but we still have a big say in the kind of person we ultimately become. We can control how we act, so I believe it is important for all of us to constantly examine and challenge what we believe in, because that's the undercurrent that drives our attitudes and actions.

Challenging our beliefs is difficult, not only because it requires reflective thought, but also because we get comfortable within a familiar frame of reference. But just as we choose what attitude to take, we can choose what to believe – and we need to take responsibility for those choices.

I'm lucky – between them, my parents gave us a good old-fashioned bush upbringing and laid the bedrock to build a sturdy and durable belief system. Against the backdrop of rural Australia in the 1960s and 70s, our parents simply shaped our beliefs and values through example, and then trusted that we had the foundation to decide for ourselves what behaviours and actions were appropriate from there.

Now, as a parent of children who have grown to adulthood, I can reflect upon and appreciate the influence of my parents and grandparents in the person I have become. I can only hope that my children and their children might do the same.

It's never too late to question what you believe but I'm acutely aware that time is precious. Don't leave it too long, don't just muddle along – if you don't know where you're going, any road will take you there.

★

My father, Jim, devoted his life to working his guts out. He was the sort of man who, even in his youth, earned a reputation for being a tough old bugger. And my mother, Edna, has always been a nurturer who thrives on putting others' needs before her own.

In essence my father was a product of the Great Depression, which no doubt ingrained in him a strong work ethic. His grandfather, James, came to Australia from Tipperary as a boy during the 1860s, in the wake of Ireland's Great Famine. James worked at the Melbourne docks before taking up farming in the tiny community of Miepoll, near Kyneton in Victoria. James's son John (my great-grandfather) and his family later relocated to Euroa, about 150 kilometres north. John's sons, Jim Sr (my grandfather) and Jack, saw an opportunity to set out on their own when the New South Wales government began opening up large tracts of the Riverina plains under a Closer Settlement scheme. The two brothers entered the ballot and were both awarded 740-acre allotments.

In late 1914 they began planning the journey to inspect their new land, which had been part of the former 15,000-acre Ungarie Station. John Oxley, believed to be the first European to explore the region in 1817, had declared 'this country will never be inhabited by civilised man'.

But that didn't deter Jim Sr and Jack, and the two brothers made the rugged 485-kilometre trek on their bicycles over a period of several weeks. Upon arriving, they found a dry and dusty property, with rocks, eucalypts, scrub and the odd kurrajong tree. The nearest water was several kilometres away at Humbug Creek and the prospect of farming this demanding terrain was not for Jack, who headed back to Victoria and joined the police force.

Jim Sr, however, settled and named his property Hillview after the farm he had left behind in Euroa. Over time he toiled away at the back-breaking work of clearing the land, removing trees with a handsaw, carting off stumps and rocks and ploughing the soil. My grandfather eventually established a homestead and married Eileen Cullen. My father, Jim Jr, was born in 1928, one of six children – Jack, Mary, Jim, Leo, Joan (who passed away seven days after birth) and Tess. Daniher Country had begun to take root.

Those roots spread when the family applied for the adjoining 740-acre allotment, which they hoped could be acquired cheaply. This prompted a surveyor to come up from town to assess the value of the block. Calling upon a bit of bush nous, the family led the surveyor into the property at a point where the land was at its most unforgiving – Dad's brother Leo reckoned 'the wattle was that thick you couldn't hear a dog bark' – and then steered him even deeper into the bush. The surveyor duly declared the allotment was of little value and soon afterwards the Danihers doubled their landholding.

In due course, my father would take over the farm.

Running a farm cropping wheat, oats and barley, as well as a fair few head of sheep, is bound to consume your thinking every day of the year, and it is not surprising that my father was not into razzamatazz and the niceties of life. That's not to say he didn't know how to find some fun in his day – he could be cheeky, social and a bit of a stirrer – but fundamentally he was of a generation that subscribed to the 'don't complain and don't explain' view. His attitude was always to plan for the worst and maybe hope for the best. Work hard and every now and then you get lucky. He was forever predicting a drought, so much so that as a kid, when we had a scattering of showers after a dry spell, I'd tip a few extra drops in the rain gauge because I thought it would make him happier. My brothers and sisters joke about identifying Dad in the lines of an old Australian bush poem: "'We'll all be rooned,' said Hanrahan, "before the year is out.'"

My father's belief system served him well on the farm, because if you do plan for the worst, when the worst materialises it doesn't bring you down. You have the capacity to deal with a drought, or switch to a back-up plan when the machinery breaks down (which invariably involves fixing the machine, cobbling together a new one or binding the parts together with wire). It also means that you can overcome the cruel disappointment when a bumper season is nullified by an early frost or a late hailstorm or by the price of your crop being driven down after harvest. On the other hand, if things turn out well, you're in front.

In the 1980s when many of Dad's contemporaries were handing over control of their farms to their sons, interest rates went to 18 per cent. A lot of farmers in the district had borrowed to buy more land and had overreached – and lost the lot. Dad was more conservative: he avoided borrowing money, didn't trust banks or governments, and it was never a good idea to get him started on the unions. He would often tell us to be careful, to not take risks with money. He wasn't one to spend money unless it was essential. For example, he rarely took a holiday, let alone an overseas trip.

'Why would you want to go overseas?' he'd ask. 'I can see it when I turn on the telly and it doesn't look a patch on Australia anyway. Always looks like drama and strife.'

If we did venture out of town on a holiday, mostly on a car trip down to Melbourne to watch the footy, there was never much thought given to dining out. Dad used to say restaurants were a waste of money 'and if you do ever go to one, steer clear of the places with candles on the table, because they'll charge you extra for the privilege'. He was a fan of tucking into a steaming hot bundle of fish and chips back at the motel room.

As children we unwittingly soaked up all of Mum and Dad's wisdom, but as an adult I challenged Dad about how farmers, for all of their conservativism, were actually the biggest gamblers going around.

'Every year it costs you mega bucks to plant a crop,' I would say, 'and every year you're just flipping the coin.'

He knew I had a point, but he just harrumphed. In his mind he would have been thinking, *You little smart alec. I knew I shouldn't have got you educated. You come back here with your high ideas trying to tell us workers how to go about it.*

★

My earliest memory of my mother is of sitting on her lap at the dinner table while she taught us to read: at, cat, mat and so on.

Mum is the most giving person you could ever meet. Edna Erwin grew up on a farm on the outskirts of Ungarie in what was known as 'kurrajong country' (if times got really desperate in a drought, the farmers would feed kurrajong branches to the livestock). Mum was one of four children: she had two sisters and a much younger brother. After finishing boarding school in Goulburn she headed south, crossing the Murray River and spending three years as a nurse in Mooroopna before home-sickness dragged her back to Ungarie, where she married Jim Daniher. Mum's older sister, Beryl, married Jim's older brother Jack, a bit of a lovable rogue who sheared all over the district. And Mum's younger sister, Dorothy, married Leo Daniher, who helped run the family farm with his brother Jim.

Yep, you're reading it right: three brothers married three sisters. Theirs was an era when you lived in the town where you were born, you married the girl from up the road, you went into the same line of work as your parents and you voted, prayed and supported along family lines. Those blokes were just lucky to find three great sisters living down the road.

Between them, the three Erwin sisters had 28 children. Mum thrived on her unconditional devotion to raising 11 kids – Terry, Estelle, me, Dorothy, Anthony, Chris, Angela, Colleen, Julie, Nerolee and Fiona – and later derived equal pleasure doting on her grandkids. Dad once told me that their agreed ideal had been a family of six children, but 'your mother just kept loving the idea of another baby in the house'.

When I was born in 1961, there was no mains power on the farm. Mum recalls hearing the shocking news of John F. Kennedy's assassination on a battery-powered radio. No mains power meant no luxuries such as a fridge or air conditioner, so to keep her babies cool, she used to drape damp towels around the cot.

Mum used to cook her heart out. Her go-to dinners made use of farm-raised lamb: roast and vegies, chops and pies. Her dessert specialty came to be known as Danihers' Delight, a concoction of stewed fruit, Weet-Bix, cream and custard. As the family grew she divided dinner into three shifts: first, the young ones would take their turn at the table, then the older ones with Dad, and if there was anything left, Mum would sit down and pick at it after we had cleared the table and done the dishes.

With the farm being 13 kilometres out of Ungarie, shopping was as carefully coordinated as a military offensive. As the family grew, we took to bulk buying in the big smoke – West Wyalong, 45 kilometres to the south. We would load up the station wagon or the ute with cubic metres of essentials such as Corn Flakes and toilet paper. Every Christmas each of us was handed a $20 note and set loose to find a dozen presents for the rest of the family.

Mum's father, Bill Erwin, bought the first colour television in the district in 1976 and when television eventually made its way to our living room, we weren't allowed to watch such morally questionable programs as *Dr Who* or *The Goodies*, and never too many cartoons. We might sneak in an episode of *Get Smart* or *F Troop* before being shooed out of the living room when the nightly news bulletin came on. It was always a battle to convince Mum to switch the channel from the ABC, and we had no hope when it was time to watch her favourite series *Bellbird*, a soapie that was set in a fictional rural town of the same name. The television reception was generally pretty reasonable – unless there were galahs on the antenna, which would prompt someone to sing out, 'The telly's on the blink, grab the slug gun.'

Any form of heating in the house involved burning wood, so hot water was at a premium. We relied on the woodchip heater for a bath, which was basically a quick dip to remove the dust before bedtime, and if you were the fourth or fifth into the tub, the water was pretty cloudy and tepid. But we didn't care: we were warm, fed and loved.

★

If Dad's belief system was grounded in the land, Mum's was very much formed by looking to the skies. She was a thoroughly devout Catholic and, despite being the most caring person you could imagine, she would still probably question whether she was doing enough and think she needed to do more to get to heaven. There were four churches in Ungarie – Catholic, Methodist, Church of England and Lutheran – and my paternal grandfather had played an active role in building the original St Joseph's Catholic church, spending countless hours carting timber to the site.

Mass was usually at 7 or 8.30 am on Sunday; we'd get a bit of a sleep-in if the parish priest held an early Mass at a neighbouring town and our service was pushed back a couple of hours. Our attendance was non-negotiable. My older brother, Terry, once asked to skip Mass so that he had time to get on the bus for the 160-kilometre trip to Griffith, where he was due to run out with the Ungarie rugby league team. He was told flatly, 'You still have to go to church.' All he could do was pray that the priest didn't have a particularly long sermon planned for that morning.

Sunday Mass was Mum's time to shine. She would be up early to make sure that we all had our Sunday best clothes organised, that we had bathed and run a comb through our hair. The arrival of each new child meant her alarm clock went off progressively earlier on Sundays, until at one stage she was rising at 4 am for 7 am mass.

'You didn't notice it as a trial or difficult because everyone was in the same boat,' she once confided, but she later wondered how on earth she coped.

Dad's attitude was simple: you work hard through the week and get to Mass on Sundays. He would invariably want to stand around and chat about farming with the neighbours for the best part of an hour afterwards. Mum used it as a chance to catch up with her sisters and other friends in the township. It was as much a social gathering as a spiritual gathering.

All of us kids would duck down the road to catch up with our cousins at Aunty Beryl's house. There would be 18 or 20 kids, and Beryl would give each of us a biscuit before we settled in to listen to the latest 45s on their record player. Those Sunday morning gatherings were the bee's knees. If we were lucky, Dad would take us into town and treat us to an ice-cream before we headed home.

As children, religion was not so much about belief, we were just doing what we were told; we were lovingly indoctrinated. Growing up a devout Catholic, I carried that denomination into my adult life but I became more inquiring as an adult, wanting to examine why I was here and what role faith had in that, and to form my own opinions.

Over the years my devotion to Catholicism has been tested and I find myself questioning many aspects of organised religion. One of the most damaging aspects of any religion is when the zealots say: 'I believe this and I'm determined to make you believe it too or else I'll cut you down.' Every religion has its own different take on what you should believe and that's OK, but I get worried when it goes to the next level where they are all convinced they are totally right and the others have got it totally wrong. I find people who insist they are right and refuse to listen to any other views to be both dangerous and scary.

★

Essentially our Catholic upbringing helped my parents set an old-school moral compass for their children. Manners were important, so was loyalty. Honesty and integrity were expected. If you said you were going to do something then you did it: your word was your bond and your word was good enough for me.

One time, I was being a real smart alec to a kid from West Wyalong, who eventually got sick of it and declared that he was going to fight me. Dad gave me a look that said, *You've got yourself into trouble, now you have to get yourself out of trouble. Don't come looking to me. What are you going to do about it?*

Mum was more inclined to offer direct advice, but always in her good-natured and tender way. I remember coming off the ground at half-time of a football match for the Ungarie under-12s and she gently suggested, 'Neale, I think you can do a bit better than that.' She reckons that I then tore around in the second half, knocking over the other kids to get the ball and then after the match asked her, 'Well, Mum, do you think I had a good enough go in the end?'

We always knew where we stood with Mum and Dad. And we all wanted to make them proud of us.

Each one of us has hundreds of beliefs and values that are either passed on to us or that we develop along the way. Some are fairly innocuous – 'I barrack for the black and white, the mighty Ungarie Magpies' – others are not so harmless and have graver consequences – 'I barrack for the white, but not for the black'. But at the top of the triangle are the core values: the ones we consider to be indisputable and non-negotiable, the ones that guide what we stand by and how we behave, and the ones that we live our life by.

One of my parents' core values was to work hard. There could be no higher praise from Dad: he might acknowledge that a man was flawed before redeeming him by concluding, 'But gee, he's a hard worker.'

Undoubtedly, some of my parents' instincts about hard work have flowed to me because, like them, I strongly value actions above words. *What are you going to do about it? I think you can do a bit better than that.*

This concept has become one of my core values, and it's best captured by a saying attributed to the Ancient Greek storyteller, Aesop: 'After all is said and done, more is said than done.'

What we think, say or feel is crucially important to what we choose to do.

However, I believe the mark of a person is not what he or she thinks, says or feels – in the end, I believe we are measured on what we actually do.

Watch and learn

There was nothing in my upbringing that emphasised what I should accomplish. Mum and Dad wanted their children to work hard, be respectful, show kindness and be humble, loyal and honest. Living by those standards was more important than striving for achievements, and the values were steadfastly reinforced, both at home and in the wider community. It was first and foremost about 'What kind of person are you going to grow up to be?' rather than 'How much are you going to achieve?'

Don't get me wrong. We were encouraged to try hard, to give everything our best effort at school or in sporting contests, but the focus was not on getting good grades or bringing home ribbons. My parents were more interested in building character than a trophy cabinet.

Mum and Dad's thinking contrasts with much of the parenting we see today, where the focus is on a child's achievements and self-esteem. That might boost children's confidence, but does it build their character?

Us kids all understood this. When you're one of 11 kids, it can't be all about you. You're not special, but you could *become* special, you could *do* something special. You have the opportunity in life, but it's up to you to reveal your character and make the most of that opportunity across your lifetime. Go out and do it.

★

Many of my parents' beliefs and values were never explicitly laid out, they were implied. Dad was a man of actions, not words. If he wanted to teach you how to complete a task around the farm, he would say, 'Watch and learn, son.' And then, 'Right, now it's your turn, away you go.' Through his example we learned many lessons: always have a real crack; don't let anyone stand over you; negotiations are all tough but fair; shake hands at the end of a game.

Not surprisingly, Mum adopted a stoic, can-do attitude. No matter how much household drudgery confronted her – against the backdrop of being pregnant every second year – her view was that you just get on with it.

As much as my parents moulded my beliefs, so too did the experience of being part of a large farming family. That taught me to cooperate and to compete, and ingrained in me character traits of responsibility to the family and consideration of others.

From as early as I can remember, we all had chores and there was an expectation that we would carry them out, rain, hail or shine. Doing our chores was simply an accepted part of our day. The eldest two children would trudge the 150 or so metres early every morning to a little shed where they had to milk the cows, separate the cream and feed the poddy calves. Any thought of a complaint would be headed off with, 'I know it's freezing out there, but we need milk on the table so off you go.' As the two eldest children moved on to other ways of helping the family, the next two stepped up, and then the next two. There was wood to be chopped, chooks to be fed, eggs to be collected, dishes to be washed.

Everyone had their role to play, although we would some-times have a blue over whose job it was to bring the cows in at night. If it was your turn, you used to pray they weren't down in the back paddock. One chore that broke up the routine was picking the fruit from Mum's garden – apricots, plums, peaches – and then taking out the stones and washing the flesh for Mum to make jam. There was no better treat than fresh bread with homemade jam and thickened cream.

Many of the chores seemed meaningless and mind-numbing, but they were essential in contributing to running the farm and the household. During the school holidays Dad might round up whoever was handy and take us out to remove rocks or wild melons from one of the paddocks.

'How much will you pay me per rock?' I'd demand and he'd have fun with it, negotiating down the price, knowing full well that he wasn't going to pay me a cent. There were no cash incentives for us to do our bit to help the family, it was simply our responsibility. Dad would hitch a trailer to the back of the ute and our job was to hop in and out, picking up anything that would get in the way of ploughing.

There are many reasons to admire my father: he was a big-hearted, hard-working man for a start. But his patience behind the steering wheel is not one of those reasons. Whenever we had to open a gate on the farm he had a terrible habit of taking off before we'd fully settled back in the car. On one particular rock-collecting expedition, he took off in the ute more suddenly than I expected and the trailer ran over my right leg. Of course, Dad reckoned I was to blame. 'You shouldn't have been buggerising around back there.'

The local doctor wasn't sure what to make of it when a 13-year-old boy presented with a trampled knee, but he decided the safest option was a shin-to-thigh plaster cast for the rest of the school holidays.

While such manual labour was character-building, it also confirmed for me pretty early that I had no interest in becoming a farmer. I enjoyed the camaraderie of the shearing shed, but putting in fence posts or driving a tractor around and around and around in 39-degree heat with flies on your face simply held no appeal to me. I used to think to myself, *There's got to be something better than this*. My father, on the other hand, was probably thinking, *What could possibly be better than this?*

Dad not only believed that he was putting food on the table for his family, he also took pride in the fact that he was playing a role in the grander scheme of things. He was helping to feed a nation.

★

The basic little farmhouse built by my great-grandfather had been surpassed by a timber and fibro-cement home comprising four high-ceilinged rooms, surrounded by a verandah, with an outdoor toilet. As the family grew, Dad gradually built in sections of the verandah to make more bedrooms. I was in one bedroom with my three brothers – a single bed in each corner, a huge wardrobe and endless shared memories. None were better than the time Terry acquired a cassette player and we were in the privileged position of being able to close the door and wail along to our favourite music.

The younger siblings maintain that us older ones received special attention. They like to refer to the 'top four' – Terry Estelle, myself and Anthony – and to point out that we were the only ones to ever go on a bona fide family vacation (we drove to Sydney, visited Taronga Zoo and got burnt to a crisp after a day at the beach). We would counter with the fact that by the time the 'bottom three' were old enough to endure the milking duties, our parents had got rid of the cows.

As you'd expect, there were numerous little squabbles between the brothers and sisters. I don't remember the day Estelle knocked out one of Terry's teeth, but I'm sure I would have been in the background barracking for her. And I was away the time Anthony shot Dorothy with a slug gun, but what surprises me more is that it wasn't me taking aim at Terry. I do know that Terry used to take it upon himself to bait us, and that he thrived on shoving and bossing me around. I must have threatened my revenge a thousand times. When I was young, Terry was too big and ugly for me to do anything about it, but as I got older I had to stand up for myself and say, 'I've had enough of you, mate.' Mind you, if I lost to him in a blue I'd go and sook to my parents, who would usually say I needed to deal with it myself.

With so many kids and so many scuffles, Mum avoided getting involved every time someone came crying for attention. She didn't have time to adjudicate and if, 'Go and sort it out for yourselves' didn't work, there was always the last resort of throwing in a line like, 'Don't make me tell your father'. On the odd occasion she would have us all lined up in the bathroom waiting for Dad to dish out punishment when he came in from the farm. If I ever raised his wrath, my tactic was to hide in the outhouse until he cooled down.

★

Dad maintains that having so many kids in the house made us fierce competitors on the sporting field. Between the four brothers we played 752 VFL/AFL games, while our sisters won countless premierships and trophies on the netball court.

'You were a determined beggar,' Dad once told me. 'You had Terry in front of you to aim at and Estelle, who was quicker than you, to try to catch.'

He believed in the principle of giving sport a go and giving it your all. He didn't particularly compliment or criticise or tell us how to go about it, he just believed in his kids being active, involved and learning our own lessons as we went along. Praise was sparing and understated and had to be earned – he was more inclined to encourage our appetite for sport through his actions rather than his words.

Dad was a driving force in starting up the Ungarie junior football club in the late 1960s and rang farmers from surrounding towns to help establish a Northern Riverina junior league. He helped facilitate and organise sport at our local primary school. On the farm, he fenced off a tennis court – admittedly, the packed dirt surface would usually only last one set and after that you had to volley; nevertheless, we spent hours volleying away. When it was athletics season he would measure out a 100-metre running track and create a long-jump pit. His high-jump fit-out encouraged success, not least because none of us wanted to land on the rigid cane crossbar that left a welt across your back.

When I was 11, Dad drove us the two hours to Griffith for the annual sports carnival. Given the effort required to get there, he was of the belief that we should compete in every event on offer. Having taken part in the 400-metres, the high jump, the hurdles, the 1500-metres, the long jump, the javelin and the triple jump, I declared, 'That's it, Dad, I'm shot. I'm not going in any more events.' He spent the next 30 minutes trying to convince me that I should enter the 200-metres at the end of the program. His view was, 'Come on, I've driven all this way, you're going in it.' I somehow managed to drag another effort out of my weary muscles, and once the race began the competitive streak kicked in and I ran as hard as if it was my first event of the day.

At the height of summer we usually opted for a later lunch to avoid the scorching early afternoon sun, followed by an hour or so watching the Aussie test cricket team on television. Inevitably Terry would suggest having a hit of our own. We would head out to the grassy strip outside the kitchen where, as left-handed batsmen, our leg-side shots would clatter into the exterior walls of the house and our drives would knock fruit off Mum's trees. I suspect it was as much to rid himself of the incessant commotion as anything else, but before long Dad was out the back of the house, marking out the lines for a little concrete half-pitch near the tennis court. Terry spent hours bowling on that narrow strip, grinding himself into the ground trying to get me out, until eventually I'd wander towards him with a mischievous grin, offering the handle of the bat.

'You about ready for a hit yet?' I'd taunt him.

'Get back in yer box, yer cheeky bastard,' he'd growl, 'I've just about got yer where I want yer.' Such was his competitive streak that he couldn't stomach the belief that his three-and-a-half years younger brother could edge him at anything. Later our younger brothers Anthony, with his improbably wrong-footed bowling action, and then Chris, like a little fox terrier all bustling with energy, would join in our games.

Then there were the times when we competed just for the sake of competing.

Getting off the school bus each afternoon we would have a race, a 400-metre dash to the trees. There was even an unofficial handicapping system, with the youngest jostling for the front position, ready for when the bus doors opened, and the older siblings lining up behind them. We were equally competitive in all of our pastimes, whether it was swimming in the dam, catching yabbies or riding our bikes around a makeshift course through the peppercorn trees. It was an exercise in finding a reason to challenge ourselves and having fun with it.

We were free-range kids: our goal was to get out of the house and enjoy shared experiences running around and laughing with our brothers and sisters. And there was a pattern to our days, a rhythm to our lives. There were set times for meals, chores and washing.

Those were different times, of course. These days, kids often have meals whenever, and their main shared experiences might be online, sitting alone in a corner with a hand-held device. That's a classic example of how the freedom opened up by technology can also limit lived experience.

★

Upon reflection, my Ungarie upbringing chiselled the shape of my beliefs and values and influenced my attitude more than I realised as a young man. My father's fortitude and grit, my mother's compassion and devotion, their honesty and integrity – they all seeped into my understanding of what is most valuable in life. The farming analogy that you work hard but you can't control everything has become one of my guiding principles. So too the rural inclination to be loyal but to also stand up for yourself. Family life taught me the importance of taking on responsibility, and showed me the need to cooperate and how to compete.

I feel blessed to have had a childhood that overwhelmingly set forward commendable and constructive beliefs. The role of the Ungarie community was also important in establishing these beliefs, not just for the Daniher children but for others. Dad and his mates set up the junior footy club, perhaps with no greater motivation than to give the youth of Ungarie something to do on a Saturday and a diversion from the pathway to propping up the bar at a pub and punting on the nags.

You could assume my parents fitted the Irish-Catholic drinking stereotype, but in fact, Mum and Dad were both non-drinkers when we were growing up. Dad had a hepatitis-related illness in his mid-twenties that made him very wary of alcohol. Later in life, he'd have a whisky and dry and these days, Mum still enjoys a champagne. Obviously their restraint wasn't passed on to their kids!

The footy club allowed any kid in the town to be part of something and to be surrounded by some good role models, male and female. We had some aimless young fellas in our town – every town has them – but being part of the footy club allowed them to see what could be. It exposed them to a sense of community and to people who were prepared to put in some long hours for no other reason than their devotion to the common cause. It was a matter of, 'Righto, son, you turn up at this time and we'll put you on the team bus and you'll be with us until you get back at 4 pm.' And their parents probably thought it was great, because they didn't have to worry about what little Johnny was up to of a Saturday.

I mean we all do it. You see the real estate agent who will drop his kids off at Little Athletics in the morning and then head off to work for the day. And all of that can only happen because of the sense of community and the volunteers who are prepared to look out for other people's kids.

Even beyond the organised activities, we also had aunts and uncles and neighbours who looked out for us, allowed us to wander in and out of their houses and kept us out of mischief in the town. Sometimes all it took was 'You're Jim Daniher's boy, aren't you?' and that was enough of a shot across the bow to make sure you pulled up and stopped mucking around.

My early schooling played a role, as well. St Joseph's primary school aligned with my parents' thinking about life: discipline, responsibility, consequences. If we came home and the teacher had chastised us, our parents would believe the teacher – they wouldn't be siding with us. And they probably knew the teacher personally, or might have played in the same footy team together. Or if it was a nun, it was as simple as, 'Well, nuns don't lie.'

That helped us develop character. Often parents are more inclined to automatically defend their children and absolve them of responsibility and consequences. In today's world, there is not enough focus on building character because there are too many excuses. People look to shift blame rather than accept responsibility. It's easy for parents to blame the teacher, the school or the curriculum, but maybe the truth is that little Johnny isn't prepared to work hard enough to pass his exams.

Our formative years are so important and I do understand that for many reasons, many families can't offer what I was given: the knowledge that there were people who loved me and that I was lovable. Kids who don't experience that miss out in a big way. On the farm at Ungarie we were loved but we weren't pampered. And it had nothing to do with how much money we had, or how many toys were in the box. By the age of six, we each knew we had to carry our own weight. And it did help us become more independent and more resilient.

I'm not judging what's right or wrong, I'm just saying that's what happened with me and I feel privileged to have had such a childhood.

At some stage, you've got to make a break

There comes a time in everyone's life when you have to leave the comforts of home, and explore what else is on offer in this big wide world. Everyone will have a different idea of what constitutes 'home comforts', but I'm not talking about Foxtel, central heating or a new car when you turn eighteen. I'm talking about having that fundamental understanding that you are safe: that you have a roof over your head, food on the table, and that there are people who love and care for you. If you're fortunate enough to enjoy these comforts growing up, it's all too easy to take them for granted.

The same applies to the values and beliefs we grow up with – most of us don't really think about them until we discover how other people live, and what they believe in.

Most learning opportunities emerge once you decide to, or are forced to, leave your comfort zone. Throughout life, we'll be faced with this challenge at many different stages – and each time, the more comfortable you get, the harder it is to make a break. That's because there's no guarantee that these learning opportunities will end well . . . We often stumble, fail, perhaps feel exposed or embarrassed, and worry that we'll look foolish or that we're not as good as other people.

We all fall short at different stages of our life. It's how we build resilience. It's how we learn to take responsibility for our own decisions.

Right from the start, when we first venture out into the world, we need to build the character trait of getting back up and going again, rather than giving up and staying put. There's an old saying that ships are safe in the harbour, but it's not what they're built for.

For each person, the first shift towards independence happens at a different age and phase of life. For me, that shift came earlier than most. I let go of the apron strings at the start of secondary school.

★

The echoes of the gleeful children have long since faded from St Joseph's primary school in Ungarie. The basic weatherboard building, where grades one to three gathered in one room and the older children were taught in another, closed its doors after my brothers and sisters and cousins reached Year 7 and moved across Humbug Creek to Ungarie Central School. The corner block was sold off and the tin-roofed school building awaited conversion to a renovated home. It is the place where I learned my times tables and grammar, always with an eye out the window, eagerly anticipating the games at recess or lunchtime.

On one side of the long, narrow concrete path leading from the arched iron front gate was an area set aside for the girls to play. On the other was a dusty, grass-tufted playground designated for the boys. Perhaps 60 metres apart were two sets of goalposts hewn from eucalypt branches and rammed into the earth. Off to one side was the concrete cricket pitch that had been carefully poured by a working party of farmers, including my father. Every Monday morning the schoolboys would pick two teams and the ensuing football or cricket match would run through to Friday with a running score diligently marked down – without any umpires.

Most of us viewed school lessons as just something you did in between these epic games, but I must have shown some kind of proficiency in the classroom, because towards the end of primary school one of my teachers, Sister Teresita, spoke to my parents about applying for a scholarship to an all-boys Catholic boarding school in Goulburn for me.

'I could see you had a spark,' Sister Teresita told me years later, 'and I didn't want it to grow dim in Ungarie.'

I was duly ordered to write an essay as part of my application; its content is long-forgotten but the words were undoubtedly tidied up and massaged by the kind-hearted nun. My mother had also attended a boarding school in Goulburn, and she was buoyed by the prospect, harbouring unvoiced thoughts that a good Christian Brothers secondary education might steer me in the direction of the priesthood. Dad wasn't so sure; he'd attended boarding school at Lake Cargelligo when he was seven, and then later at Forbes, and hadn't particularly enjoyed being away from home. In the end, the application was posted off and I thought no more of it.

The time of the farming year I loved most was when the shearers descended on our shed, with their cursing and yarns and laughter during smoko. There would be jovial but robust exchanges; the shearers lamenting the labourer's lot, my father countering with the constant hardships faced by land-owning farmers. It was my first exposure to the cut and thrust of workplace relations. My Uncle Jack and one of his mates, Athol Apps, were two of the larger-than-life shearers who regaled us with yarns from shearing sheds to the north, south, east and west. I was only 11, but I felt included in some special adult fraternity and I industriously went about my designated role as a roustabout, clearing shorn fleece from the shearing board to the wool table, tending the wool bins, sweeping up and running errands.

So it was that I happened to be in the shed when the phone call came through to the kitchen from one of the brothers at St Patrick's College, informing Mum that my application for a scholarship had been accepted. She was thrilled. Dad felt that I was too young and would be better waiting.

I didn't know what to think or say, but sensing how enthusiastic my mother was about the opportunity, I declared that I wanted to give Goulburn a go.

★

On a stinking hot day towards the end of January 1973, Mum and Dad piled Terry, me and my bags into the station wagon and we headed off on the 340-kilometre drive east to Goulburn.

The school was huge. We wandered up the driveway, past statues of St Patrick and Edmund Rice, the Irishman who had founded the Congregation of Christian Brothers in 1802. Once we had completed the formalities, my parents were ushered in to a meeting with one of the brothers, leaving me and Terry free to stroll around the college. Inevitably we were drawn to the manicured sporting fields, a sharp contrast to the Ungarie Recreation Reserve. None of the posts were made from eucalypt branches and they all had crossbars. This was rugby union heartland.

We made our way up to the spartan dormitory, with its scarred wooden floors, lancet windows and three rows of 15 basic beds. I threw my bags onto one of the bunks, and Terry raised an eyebrow.

'Geez mate, how're you going to go living here? I'll bet it's going to get a bit nippy come winter. Thank god it's you going in here, not me. I'd rather be home eating Mum's tucker and putting up with a foot up the arse from the old man. You can have this.'

When my parents returned from their meeting, satisfied that the college would look after their boy, their thoughts turned to the long journey back to Ungarie. Mum would confide years later that she wept all the way to Yass, an hour up the highway.

'I couldn't believe I'd actually left you there,' she said.

Watching them drive off, Terry grinning out the back window, I felt as alone as I had ever felt in my life. Back in the dormitory, I packed away all my gear and lay on the bed, wondering what on earth I had agreed to. It was a bit of a shock to the system and I went into survival mode, not knowing what to expect.

The next morning was the first day of term. There were baked beans on toast for breakfast in the dining hall and plates and cutlery to place on the rack of a big dishwashing machine. Then it was back to the dorm to make your bed and brush your teeth before you entered the fray of the school day proper.

I tentatively descended the stairs and walked into a vast cloister bustling with boys, excited to be with their mates after the holidays, joking and wrestling and catching up on each other's news. I stood there gripping my books, not knowing a soul, completely out of my comfort zone. I thought to myself, *You're on your own here. No mummy's boy now, mate.*

The peal of the school bell had all of the boys instinctively lining up like something from a Dickens novel. Once we had all filed into class, I found that the familiar structure of the classroom came as a relief. I sat there thinking, *Get on with it, it's not that bad. No one's feeling sorry for you, so take your feelings out of it.*

Soon enough I connected with Donald McKenzie, a kid I vaguely knew from West Wyalong and struck up a few other friendly conversations. But in that first year the strongest connections were not made through the classroom; the academic demands posed no problems, but I only devoted enough energy as I needed to just get through. Rather, the connections were made through sport, where I was skilled and confident enough that I could gain some acceptance and acknowledgement.

It helped that I was a more mature, bigger-bodied kid than most. When cricket training got underway a few days into the term, I began to feel genuinely comfortable for the first time, knowing this was a field on which I could more than hold my own. As the weeks passed, my apprehensions eased, although I still felt like a free-range chicken that had somehow found its way to a cage farm.

When I returned to Ungarie at the end of that first term in 1973, I was still angling for a return to the nest. I knew that Dad was of the view that once the decision had been made to send me to Goulburn there was no turning back. He would have been thinking, *We've made the call, now off you go. Don't come crying when it all gets a little bit hard.* So I had to work on Mum. She softly urged me to give it another go.

My cricketing prowess had helped me to feel welcomed among the St Pat's cohort (by the time I was 15, I would find my way into in the first XI). But with St Pat's being a rugby union school, the real sporting spotlight was at its fiercest in winter. Simon Poidevin, who would go on to become a member of the 1991 World Cup-winning Wallabies outfit and later Australian captain, was two years ahead of me in school. I played as an inside centre which allowed me to have a playmaking role and kick the ball. I did reasonably well, but I found the game a bit one-dimensional. I yearned for a game of Aussie Rules.

The Christian Brothers could be harsh. Our weeks were highly regimented and fully scheduled, designed to keep idle hands busy. There were curfews and strappings; it was an oppressive environment. Boarders were only allowed to make an accompanied visit to town between 3.30 pm and 5 pm on Fridays, with 60 cents spending money drawn from our bank accounts. The brothers made sure we wrote a letter home every week. Mum always wrote back, and would also mail me a birthday cake placed inside a tin each February.

Fortunately the boys in my dormitory were a great bunch of fellas – I still occasionally catch up with some of them, decades later – and living in that space broadened my experience when it came to one of the great joys in my life: music.

At one end of the dorm would be the easy-listening crew, playing songs by the Doobie Brothers, America and The Eagles. In another corner would be the farmers' sons listening to John Denver and Creedence Clearwater Revival. Then we had the headbangers section, blasting out Deep Purple, Black Sabbath, Led Zeppelin, Status Quo and Slade.

I would absorb this teenage symphony, finding myself exposed to songs that had never made their way onto AM radio back in Ungarie. And by Year 8, I had managed to get hold of my own radio cassette player, which allowed me to make a mix tape of tunes recorded off the radio (my pet hate was when DJs talked over the start or end of a song I wanted to capture). The way I would escape any harshness of those years in Goulburn was to lie on my bed, slip on my headphones and drift away on my favourite music.

As boarders we also found other ways amuse ourselves, testing how mischievous we could be without getting caught. A few of the boys somehow found out that one of the brothers used to have a smoke while playing golf, and suspected he kept his cigarettes in his golf bag. If we were looking for a random, risky dare, someone would spring up and say, 'Who's going to sneak in and pinch a few fags from his golf bag?' Someone would always be up for it, including me, but we were smart enough to never lift the whole packet, we'd just siphon off five or six. He must have wondered what was going on.

And there was our awakening to the charms of the opposite sex. We used to go ballroom dancing with girls from two of Goulburn's Catholic sister schools: Our Lady of Mercy (my mother's alma mater) and St Joseph's. Mind you, the Christian Brothers and the nuns watched like hawks to make sure that we didn't get too close while dancing, and that our hands always rested well above the waist. But it did open the lines of communication between the dancers.

Occasionally day students would hand-deliver perfumed letters from the girls, and if you trusted the messenger you would call on him to dispatch your reply. It was not uncommon for some of the older boarders to doctor up a love note to a young, unsuspecting rookie and watch gleefully as he tumbled into the trap. I received one of these faux letters but quickly spotted the ruse, thinking to myself, *Nah, this hasn't been written by any 15-year-old girl. Someone's setting me up here.*

During my time at St Pat's, I did meet my first sweetheart, a nice girl from Wollongong. One afternoon as we were strolling along the street in Goulburn, a few metres in front of us a door swung open and out of the pub appeared Athol Apps, the gregarious shearer from back home in Ungarie. A cheeky grin crept over his big balding head.

'Hello Neale,' he said with unwarranted enthusiasm. Then to my friend, 'Hello darling, what's your name?'

Perhaps sensing my awkwardness at being sprung holding hands with a girl, Athol didn't prolong the moment. But as I went to shuffle off, he nudged me and offered quietly, 'Don't worry, I won't breathe a word to anybody.' And he was true to his word, although the next few times I saw him in the shearing shed on the farm, he would playfully ask me how the weather was up in Wollongong.

★

Boarding in Goulburn was a watershed in my personal development. It was a clarion call that you can't go through life relying totally on others; you need to learn to be self-sufficient. I had to join in, meet new people, make an effort and generally just find a way to cope.

Terry maintains that there was a shift in my persona after my stint in Goulburn. He says I was 'a typical young fella, happy with life and full of zest, but I suppose the time at boarding school helped you grow, stand on your own two feet, made you a bit more independent. You had to make your own decisions, be responsible.'

He did see some similarities between me and my younger

sister Colleen: 'She's got some of the same traits. A thinker, a bit sarcastic, switched-on, self-assured.'

Funnily enough Colleen, who would have been five when I went to boarding school, once said to me, 'It's like you were from another family.' Chris, who is five years my junior, suggested, 'It was like you were always ahead of the game, even if it was a pain in the arse for the rest of us.'

In childhood you learn about resilience from the people around you. Terry reckons that my 10 siblings were 'pretty casual . . . well, until you trod on our toes', and that's not a bad way to look at it. We all absorbed the lessons of our farming environment, because there's no shying away from failure. Sheep die, crops fail and it has a real impact on your life. You live through it and you have to get on with it. That's just part of your DNA.

At some point, everyone has to leave the fold. Sooner or later, we all find ourselves exposed to challenging times and when you come through them you think, *That wasn't too bad, I came through that all right.* And you start to think that maybe you're better equipped to face life's challenges than you gave yourself credit for. I think everyone has the capacity to cope, but it's not until you're tested that you realise it. Then when greater and tougher challenges present themselves, you can start to draw upon those previous experiences and remember that you got through them. You build up wells of resilience.

The end state of resilience is the ability to grow and flourish despite setbacks and adversity. It is not about recovering to where you were before adversity; it is about growing because of it. It is about getting to somewhere better than where you were.

Resilience is perseverance, the belief and resolve that setbacks and adversity won't beat you. That is largely a mental exercise, and it can be hard work in the moment. It's multifaceted but the outcome is that you end up at a better place, stronger and wiser. Resilience is developed.

It is difficult to know whether that time at St Pat's rewired my character, but I agree with Terry that it certainly taught me to stand on my own two feet.

As you grow older and wiser you develop an ability to deal with adversity. You've had more of it and you've endured it and you have developed your own template on how to deal with it that you didn't have at 11 or 24, and might not have at 37 or 57.

Each time you get through a challenging experience, you add a layer of resilience. You can be like the farmer who saddles up again and sows another crop with the hope and faith that the next one will be a bumper. Each time you fortify your coat of armour for the next time you're thrust into survival mode.

★

Towards the end of Year 10, in 1976, my St Pat's scholarship was up for renewal and I asked Dad to consider whether I could make the switch to another Catholic boarding school: Assumption College in Kilmore, about 200 kilometres south of the Murray.

I knew of Assumption's reputation as breeding ground for Australian Rules footballers and it helped that it was on the road to Melbourne, where Terry was now living. The family had occasionally driven past the signposts to the Marist Brothers college while undertaking our annual pilgrimage to the MCG to watch a VFL final. Dad would get tickets through his role as secretary of the Northern Riverina League, and as many as could fit would pile into the station wagon and head down the Hume Highway for a weekend in the big city.

Even though my Aussie Rules outings were largely limited to appearances for Ungarie during the school holidays, I had shown enough promise to play some representative football and was craving the chance to shift to an Aussie Rules environment. My appetite was also whetted by knowing Terry had joined South Melbourne that year and had cracked it for a senior VFL game against Hawthorn at Princes Park. He got a late call-up on the Friday when Norm Goss pulled out injured, and rang the Ungarie pub to urge his mates to make the journey down to Melbourne in case it was the only game he ever played.

This time around, the toughest part of the drive to the new school was the two-hour detour via Hay to collect a former student's second-hand blazer. Once again, upon arrival I found that the dormitory was hardly a snuggle in front of Mummy's fireplace, but there was an easy affinity. The boarders were from Riverina farms and Victorian towns like Rushworth, Numurkah and Colbinabbin, and they would chinwag about kicking goals and lining up as a ruck rover rather than scoring tries and the intricacies of rucks and mauls. There was not much need to lower the bucket into the well of resilience.

Assumption had a proud sporting tradition, and that allowed me to settle in and belong. Within weeks I was opening the batting for the first XI in our first home game of the summer, against Ivanhoe. I scored 157 not out. Brother William, an old Englishman, was convinced that the innings was in no small part due to the fact that I used a bat he had handcrafted from willow; he was delighted to see 22 boundaries come from the blade.

That evening there was plenty of backslapping in the dormitory, but I made sure I chipped in, 'You know I'm better at football.' Any delusions of cricket superstardom were obliterated the next day, when we had an informal Sunday match against a bunch of locals, a team they had cobbled together with some bushies from the hills. I confidently strode out to face the first over and started my innings like I was resuming on 157. On the fourth ball I faced, I produced an expansive drive and was bowled without scoring.

The learning was that the day before I had shown respect to the bowling early in my innings, had worked the ball around for a few singles until I got my eye in, and that led to a century. The bowler would have thought it was a jaffa, but it was more about me not showing enough respect. That's cricket.

I remember that duck every bit as vividly as the century.

★

One of our dormitory supervisors and teachers, Ray Carroll, was the sports coordinator at Assumption and coached the senior football and cricket teams – a role he would hold for 53 years until he retired in 2011. During that time he coached Assumption teams to 45 premierships.

Ray was a man of great integrity, humility and generosity of spirit, and cared deeply about the welfare, education and personal development of his charges. He would become one of the great mentors in my life. Ray was a firm believer in the college credo of *Quae Supra Quaere*, which means to 'seek the things that are above'. In a sporting sense, that meant elevating pride in the team above self-interest. The game was not about the individual, we were just bit-part players. He also relentlessly reminded us that we were following in the footsteps of champions who had played on this oval. If we ever lost at Assumption, it would be etched in our memory. Ray used to drive us crazy with the way he always reinforced what had come before and the boys who had built this tradition. Our responsibility was to uphold that tradition, to build on it. While we were representing the school, that was our purpose and when we graduated we would have to go and find our own. It inculcated in us a sense of being a part of something bigger than ourselves.

Those ideals were all-pervasive when I captained the cricket and football teams in Year 12. It gave me great satisfaction and pride to lead the cricketers to Assumption's first premiership in a decade and to be part of a football team that went through the season undefeated.

For all of the focus on sport, my time at Assumption was not only enjoyable because of what happened on the ovals. I found the Marist Brothers approach far less autocratic than that of the Christian Brothers, and more aligned to the way I'd been brought up. The Marist philosophy is that 'to educate children you must love them and love them all equally'. The college lived up to those ideals. And the friendships I formed during those years endure to this day.

The college also gave me ample academic opportunities, although my attitude towards formal education was similar to my attitude to digging holes for fence posts or ploughing the paddock: it was a bit of a grind, but something that had to be done. Conscious of the knowledge that there had been a financial outlay by my parents to get me into Assumption, and knowing I was the first in the family to go beyond Year 10, I felt a responsibility to graduate, but I simply did what I needed to for pass marks in order to get my name on that certificate. When it came to learning, I was more interested in acquiring knowledge about issues that captured my imagination, whether they be social issues, current affairs or an interest in people and what motivated them.

One time my maths homework did come in handy was when three-time Richmond premiership player Kevin Sheedy visited the school to conduct a sporting clinic in 1978. Knowing that he was also a handy leg spinner who had represented Richmond Cricket Club's First XI, I asked him about choosing between the two sports. He replied, 'If you want to play cricket for Australia, you've got to be in the top 15 players in the country. If you want to play VFL football, you've got to be in the top 300 players.' I might have only managed a C+ for statistics but I understood how those numbers stacked up.

On my last day at Assumption I walked out the door quietly confident and daring to dream that I might make it as a footballer. I'd been tested in all kinds of ways since that first day at St Pat's when I'd watched Mum, Dad and Terry drive off. I might not have used the words, but in leaving the comfort zone of the farm, I'd discovered the strength that accompanies independence – I'd started to fill my well of resilience and I'd begun to spread my wings.

What I learnt in those six years would stay with me forever.

Grow through what you go through

A wise man said, 'Life can only be understood backwards, but it must be lived forwards.' I understand the wisdom of that observation, particularly because right now, I don't have much 'forwards' left.

I would love to be able to have a chat to younger Neale and tell him that he was living some of the golden days of youth and didn't even realise it. But younger Neale wouldn't have had time to listen: he was too busy working out which mountain to climb next.

I have always wanted to wring the last drop out of myself and make the most of every opportunity that came my way. There's nothing inherently wrong with that; discovering your strengths and using them to accomplish things gives great satisfaction. However, we all have times when we get so caught up in striving for our goals and aspirations that we don't realise we have given free rein to our ego. The problem is that when you hand the keys over to your ego, whatever you accomplish is never enough and that yearning to keep on achieving can never be satisfied.

The challenge is to get to a point where you can really begin to appreciate what you have and not be constantly on the treadmill of chasing what you think you want.

It wasn't till later in life that I worked out that the quest for a good life is tied up in what I believe to be our existential passage in and out of four modes. My homespun names for these modes are: survive, strive, thrive and arrive.

I'm not one for regrets, but I wish I'd understood earlier that life isn't a sequential journey with incremental movements onto the next phase, culminating in a final single moment when you're an old man looking back proudly, knowing you're ready to check out because you've ticked all your boxes – you've made it. I know only too well that you can experience the slog of survival, just putting one foot in front of the other, over and over again throughout different periods of your life. I also know that striving for that elusive 'success' can wear you down, and that when you're thriving – when you're engaged in pursuits that are about more than serving your ego – the internal rewards are greater than you can imagine. I also know, somewhat belatedly, that you need to take time to appreciate the remarkable moments of now – arrival.

When you can recognise the different modes you're in, you put yourself back in the driver's seat and regain the power to decide what turns to take. It's then that you're in the best position to get the most out of this precious thing called life.

★

My determination to become a VFL player had seriously taken hold during my time at Assumption College. In 1977, when Terry was in his second season with the South Melbourne Swans and regularly performing well at VFL level, a confidence evolved that maybe I could make it too – after all, I used to rib my older brother about how I had him covered as a footballer.

Whether in the dormitory at Assumption or back home on the farm during school holidays, I used to listen on the radio to broadcasts of the 1977 Swans games when Terry was playing and it was like getting a glimpse of Hollywood. There was something magical about hearing your brother's name being called during the commentary. In the family kitchen we would listen as the experts gave a summary after the game and if Terry's name came up the whole family would swell with pride.

Because South Melbourne wasn't a high-profile club with a large supporter base at that time, Terry's games rarely got much of a look-in on the television replay, so the only way to watch him play was to be at the ground. Sometimes that opportunity arose when Assumption College played at a Melbourne school on a Saturday, as the team would be allowed to stay in town before heading back on the chartered bus later that evening.

My schoolboy football career had progressed well. In Year 11, I represented New South Wales in the under-17s Teal Cup competition and was selected in the All Australian squad. Later that year, in a match playing for an Associated Grammar Schools team against a Ballarat representative outfit, I had a day out, kicking eight goals. A host of VFL scouts were watching on, including Essendon team manager Kevin Egan.

With Ungarie being part of South Melbourne's Northern Riverina recruiting zone, the Swans invited me to play in a 1978 intra-club practice match at one of the ovals near Albert Park Lake. My only memory of that day is of being taken aback at the size of the powerfully built VFL players and being grateful when South captain Ricky Quade doubled back and ran away from goal, dishing off a handball to make sure I got a touch of the footy.

My path to the VFL looked like it was heading towards the gates of South Melbourne's Lake Oval home ground. Then detour signs appeared on that road later in the summer. Determined to bolster their playing list and push for a tilt at a flag, South's backroom powerbrokers began pursuing trades for proven senior footballers. One of those was decorated Essendon centreman Neville Fields, and as part of the deal to acquire the classy left-footer, the Swans agreed in principle to release Terry to Essendon. When South looked to finalise the deal, they put in a phone call to Ungarie to speak to Dad, who was managing Terry's affairs. True to his word that all negotiations are tough but fair, Dad insisted that Terry's transfer was conditional on South also relinquishing their hold on my playing future, which was tied to the Swans through zoning regulations.

'We only get down to Melbourne twice a year and we want to see them both play when we get there,' he rumbled down the phone.

Mum, realising what was happening, suggested that my 15-year-old brother Anthony be included in the package deal. But Dad, glancing at Anthony sitting at the kitchen table tucking into a huge bowl of dessert, ignored the proposal. *The kid might never play bloody football,* he thought to himself.

South Melbourne general manager Oberon Pirak agreed to the terms of the ultimatum and – at Dad's insistence – committed the pact to writing. A letter, dated 6 March 1978, duly arrived at the farm stating that I was released to join Essendon 'free of any encumbrances'. Now the path to the VFL would lead me to Essendon's Windy Hill home base.

The first glimpse of what it meant to play for the Bombers at Windy Hill came a few weeks later when I headed to the heaving suburban ground on a Saturday afternoon with a few Assumption schoolmates to watch Terry play against Richmond. Terry booted five goals in the Bombers' 21-point win. One of his opponents that day was Tigers defender Kevin Sheedy – it was inconceivable that within a few years, the two of them would be standing alongside one another again, but this time at the MCG, accepting the premiership cup as Essendon's captain and coach. But it was conceivable, to my mind, that one day I would be proudly running onto that Windy Hill turf alongside my older brother.

In terms of what I wanted to achieve, things began to fall into place in the months after I left Assumption College at the end of 1978. Soon after I returned to the farm, the Essendon Football Club contacted me about coming down to Melbourne for their 1979 pre-season training. I would get the chance to train and maybe play alongside Terry, who had impressed during his first season with the Bombers, on the back of a couple of patchy seasons with South Melbourne.

There was also a letter in the mailbox informing me that I had passed my Higher School Certificate, followed not long afterwards by an offer to take up a place studying science at Melbourne University. Both of these developments were uncharted academic waters for the Daniher family and, for Dad especially, the concept of tertiary study was somewhat mystifying. Why would I want to go and listen to some boffin lecture about science when I could be out earning an honest dollar? Still, the fact that the Whitlam Government had abolished university fees a few years earlier probably made the prospect slightly more palatable for him.

After a Christmas spent in Ungarie, enjoying the moment and yet equally eager to bring on my new challenges, I headed down to the big smoke to take up residence at Newman College, the university's Catholic residential college. This would be a boarding experience unlike Kilmore or Goulburn: rather than a dorm I would share a room (with a good fella called Chris from western Victoria) and there would be considerably more freedom and independence. With my eighteenth birthday just a few weeks away, I certainly felt like I was on the brink of adulthood. Nobody would be telling me what to believe or what to do; for the first time I would be working it all out for myself.

Lurking in the back of my mind was a little voice of self-doubt that sprang from knowing I was a bit of dag from the backblocks who could not possibly be as smart or enlightened or as polished as the city kids. How could I hope to match their self-assuredness, their ability to be cool and sophisticated? In the 1970s, many kids from the bush struggled with that complex internal tussle, the pull between wanting to remain humble and the drive to show we could match and even outdo anyone. Mr Negative was on one shoulder saying, 'Of course you'll fail' and Mr Positive on the other saying, 'No you won't, stick it up 'em'.

I turned up at one of Australia's most revered and prestigious learning institutions with a wide-eyed naivety . . . and a quiet determination to succeed. I turned up to Windy Hill – another revered place of a completely different kind – with quiet confidence that my destiny was to be a footballer.

★

You may have heard the story about the two young fish who were swimming up the river one morning when they happened upon an old fish coming back downstream. The old fish glanced over at them and said, 'Morning boys, how's the water?' The two young fish looked at each other with puzzled faces, until one said, 'What's water?'

This little fish tale is a way of saying that sometimes we take the most obvious but important things for granted. At the risk of coming across as 'old man trout' trying to lecture the small fry, I would love to grab teenage Neale by the scruff of the neck and tell him about the water ahead: all of the wild rapids, the gleaming smooth patches, meandering twists and turns, the ragged rocks and the hooked lines dangling from the banks.

I have always tried to make some kind of sense of the world – and walking through the arches of a grand seat of learning such as Melbourne University may have seemed like an ideal opportunity for some deep reflection about meaning and purpose – but in reality I didn't have the time or space for such contemplation. When it came to searching for meaning in my studies, I knew I was simply trying to get by, usually sitting up the back during lectures, sometimes thinking, *What the hell is he talking about?* And when I did have pause for thought, it rarely extended beyond mulling over why on earth I had elected to pursue a science degree without any grounding in similar subjects at high school.

As for my purpose, well, that didn't extend far beyond trying to make it as an Essendon footballer. That was my primary focus. Any spare time that was left was devoted to jugs of beer and mingling with guys at the Clyde Hotel. If I was of a mind to eke out some time for deep thought, it usually came from ruminating on the issues explored in the pages of *Newsweek* or *The Bulletin* that I had come across on campus.

Four decades on from those times, I want to dip my toe in to explain what 'water' is, even if it's just for the benefit of my grandchildren getting to know a bit more about their grand-father. And I do so knowing full well that while they might gain the odd insight from reading about the philosophy I have arrived at late in life, they – like my younger self – will still need to embark on their own odyssey and work out what philosophical construct helps them make sense of this life.

★

So what is water? Let's have a look at those four different modes in life: survive, strive, thrive and arrive.

In essence, 'survive' is when we are consumed by the most basic of struggles, with problems and challenges; 'strive' is taking on the world, finding our place in it, accomplishing and finding significance for ourselves while pursuing largely self-centred goals; 'thrive' is when we find meaning and purpose through pursuits that transcend our egocentric motives; and 'arrive' is about being present and enjoying the moment.

These modes intersect and overlap at various times throughout our lives; they are not linear, they can coexist. At any one time you could be in all four modes. You might be really struggling at work in a job you don't like much, but thriving at home with the family. You could be striving to win your club's singles championship, and spending quiet one-on-one time with your ailing favourite aunty, experiencing 'arrival'.

I have found myself in survival mode at various stages of my life: when I lobbed up for my first day at boarding school, or when I was sacked from my AFL coaching gig at Melbourne. Or when I was diagnosed with a terminal illness. I was *surviving* when I was grinding my way through the academic part of first-year science at university, while simultaneously *striving* to make a name for myself as an Essendon footballer.

On our first day at school or when we walk through the door at a new job, we might feel like a bit of a fraud because we don't really have any idea what we're doing. But each time we get through one of these 'survival mode' experiences, we add a layer of resilience and fortify our coat of armour for the next time we're thrust into survival mode. So that by the time a nasty circumstance comes along – such as being diagnosed with a terminal illness – life has given us enough survival lessons to think, *Right, this is a bad one, but I've got the mechanism to work my way through it.*

We weren't born to spend our time just surviving, and moving beyond that is a combination of choice and opportunity. Life doesn't promise to be fair but it does offer opportunity if we choose to look for it, adopting a proactive attitude and approach that gets us through the grind. Some people hope that something comes along to rescue them – they are reactive. I can safely say that hoping for the winning lottery ticket that's going to rescue you from survival mode is probably going to lead you down the path of disappointment.

The key to getting out of survival mode is to choose to be hopeful, to be optimistic, to draw upon whatever resilience you have in order to persist. It's about deciding against staying in the pit of anxiety, stress and fear, and instead working out how to claw your way forward. Being in survival mode is tough, because you are consumed with your own problems, but it's important that you keep your mind open to finding a way to get through it, and keep looking for the next opportunity.

Moving beyond survival mode, we typically find ourselves striving and/or thriving.

All of us have a natural urge to move forward in life, to begin to understand ourselves and our place in it. We look to identify our strengths and build on our competencies to achieve goals and to be seen as successful in life. Striving has a very valid place in this world; if we don't strive towards achievements, we would never put man on the moon, produce world champions and create celebrated works of art.

But here's the thing that matters to me. When we are striving, the focus can easily become too self-centred. Our ego has its hands on the wheel and life is all about achieving, competing and conquering. The major difference between striving and thriving is intent. Striving's main intent is self, thriving is beyond just self.

For most of us, when we are striving we are driven to acquire, to look good and to be seen to be successful. It's all about the next accomplishment, the next attainment. Or how our house is never grand enough. It's all about I, me and mine. The sense of fulfilment that is reached through striving is lessened because it is not linked to an underlying purpose – if you never move beyond striving, there's every chance you will never find fulfilment. Striving is never being satisfied.

Some people chase happiness as an outcome. Sure, happiness is something we wish for ourselves and all those we love, but it's only a small part of the picture. There's more to living a good life than experiencing a particular emotional state. I tend to agree with Martin Seligman – we should aim to flourish in this life, to be fully engaged in what we do while creating and maintaining positive relationships. Aligned closely with this is finding meaning and purpose to guide us to noble accomplishments.

Thriving, on the other hand, is about contributing to something greater than ourselves, something that feels worthy of our time and effort. It's not dependent on you being at the centre of your own universe, the cause becomes the central focus. It helps us to think, *I know what I'm doing and I know why I'm doing it and it's bigger than me!* When we are thriving we are still accomplishing, but the intent is beyond just self. You have committed to a cause that you deem honourable and worthy, and that brings meaning and purpose to your life. I think it's what Albert Einstein meant when he said, 'Do not try to become a man of success but try to become a man of value.'

And it can be something simple. My mother gained meaning from being a person who raised 11 kids. My father gained meaning from being a farmer who helped provide food for the world. Some people survive at work Monday through Friday just to pay the bills, and what gives them some meaning is the volunteer work they do on the weekend, or helping out at the community garden or coaching their daughter's netball team. That's what gives them a reason to get out of bed in the morning, to look forward to the weekend. It's something beyond just self, beyond the individual. It can be a passion, but the passion is sparked by being part of something bigger than just reducing your golf handicap. Thriving allows us to nurture a family, build a respected business, volunteer for a worthy cause, take on MND, whatever it may be. Thriving is about knowing that we are a part of an endeavour that is going to improve circumstances for other people, not just ourselves.

In order to thrive we all need to unravel what it is that will bring meaning to our lives, not just tick the boxes that society equates with personal success. It's not necessarily about identifying just one meaning or purpose and working away at a grand vision the whole time we're on this earth. Rather, it's asking what are the ways to add some substance to what we do, to bring something to someone else rather than focus on what we can get out of life.

How do we know whether someone – a friend, teammate, politician, business leader or a coach – is driven by self-interest or a bigger cause? Sometimes their actions and behaviours are self-evident, sometimes not. The truth of whether a person is striving or thriving is only ever known inside the heart of that person.

The other mode in life – and it's a vitally important one – is arriving. It's easy to think of this as 'the end', but arrival mode is allowing ourselves to accept that you can't change the past, the future doesn't exist and all we have is the now. It's all about enjoying today; we can't enjoy tomorrow, it's not here.

We don't necessarily have to have progressed from 'thrive' mode to get to 'arrive', because on a smaller scale we can always enjoy the moment. When I returned back home from boarding school to the farm I could step back and think, *How good is this?* However, as I've matured, I can see the benefits of getting yourself to a point where you are in arrival mode most of the time.

I'm working on mastering the art of arriving; my capacity to reach arrival mode has undoubtedly increased through losing things I took for granted, forcing me to contemplate what it is that I really appreciate in life. Having MND has helped bring 'arriving' into sharp focus and has made crystal clear the importance of the simple things: friendships, laughter, nature, the changing seasons. I can tell you right now, on my deathbed I will not regret that I didn't strive more.

Don't wait until you're dying to want to get into 'arrive' mode. Arriving can act as an antidote to incessant striving. Arriving helps us appreciate people more; it helps us show respect by really listening to others; helps us have more empathy and be less judgmental; helps us to look at people and wonder what challenges they've had along the way. When you are in arrival mode, there is a lot more love in life because you are more open to it. People have a fundamental need for others to acknowledge that they are there and that they are worthy of our attention. Sometimes, arriving is just doing that: giving people the time of day, paying attention to them and taking judgement out of the equation.

★

So, as a young fish of 18, would I have been interested in hearing what some dilapidated old cod had to say about trying to make sense of life? I reckon I would have been only half listening, probably turning the sound up to Skyhooks' 'Ego Is Not A Dirty Word'. I would have been too busy making plans to become a footballer, thinking the world was my oyster. I reckon I would have said, 'I'm just trying to survive this semester. I'm supposed to be meeting the gang over at the Clyde Hotel for a cold beer and I don't really have time to take in all of this "thrive" stuff you're rattling on about. I'm just striving to arrive at the pub before Happy Hour is over.'

Balance is not something you find, it's something you create

These days, there's a lot of talk about living a balanced life, but it's hard to know what that really means. Too often we're too busy striving to make our mark on the world to think about it.

One of life's greatest challenges is how we achieve balance in the fundamental dualities in human nature, ones that at first glance might appear contrary but are actually complementary. Things like: when to speak and when to listen; when to lead and when to follow; when to be firm and when to be flexible; when to reflect and when to act; when to be caring and when to be ruthless; when to be independent and when to be interdependent.

With all of these questions, the perfect balance is also dependant on the situation you find yourself in. The answer lies in creating some sort of equilibrium, not operating in the extremes. We are operating in an extreme if we always question and never believe. And we are operating in an extreme if we always strive and never thrive or arrive.

In your youth it is difficult to understand these dualities within; there's a strong dose of ego, which always wants to tip the balance towards what is best for you individually, and it's usually about short-term gain. Ego has its place, but if you allow it to be a runaway horse then you need to find a way to grab the reins and regain some control over the direction you're heading in.

Maybe getting the perfect balance is more obvious than we first think, as Sister Teresita tried to explain to me in grade six: 'Neale, there is a reason God gave you two eyes, two ears and one mouth. You should observe and listen twice as much as you speak.' Good advice is often not recognised at the time – instead we learn the hard way.

As a player and as a coach, I didn't get the balance thing right all the time. Striving to get the most out of myself demanded all my focus and I didn't recognise – let alone know how to balance – the dualities of my own nature.

Balance isn't waiting in the wings for you to find it. It's up to you to create it.

★

As soon as I headed down the Hume Highway to live in Melbourne, I was in 'strive' mode. My driving ambition was to carve out a successful career as a league footballer well before I'd kicked a football at my new club.

Terry jokes that the club nearly lost me before I'd even played a game. Essendon's way of welcoming me to the fold late in 1978 was to send me on the players' end-of-season trip to Hawaii. While bodysurfing at Sunset Beach, I was dragged into deeper water by a rip and drifted a few hundred metres further down the beach. Back on the shore, Terry did a quick headcount and realised someone was missing – his younger brother. After returning to dry sand, I strolled back up the shore to the group, unaware that panic was starting to set in.

'Where the bloody hell have you been?' Terry demanded. In my teenage naivety I was oblivious to the agitation my disappearance had stirred.

Despite the tranquil setting and the relaxed mood during that trip, I was relatively earnest, impatient to get into a real league football environment. At one point I discussed the upcoming season with Terry. By his own admission Terry found playing football 'a bit of an escape' from the farm, and having a few beers with his club mates was as much of a focus as getting a kick. 'I was there for a bit of a good time not a long time and was just rolling along,' was how he described his first two seasons with South Melbourne. So, over a beer at Waikiki, the 17-year-old rookie decided to challenge his 21-year-old brother who already had 39 VFL games under his belt.

'Come on, Tez, you've already had one go at it,' I told him. 'Why don't you pull your head in a bit and we can work at this together and see if we can make a fist of it.'

Terry studied me with a cocked eyebrow. 'Fair enough, mate, but settle down a bit. We're here to have a good time, too, let's not get too serious about life.' This would be something of a recurring theme during our football careers: Terry's laidback style and my diligent intensity helped each of us level out the other at times, although we were both often too stubborn to change. Regardless, both styles came with an ultra-competitiveness and desperation to win.

Back in Melbourne at the club, I lapped up that first summer of pre-season training. We ran through our paces on the main arena at the Melbourne Showgrounds while the Essendon cricketers took priority at Windy Hill. During the Christmas break, Terry and I undertook our own training program back at the farm. We worked the speedball during fitness sessions in the garage and Terry, an endurance-running beast, led the way as we pounded the dirt tracks and did interval running on the dusty lane beyond the front gate.

When we returned to Windy Hill in the early part of 1979, the aura of the club's history and tradition felt palpable. For all of my flinty resolve to make it as a senior player, I walked through the doors as a quiet and respectful country lad, hoping not to stuff up and embarrass myself. I didn't want to let the club down, let my family down or let myself down, and knew I had my work cut out to prove myself. *You've done nothing, you deserve nothing, earn your stripes.* I was determined to listen and learn and in the changing rooms I spoke only when I needed to. Picking up on my reserved manner, Alan Reid – a wingman from Western Australia and self-appointed bestower of nick-names – dubbed me 'Rowdy', a tag that would stick throughout my playing career.

In underage football I had always played as a forward or on-baller, but after a couple of pre-season matches on a forward flank, coach Barry Davis decided to try me across half-back. Everything seemed to click and I worked my way into the Bombers' best 20.

★

Every elite footballer has a moment from his first senior game stamped in his memory. Dozens of games might be a hazy blur, but there will be a vivid – and often slightly romanticised – memory of that first scrambled kick, a first opponent, a rattling bump or simply the joy of running onto the ground with the team. My first game for Essendon was against Carlton at Waverley Park on the last day of March 1979.

My first memory of playing for the Bombers is not a passage of play, or of having to pick up one of Carlton's dangerous forward flankers such as Trevor Keogh or first gamer Wayne Johnston. It is of the huddle at three-quarter time. We gathered on the wing, four goals down, waiting for coach Barry Davis to deliver his speech. I looked around and sensed in my teammates a universal atmosphere of defeatism. Heads were bowed, there was no enthusiasm, no drive to turn momentum around. The general mood of 'we can't win this' hit me like a slap in the face. It was such a foreign feeling.

At Assumption College our teams always believed we could win, no matter the state of the game. Each loss was regarded as a mini-disaster. But no matter how quietly determined I felt, as a pimple-faced teenager I wasn't going to pipe up in the huddle – I was trying not to embarrass myself in my first game, conscious of wanting to get another game the following week. Essendon lost by 21 points that day.

My second game for Essendon unfolded in a similar way: down by 22 points at three-quarter time against North Melbourne at Arden St Oval, and losing by 20 points. I lined up on one back flank and Neil Besanko, a miserly 165-game defender, was on the other. The way our backline was set up, the task fell to me to play against high-profile North recruit Graham Cornes, who at age 31 had shifted across from South Australia after a highly acclaimed career with Glenelg. But by midway through the second quarter, North champion Malcolm Blight was tearing the game apart at full-forward and our runner approached me with a message: 'Go back to the goalsquare, you're on Blight.' I trotted back, only to have the reigning Brownlow Medallist kick another two goals against me over the next five minutes. I wasn't on Blight for long.

After the match I was keenly feeling my contribution to the loss. Later I spoke about it to Barry Davis, who was a calm and considered coach, a university lecturer who was more inclined to develop and teach players than rant at them.

'Don't worry, not your fault,' he said. As it turned out, our coach – who preferred to call the players by their first names – had phoned the interchange bench and told the runner to 'shift Neil onto Blight'. He had meant Neil Besanko but the runner had delivered the message to me.

The fact remained, though, that I had played in two losses in my first two VFL outings and that did not sit well with me. Despite having just turned 18, I had a single-minded determination to be one of the best players in a successful team, and I was in a hurry to get there; that inner drive to excel was consuming me and not necessarily in a healthy way.

As a young footballer I was operating in the extremes. I was so determined to succeed that I had not fully savoured the experience of playing my first VFL game. Instead I had latched on to the joylessness of being in a losing team. The enduring impression I had taken from my debut was that this mighty club, steeped in premiership success, had lost its ruthlessness over the 13 years since its 1965 flag.

There were balances I needed to find: between being earnest and carefree, between being selfish and selfless, between being taciturn and speaking up. But at that time, in the callowness of youth, I was intent on piling more weight onto one side of the scales.

★

When you're striving to make it in your chosen field, you can become so intense that your ambition gives you a bad case of tunnel vision, preventing you from seeing the bigger picture. You lose perspective on what's going on beyond your own little space. That can catch up with you, especially when those goals you're desperately wanting to achieve don't happen.

Much has changed in the modern era of the totally professional footballer: some changes for the better, some for the worse. One aspect of the players' lifestyle that I don't envy is that they now have less time away from the game during the week and fewer non-football outlets, which limits their ability to gain perspective and create balance.

In 1979, football wasn't a full-time job option. I would rock up to training after lectures, I would throw my bag into the number 6 locker and change into my gear alongside guys who had spent the day teaching at high school, digging ditches, hustling through the law courts or connecting electrical cables. Running around kicking a football was a welcome release from their daily grind. Not only that, but for a teenager from the bush, a VFL club was an environment where I got to mix with players and staff with a diverse spectrum of ages, backgrounds and experiences and it allowed me to gain an appreciation of their views of the world. My focus and purpose were very much wrapped up in making it as a league footballer, but at least there was something other than a Sherrin to occupy my mind during the week. I hate to think how intense I might have been if perspective hadn't been forced upon me to the extent that it was.

During the early weeks of my first year at Newman College, the senior students subjected the first years to an initiation ritual, a form of hazing. They would call out a new student's name and subject them to a humiliating prank, essentially making that person the butt of their entertainment. Eventually I had to take my turn and it involved spending the afternoon wearing a jock strap on my head. I reluctantly agreed to the absurd demand, but did so convinced that this was simply bullying by a different name. The smirking seniors came across like a pack of mongrel dogs; they wouldn't behave that way as individuals, but felt secure doing so as part of a pack.

There were, thankfully, many times when the college camaraderie was more constructive, welcoming and simply fun. There was shared study, social gatherings, card nights and full-blown parties. We also enjoyed conviviality of the inter-collegiate sport on Wednesday afternoons, and inevitably it was not easy to escape being typecast as 'the football guy'.

I was called upon to pull on the Newman jumper when the block of university football matches came around. Playing in those games wasn't particularly appealing to me, but I knew it meant a lot to my college mates and I didn't want to come across as a snooty flog. The schedule didn't clash with Essendon training so there was scope for me to help the team out. The understanding became that I would start on the interchange bench and if the team was struggling I would trot down to full-forward and try to kick a few goals. In one match I kicked a lot of goals, and in the grand final against Ormond I bagged a few to help Newman come from behind at half-time to win. The beers flowed freely in the Clyde Hotel that evening.

At 18, I wasn't exactly throwing myself into my first year of university life. When my attention did drift to study, I was starting to realise that a science degree had not been a particularly good fit for me, however there was one subject within the course that piqued my interest. At that time computer science involved punched cards, reams of folding paper and a computer the size of a walk-in robe. I struggled to get a single program to work, but it did appeal as a way of the future. I thought there might be a career in it but Melbourne University didn't offer a specific computer science course. I looked into transferring to RMIT in 1980.

★

After those opening two losses of the 1979 season, Essendon eventually got on something of a roll, at one stage winning nine games in a row before we tailed away late in the season and lost an elimination final against Fitzroy. My own form was sound enough to earn an award for the VFL Recruit of the Year.

Everything that goes with being a league footballer in the fanatical heartland that is Melbourne was great for the ego and self-esteem. We felt important, felt the game was important. You had a lot of eyes on you. On Sunday mornings you might get invited to go in to Channel 7 to appear on *World of Sport*, talk about the game and come away with a bag of goodies. Sometimes I'd tune in and hear legends of the game say, 'Young Daniher is going all right.' It was a real buzz. I would look for my name in the Sunday newspapers, the *Observer* and the *Press*, and if only one of them named me among the best players I thought, *Well, this is the better paper, I'll make sure I buy this one from now on.*

Those personal accolades and that individual attention reinforced the idea that success came from building a good resumé and that all I had to do was continue to play to my strengths. In among all of that attention, it was difficult for this immature young man to pause and consider that I also needed to work on my weaknesses. Outside my football skills, I don't remember giving any airtime to other areas where I needed to develop or improve. I was driven, but I don't think I was arrogant. Maybe there were moments, but you need to factor in that my upbringing had laid the foundations of my character, and we were never allowed to get ahead of ourselves.

Going into the 1980 season, Essendon had a belief that we would play in the finals, but by the middle of winter our prospects were slipping. Barry Davis publicly stated that if we missed the top five he would resign as Essendon coach in favour of someone who could elevate the team to the next level. We finished seventh, four-and-a-half wins behind fifth-placed Collingwood, and Barry honoured his vow to stand aside. I found the team's inconsistency frustrating, but from an individual perspective, I was doing pretty well, earning two Victorian guernseys and placing third in the club's best-and-fairest award.

But neither the team nor I could have predicted that the game was about to change immensely for us all in 1981.

★

Kevin Sheedy blew into Windy Hill like a bracing southerly change. In his 13-year playing career with Richmond, he had experienced 20 finals and three premierships, captained the club and won a best-and-fairest award, and upon retiring in 1979 he had worked as an assistant coach to Tony Jewell, helping guide the Tigers to the 1980 flag. Now he set about bringing some of that ruthless polish to the club he had supported as a boy.

Under his watch, the Essendon changing rooms were immediately painted and renovated, the start of pre-season training was brought forward from December to mid-October and sessions were ramped up to five times a week, sometimes scheduled to include a sprint session that started in darkness at 5.30 am. 'Sheeds' led the VFL trend towards full-time professional coaching and was an avid student of the successful methods employed in other sports in Europe and North America. He was determined to ingrain a hard edge into the team, to iron out the fluctuations in form and to build among the Essendon players an innate confidence that they could match it with the best. He would refit the team, investing in footballers he thought could meet his demands.

Years later, he would confide that he was drawn to Terry and me because we were young, hungry and both of us, in our own ways, were obsessed by football. Sheedy's appointment gave me a green light to shift the dial even further towards the driven and intense side of my nature. So much for balance.

When Essendon made a tentative start to that 1981 season, winning just one of our first six games, Sheeds threatened to pull the boots on and come out of retirement. Fortunately, we responded to that disconcerting prospect with a home win against St Kilda the following Saturday and launched into a 15-game winning streak.

Late in that stretch was a match against Carlton at Princes Park that many people now like to identify as the high-water mark of my playing career. In reality, I was having a pretty average afternoon at half-back and Sheeds shuffled the chess pieces around at three-quarter time in an effort to get us across the line. I switched to the forward half, while Terry went back the other way. I managed to jag a goal early in the last quarter but the game looked to have slipped away when Carlton's Jimmy Buckley bombed a running goal at the 20-minute mark to extend the Blues' lead to 26 points. He was hoisted into the air by a cluster of teammates, who celebrated like they had won.

A few players in red and black didn't like the look of it, and we responded. Goals to Roger Merrett and Paul Vander Haar got it back to a couple of kicks. With about two minutes to play, I managed to take a contested mark to reduce the deficit to five points and from the next centre bounce, Glenn Hawker cleverly paddled and gathered the ball on the wing before tumbling a funny old mongrel punt that allowed me to run onto a chest mark.

The idea of missing the 35-metre shot never entered my mind, all I was concerned about was adjusting my run-up slightly so that I didn't have to kick from a boggy patch of turf. The goal put us a point up and with a few seconds to play, Ron Andrews – kicking in his socked foot after his boot was wrenched loose – launched a torpedo that I flew for, attempting another mark. I spilled it, dislocating my finger in the process, just before the final siren sounded.

Although it was not my most complete performance, the three goals in the final quarter drew a shower of plaudits, particularly because we had knocked off top team Carlton – the power team of that era – on their home patch for the first time since 1968. Well-wishers swamped us after the siren and everyone wanted to slap me on the back. Worse, they wanted to shake hands, not realising my dislocated finger had not been put back in. They must have wondered why, even after the most stirring of victories, this serious young man struggled to muster a smile and savour the moment.

Truth be told, even without the dodgy finger I probably would not have uncorked my emotions, because my mentality was that there were two more games in the season and a finals series to conquer – best not to get complacent. I was more driven by a fear of failure than the spoils of success. The euphoria of victory was never really something I got to. I used to think, *Right, let's move one to the next one.*

I found an interview I did with Mike Sheahan in the *Herald*, where I explained this: 'I'm really tense after the game. I bite at people sometimes and it takes me a while to settle down. I go home, rip the top off one and whack the telly on Channel 2 to watch the footy [replay]. I go back to the club about 8 o'clock when everything has settled down.'

As it turned out, I would have been better cherishing that Carlton win, because the following Saturday the bottom fell out of my season. We were playing in a home game against South Melbourne and Sheeds started me in the midfield. Just a few minutes into the game, Justin Madden palmed a beautiful tap straight to me. As I ran forward and kicked the ball, one of the Swans pushed me from the side and my right knee buckled.

I felt something clunk inside the joint but didn't go down screaming. The knee felt a bit numb but I pushed on. The next time the ball bounced towards me I gathered it up at half-back and went to do a little shimmy, like I always did to buy myself a little space. It was an innocuous little side step, but as I lightly put my weight on the right foot it was like stepping off a ledge and the next instant I lay crumpled on the Windy Hill mud. I eventually managed to hobble off the ground, but I had no strength in the leg to run and sat out the rest of the match. The hopeful early diagnosis was a jarred knee.

With a crucial match against Geelong in the final round, leading into the finals, I fronted up to training on Monday, but as soon as I pushed off on the leg, I knew there was no power in the knee. I consulted a specialist and was crushed to hear the words 'the anterior cruciate ligament is gone'.

My intensity and drive to be the best footballer I could be, my single-minded focus on that one aspect of my life, was now causing me more pain than the leg encased in a plaster cast. My whole identity was wrapped up in being number 6 for Essendon and to a degree I had allowed myself to accept that my worth as a person was in part measured by my worth as a footballer.

When we are consumed by striving for that sole sense of purpose and it hits a brick wall, the crash hits twice as hard because there is no balance in our life. We are left asking, *Is that all there is?* It is a rude shock that is not limited to league footballers, it can be a slap in the face to a Year 12 student or a 35-year-old stock-broker. Or it can take the shape of a midlife crisis.

Because I was so caught up in seeing myself as a footballer, I was desperate to get back out on the field as soon as possible. I had played 66 games in a row, had never even played a reserves game. Now 'the football guy' had to try to make sense of what it would mean to sit out a year of football.

In some ways my knee reconstruction was probably a wake-up call. I might otherwise have run the risk of ending up as one-dimensional as my footy card.

Sometimes being smart is admitting you don't know something

There's an old saying that we can use other people's knowledge, but we can't use their wisdom. Wisdom is what we do with the knowledge we've acquired through experience, education, self-directed learning and from mentors, colleagues and others we've opened our minds to.

Coming out of my teenage years, the saying 'you don't know what you don't know' was very appropriate for me. I've always been interested in learning, but at school and university it felt as though we studied to acquire knowledge, commit it to memory and spew it out in an exam . . . and then two weeks later, we'd forget the lot. There's a formality and discipline to that sort of education that I appreciate more in retrospect than I did at the time, but I place a much higher value on being curious, on asking questions and being prepared to listen to answers. I like to evaluate knowledge and work out what I believe, what *my* take is.

I've been lucky enough to work alongside people who have different opinions to mine. Who wouldn't want to know more today about the world than they did yesterday? As humans, we have accumulated a vast well of knowledge over the generations and yet there's still so much that each of us doesn't know.

There's a lot of on-the-job learning in life, of course, and here's where wisdom comes in. A wise person doesn't make the same mistakes over and over again; they reflect on what happened, consider their options and work out what course of action to take next time. Life throws up plenty of lessons you learn the hard way, but the experience is not wasted if you use it to strengthen your character, for example, or load up on resilience.

None of us likes to admit that we don't know something, or that we are wrong. An important part of moving beyond acquiring knowledge for the sake of it and towards gaining wisdom is to know yourself, and to understand what you do well and what you could do better. That's about ongoing self-reflection and checking in on where your ego is sitting on the arrogance dial.

My parents' wisdom didn't come from knowledge acquired through schoolbooks; it came from living a meaningful life full of purpose. Mum thrived on nurturing others, Dad understood that he wasn't just ploughing a field, he was feeding a nation. What matters to me may not be the same as what drove my parents, but I'm the beneficiary of their lived experience. If I have half their wisdom, I will die a happy man.

★

All of us can identify specific years in the timeline of our lives that take on extra significance, years that help define who we are and who we become. And 1981 is one of those years for me, where life dished up great joy alongside some unexpected opportunities to test my mettle.

In a football sense, it was a season of contrasting emotions. I had begun to feel I was making real progress in achieving my goal of being a VFL footballer and took pride in winning the Crichton Medal, which is Essendon's best-and-fairest award, and in being voted *Inside Football*'s Player of the Year. Against that was the dismay of knowing I faced months on the sidelines after rupturing the anterior cruciate ligament (ACL) in my knee late in the season.

Off the field, my university pathway was beginning to make more sense since I had switched to studying computer science at RMIT. At that time, the computer world was changing as fast as we were learning it, so much so that personal computers were only starting to emerge and by the time I graduated much of what I'd learnt would already be superseded. But I was taught to program computers and was beginning to understand their architecture, which gave me a degree of confidence about the prospects of a career in the industry.

With the money earned from my first football contract I had bought my first car (and what would prove to be the only new vehicle I ever purchased): a Toyota Corona that cost me $7660. At a time when the Melbourne CBD was nowhere near as busy as it is today, I would drive to RMIT and park on a vacant block across the road in Swanston Street. It cost me two dollars a day.

Midway through 1981 came the most pivotal day of all. A group of young Essendon players headed up to Noradjuha, a humble little town just outside Horsham in country Victoria, for Peter Light's 21st birthday. Mention his name to most Essendon fans and they might struggle to conjure up an impression of his VFL career at Windy Hill. 'Lighty' was a midfielder/forward who played two senior games for the Bombers in 1980 and a season in the Melbourne reserves in 1982 before heading back to the bush. He had a decorated amateur career that included premiership success with Horsham and Wimmera Football League best-and-fairest awards. But Lighty definitely had an impact when it comes to our family.

Lighty's birthday was a good old-fashioned gathering, draining a few beers and chatting around the bonfire. That night I met a friend of the Light family, a cheerful, pretty young woman named Jan McCorkell.

We discovered that there was a bit of an overlap in our friendship circles back in Melbourne. Jan was a keen netballer and regularly used to head out on a Thursday evening with her East Burwood teammates to the New Boundary Hotel in East Melbourne, one of my mates' regular haunts. 'But all the netty girls think the footballers are up themselves, so we steer clear of them,' she chuckled. There was an easy rapport between us and although it was not the proverbial arrow from Cupid, she definitely caught my eye.

A few weeks later, after my knee had crumpled, Jan came to visit me in hospital. She maintains that it was because she felt sorry for me. I dropped some goofy line about how she was the tenth girl who had come in to the ward that day to show some me sympathy and, typically, I laughed longer and louder at my own joke than the intended audience did. Fortunately, she took the wisecrack to be more lame humour than arrogance and we agreed to catch up once I was back on my feet.

We were both studying at the northern fringe of the city at the time: Jan was doing a Bachelor of Education at Melbourne State College, just up the road from RMIT. I suggested a lunch for our first date and came up with the brainwave of a counter meal at the Oxford Scholar Hotel in Swanston Street. You would be hard-pressed to pick a less romantic venue. Dark and dingy, the pub's menu only extended to sausages, chops and a handful of other dishes that all seemed to involved kidneys, liver or grilled meat. Subliminally I reckon I was testing her out to see if she was the sort of woman who would run a mile from a bloke who would invite her out for offal. Despite the venue, the company was great, we chatted for ages and from that inauspicious beginning we began going out together.

Looking back, I gave Jan plenty of reasons to break up with me in those early months, to turn around and say, 'Up yours, mate'. Initially I didn't go to great lengths to build the relationship. I was a selfish 20-year-old footballer caught up in my own aspirations and I didn't budge far from my comfort zone to warm to her friends or her interests. Jan was the one who made the effort to keep our bond strong and I am forever grateful that she did.

★

During the final months of 1981, as the indignation of having my first knee reconstruction smouldered inside me, the ever-unconventional Kevin Sheedy added an unexpected dimension to my rehabilitation. He announced that the club captaincy would shift to my shoulders from 23-year-old ruckman Simon Madden, who had led the club for the past two seasons. I didn't know the appointment was coming. To that point in league history, only two footballers had ever been appointed captain at the age of 20: North Melbourne's David Dench and Fitzroy's Haydn Bunton Sr.

I suspect that part of Sheedy's reasoning was that he wanted a player who was patently ambitious and determined for the club to rise above the mediocrity that had settled over Windy Hill during the past decade. He was looking for an agent of change – generational change – and was trying to send a message to some of the established players who enjoyed a good time socially and were not necessarily fussed about making the slight changes required to become elite. Sheeds would have thought, *I'm going past all of you reprobates and I'm going with a guy who's intense and driven to be the best, and he'll shake the place up a bit.* He didn't give me any advice on how to handle the role; he would have just thought I could work it out for myself.

When I decided to write this book, I asked Sheeds his ratio-nale for appointing me captain for the 1982 season. 'There were a bunch of cowboys there, some real scallywags, but I thought you could be the sheriff on the horse,' he said. 'I thought you could just go "crunch" and shake things up.' Sheeds said his other motive was to put a bit of a rocket up Simon Madden: 'He was just rolling along, and I wanted to get some emotion into him.'

That I would miss the start of the season because of the knee injury didn't bother Sheeds. 'I'd done my knee as a young bloke and come back,' he said. 'The only reservation I had was appointing you ahead of your brother Terry, because I knew that wouldn't go down well in an Irish-Catholic family.'

At the time, I viewed my busted knee as a speed hump on the road towards leading the Bombers onto the field at some stage in 1982. I knew that Hawthorn's Barry Rowlings had missed the 1978 premiership after doing his knee in July. At age 28, he was traded to Richmond and was back playing on the MCG in round 5 of the next season, on his way to winning the 1979 Tigers' best-and-fairest award. The following year he was a part of their premiership team. I had no reason to doubt that would be my path.

Instead of just taking some time out back on the farm and easing my way through rehabilitation, I resolved to return in a similar timeframe to Rowlings. The full-length plaster cast was sawn off by November and I spoke to the medicos about the possibility of an early season comeback: my knee would not be at full strength, they cautioned, but the timeframe was plausible. To a young captain desperate to get back on the field, that was as good as a rubber stamp on an accelerated timeline.

Unable to have an impact on the team as a player, I felt it was important to exert influence as a leader. But in truth, I was not a great captain; I wasn't even a great teammate.

On the football field, I preferred to let my actions speak louder than words. I had always played in an emotionless state. Maybe it was something to do with my time in cricket as an opening batsman, but one of my strengths was my ability to concentrate and not get distracted; to get into the zone. I found that playing football with emotion was both energy-sapping and distracting, and prided myself on being able to concentrate over the duration of a two-hour game – and that was back in the days when you rarely came off the ground for a spell on the bench. I didn't get angry when someone whacked me, didn't get upset by umpiring decisions. The footballer whose game I most admired was Carlton's unflappable defender Bruce Doull. I related more to the Zen-like style of Björn Borg on the tennis court than to John McEnroe feeding off tension and conflict to elevate his game.

Now as captain, a long-term injury meant that I was in the problematic position of not being able to lead by example. I was sitting out most of the team's training time in favour of physiotherapy, swimming and gym sessions. At that time rehabilitation was very basic and boring, with injured players generally just trying to find ways to occupy their time. And while I may not have shown much outward emotion, inside I was wrestling feelings of frustration and irritation.

Ego and a desire to influence the group told me that I needed to use words in the absence of actions. As skipper I became more outspoken, challenging teammates at training or in social settings to pull their finger out. At 18, when I had been dubbed 'Rowdy', it would bother me when teammates showed what

I considered to be signs that they were anything less than fully committed to chasing success. But back then, I would say nothing. Now, just a few years later and feeling enabled by a position of authority, I went from thinking it to saying it. And that was very unwise.

Everyone loved Paul Vander Haar, a prodigiously talented footballer who at the age of 23 had already shown a capacity to change the outcome of matches. He was a bit of a rogue who loved a drink and cadging a cigarette from the dressing-room doorman after a game, and I remember telling him, 'Come on, mate, that will get you and us nowhere.' He didn't take it well.

There were other senior players who struck me as simply happy to go with the flow, guys who could be a bit offhand about how they approached training. Our routine was to warm up with two laps of the oval and when I saw a group of experienced players pulling up after ambling one lap, I had a crack at them. They fair dinkum looked at me like I had a square head.

There was nothing tactful in the way I challenged teammates; I thought that was the way to change the culture of the place, but it was an emotionally unintelligent approach and there were better ways to go about it. I made the incorrect assumption that I needed to push people rather than pull them along with me. I didn't think to put myself in their shoes – I look back now and wonder what the hell I was thinking.

I'd captained teams, but I didn't know how to lead. And more importantly, I wasn't prepared to acknowledge it. At that time there were no leadership development programs on offer, it was just a matter of working it out as you went along.

I was a classic example of a young fella operating in the extremes – striving – and not understanding the dualities of human nature. My method was inappropriate and immature. Over time, I would come to understand that 'honesty is the best policy' is more nuanced than it sounds. You have to be equipped with the means to deliver honesty in the right manner. With direct feedback, it is not about how you think you've delivered the message; it is about how the listener hears it. Instead of justifying the way you delivered a home truth by saying you had the best intentions, you are better judging its success by the outcome.

I like to think I'm fairly smart, but I'm not as smart as I think. Sometimes being smart is admitting you don't know something and letting others show you the way to the answers, and I had to learn that the hard way. In some ways I'd grown up quickly, determined not to show any vulnerability, subscribing to the theory that 'if it's to be, it's up to me'. That attitude had stood me in good stead, made me pretty resilient, but I needed to acknowledge that life isn't a one-size-fits-all affair. Not everyone was an intense unit like me. I needed to heed Carl Jung's wisdom that 'the shoe that fits one person, pinches another'.

As a player and briefly as Essendon captain, my ego told me not to show vulnerability. Now I know it takes courage to be vulnerable, and while I still struggle with this, I've slowly wised up a bit with age.

★

As much as Kevin Sheedy gambled on a change of captaincy in the hope of recalibrating the players' collective approach, I am sure he was also curious to see how his rising star would cope. Would this serious young insect soar or stumble under the added responsibility?

Sheeds is a bit of a maverick, a mad professor. He has always been a great ideas man and right from the outset was a lateral-thinking coach. His style was to be unorthodox and to take risks, and he could be impulsive and avoid structure, which could frustrate those who worked alongside him. Sheeds could infuriate the Essendon staff by skipping from one idea to the next; he could latch on to an idea and ride it through all manner of antagonism and then simply drop it and move on. Like many big-ideas people, he wasn't so great on the execution; it was often left to other people to run around and make the ideas a reality.

For a structured computer-science kind of thinker such as myself, who relied on logic, planning and process, Sheedy's mercurial approach could be challenging. He would be at A and aspiring to go straight to F, whereas I needed to understand how to work through B, C, D and E to get there.

Personally, being exposed to Sheedy's way of operating was a timely opportunity to see how someone completely different from me went about things. His insatiable curiosity, willingness to consider new concepts and push the boundaries meant that his mind was always open, and in turn that gradually opened my mind to the possibility that there were other ways to approach not just football but life itself.

Kevin Sheedy is an enigma and it is almost impossible to get a read on where he sits between the extremes. He could be scarily serious, but he also had a mischievous twinkle in his eye and a sharp sense of humour. He enjoyed nothing better than a scrap, but often avoided direct confrontation, leaving it to his right-hand man, chairman of selectors Brian Donohoe, to deliver bad news to players. Sheeds could be ruthless, cutting adrift several Essendon fan favourites when they still looked to have some fuel in the tank, but was also a romantic who loved playing footballers who were a feel-good story: bringing Paul Salmon and John Barnes back to the club, coaxing Tim Watson out of retirement, recruiting the sons of former players and playing us four Daniher brothers in the same team in 1990.

I once asked Brian Donohoe what made a great coach. He replied pragmatically, 'Winning a lot.' Sheeds did plenty of that, but his genius extends far beyond his win-loss record. He is one of Australian football's legendary innovators, warriors, dreamers and ambassadors. He operated in the extreme when it came to his love of Australian football, and the game is infinitely better for it.

Sheedy was an inner-suburbs boy who grew up in the southern shadows of the MCG, selling newspapers on the streets and relying on his wits and a touch of cunning to make his way in life. He left De La Salle College after Year 10 to take up a plumbing apprenticeship, but always retained a thirst for learning along the way. He relished any opportunity to travel and to experience unfamiliar surroundings and became a voracious reader. When others were interested in what was happening, his mind wanted to know *why* it was happening.

I'm not saying that I didn't pick up a few canny traits growing up on the farm, but my regimented experience of education led to a vastly different mindset to Sheedy's. Being coached by him demonstrated the value of being curious, of challenging the status quo and looking for answers. Where I am generally impatient, Sheeds believes that everyone has a story to tell and that those stories are worth hearing. He has no concept of time and he is generally running late, which can leave people thinking he is being rude, but he's actually just caught up in his own – or someone else's – world.

In essence, being around Sheeds was a vibrant reminder about the difference between acquiring knowledge and gaining wisdom. I had always considered myself someone who was prepared to stop and think about life, and who had tried to learn as much as I could to help me make sense of the world. But sometimes it doesn't hurt to have a prompt to remind us to be more open and inquisitive about how things work, and to not be so black and white in our thinking.

The other great certainty with Sheedy was that he was never predictable. Having appointed me – the serious and conscientious 20-year-old – as the club's captain for the 1982 season, he then turned to Ron Andrews – one of the rough and ready cowboys and among the oldest players on our list – to captain the team on game day in my absence.

As it turned out, the fundamental lesson I learned as a young captain was that my way was not the only way – and that my approach to the role wasn't working. I didn't have any real impact. But before I could consider how to reconstruct my leadership style, the issue was taken off the plate.

Circumstances would dictate that I could park these issues in the short term, but they'd resurface later in a different guise. But I'd be better equipped to handle them next time, with the benefit of hindsight, which in its own way can equate to a kind of wisdom – if you look backwards you can find answers.

All you can do is barrack for the coin to land on heads most of the time

When things are going along pretty well, we like to take credit for achievements and claim them as the result of our hard work, our intelligence, our talent. Our sense of self-importance doesn't like to acknowledge luck and good fortune until we hit a few wobbles, and it's then *all* Bad Luck's fault. Yet if you reflect on what's happened in your life, you realise that a lot of things – a big chunk, in fact – are simply a matter of luck or fortunate timing.

In life, we all get a share of bad luck, some more than others. The farmer can't control the weather. The mother-of-three can't control the drunk-driver in another car. The coach can't control the players' injuries. But wisdom is about taking luck out of the equation. It's about understanding that some adversity is self-inflicted, which is within your control. And it's also about appreciating all the *good* luck you've had.

Inevitably all of us will face setbacks and hardship – whatever label you want to give these life events, they come in many shapes

111

and sizes – and how we view the severity is often connected to our particular stage of life. A big dose of bad luck with a knee injury seems devastating to a young man who believes he has the world at his feet. But that becomes a mere blip on the radar – *What was the big deal?* – when the same man is faced with a terminal illness thirty years later.

The darkest shade of adversity is grief, the deep, wrenching sorrow of loss. Grief rarely gives us any warning, it pounces on us. It arrives in an instant: a blocked artery, a missed stop sign, a coward's punch, a split-second error of judgement. Grief usually just jumps out and mugs us. It is acute.

We don't choose grief, or setbacks, or any kind of adversity, but how we deal with these episodes often defines our lives, more so than how we handle the good times and the successes. You don't necessarily know it at the time, but you find out what you're made of. You test your beliefs. You build up resilience. You learn to handle the bad and appreciate the good.

We grow through what we go through.

★

If I'd thought about it at the time, I probably would have said I'd copped a bit of bad luck, doing my knee. I was optimistic about taking the field again in 1982 – in fact, it didn't occur to me to think otherwise.

Initially Essendon set a target for me to return to football in round 4, but later pushed that date back about a month. We ramped up the competitive work at training: on the Thursday before the round 7 match against Collingwood, I roped in teammate Kevin Walsh for a contested-marking drill. We jostled and shoved under each incoming kick and the knee felt strong. After half a dozen contests, I was convinced I was about ready to play again.

'One more,' I shouted as I flicked the ball to the kicker, jogging back to stand shoulder to shoulder with Kevin. As the Sherrin came spinning in, I went to nudge him under the ball and as I put my weight on my right knee, it just went 'clunk' and buckled. I swore in disbelief, knowing full well as I trudged off the oval that I had done my knee again.

What I experienced was an acute sense of loss, because playing VFL football was my dream. In fact, it was more than a dream, it felt like I was almost there. Imagine the thing you wanted most dangling in front of you, so close you could just about touch it, and then it's snatched away. It knocks you for six.

This time I knew only too well what lay ahead of me: more surgery, more crutches, more lonely hours in rehab, more grind without measurable reward, and more doubts that I would ever return as the player I aspired to be. Heartache has many guises, and at times it can be difficult to appreciate the difference between what we will later look back on as adversity and what is a more enduring grief. This was certainly not loss on the level of losing a loved one or being told that you have a terminal illness, but nevertheless it felt like I'd been tossed into the washing machine on the cycle of grief, although the stages were not as simple as the markings on a dial.

After my initial disbelief that I was facing my second torn ACL in less than a year came anger about the unfairness of it all. I had some dark moments and the rest of the Essendon players – who were upbeat about a season that looked destined to include finals football – would not have wanted to spend too much time in my company. Terry reflected later, 'You knew you were in a spot of strife, so you were a bit cranky from time to time. You were burning deep down because you'd set the bar pretty high.'

The bargaining stage brought with it the need to look for someone to blame. Blaming yourself and feeling shame for causing your own situation is a tough lot, and instead I wanted to blame the club for allowing me to come back too soon. Surely they knew that I was pushing the limits and that an abridged rehabilitative program meant there were questions about whether the joint was strong enough to cope with the rigours of football. At 21 and with a decade of football ahead of me, couldn't they have just told me to take 12 months to get myself right? The problem was that I only wanted to hear about the possibilities of a rapid comeback, not the risks.

Predictably, there were also periods of sorrow and anxiety. I felt lost, detached from people. Something that all of us need to understand is that as we work our way through grief, sometimes it's OK not to be OK. That can be difficult for elite athletes to accept, because they are essentially self-centred, which creates an all-or-nothing environment: everything is rosy when they are succeeding, but there is a void, an emptiness, when it all goes wrong. Managing a long-term injury is a lonely journey and you don't feel part of the team. You miss out on a lot of the banter, the camaraderie and the shared experiences of competing.

Fortunately, I had dependable and supportive people around me at the football club and beyond it. At that time, I was boarding with Peter and Lorraine Bateman, two big-hearted Essendon supporters who were like second parents to me and the many other players who subsequently lived in their Oak Park home. There was the unconditional love of my family, felt most keenly when I was best man at Terry's marriage to Gaynor that June (we had to send for a new pair of suit pants to accommodate the full-length plaster cast on my right leg).

But with time, I began to hear opportunity knocking. While I was sidelined, I spent more time around the coaching staff, occasionally sitting in the coaches' box on game day, observing their methods and enjoying a bit of the analytical side of footy. It gave me a greater understanding of the game and allowed me to consider the possibility of getting involved in coaching one day.

But first and foremost, I was determined to have another shot at resuming my football career down the track.

★

I write about the grief associated with football injuries, but looking back, it's simply adversity, experienced as a very sharp loss at the time. In all honesty, I've had precious little acute grief to process throughout my journey. The way I see it, I've had more than my fair share of good luck and fortune.

For a start, growing up on a remote farm, where there's a lot of potential for deadly hazards – it's a wonder we all survived. As kids, we used to run down to the dam unsupervised for a swim and at one stage or another, I'm sure we all pulled each other out of danger. And I can clearly remember when I was a young man helping Dad fix a water pump down at the shearing shed, and he yelled out, 'Righto, plug her in.' As I jammed the power cord into the socket, electricity charged through his body sending him reeling. Instinctively I yanked out the lead and Dad got up, dusted himself off and muttered, 'Hmm, better fix that.'

The point is that serious trouble was only ever inches away and we were lucky that grief never paid us a visit on the farm. Although I did get a letter during my time at boarding school about a time when grief poked its head through the front gate.

To catch the school bus to St Joseph's, we kids needed to get to a corner that was about a kilometre down the dirt road (since renamed Danihers Lane) from the end of our long driveway. When we were young, we would ride our bikes down and leave them in a tin shed that Dad had built. But when Terry reached high school, he used to cram us into a battered old green Holden ute and drive to and from the bus stop.

One afternoon after school it began to hail as a wild storm came sweeping across the paddocks. Terry told the others – Estelle, Anthony, Dorothy, Colleen and Chris – to take shelter in the ute and he'd bring it around to the shed. They all piled into the cabin and just as Terry was letting out the clutch, a huge gum tree came crashing across the roof of the cabin. Had it fallen 30 or 40 centimetres to the left, it would have crushed the lot of them. As it was, Terry was pinned against the steering wheel and Colleen, kneeling behind the bench seat looking out the rear window, was trapped under the roof. Anthony clambered out through the windscreen and dashed across the paddock to get help from the nearest farmhouse, the McGranes, while Estelle, who had a gashed foot, scrambled back towards our farm. My father, two uncles and Tom McGrane managed to cut off the steering wheel to free Terry, but they had to wait for a crane to arrive from Ungarie to carefully lift the fallen eucalypt, which was resting only centimetres from Colleen's head, before she was safe. Miraculously, all six kids emerged from the ordeal with no more than a few stitches and bruises.

That's why I maintain that I have been charmed: wrecked knees, being sacked as an AFL coach, being diagnosed with MND – at the time these things happened, they affected me deeply but they're all inward-looking hardships, all about self. Worse than all of these instances was the time Jan had an irregular spot on her back examined and was told it was a melanoma. My mind was racing about life without her; I was thinking, *Shit, I'm going to lose my girl.* Luckily a doctor could cut it out. The wait to get the all clear felt like forever and I was as anxious as I have ever felt in my life.

Hardship is easier to deal with when it revolves around your own adversity, rather than around your nearest and dearest. That is why the most difficult part of my MND diagnosis is not the knowledge that it will ultimately kill me, it is contemplating the grief that it will bring to my family.

★

In more recent years, as circumstances have allowed me a less frenetic lifestyle, I've savoured the freedom to get back to Ungarie more regularly to visit Mum and Dad at the farm.

On these occasions, Dad and I would often putter around the property in the old ute, discussing life. Dad had struggled with a few heart problems as well as gout, and his feet didn't work too well, which meant he grappled with lifting his foot from the brake pedal to the accelerator. 'Listen, son,' he would say, 'you either rot from the head down or the feet up. I'm rotting, but at least I've still got my marbles and I'm only rotting from the feet up.'

In between those visits, I would phone from Melbourne but the conversations were always a bit tricky. The phone line was usually a bit faint, and in his old age Dad struggled to hear, while MND meant I struggled to speak clearly. Basically, I couldn't speak and he couldn't hear but other than that, we were fine! Often, after persevering for a while, Dad would end up calling Mum over to the phone and we'd conduct a three-way conversation where she would relay questions and answers between Dad and myself.

In April 2019, I rang the farm at lunchtime, and, after our usual struggle, I asked Dad to put Mum on the line. 'She's over at the dam taking a look at the water pump,' he said. 'There's something wrong with it – the damn thing always seems to be playing up these days.'

It frustrated him that, at 90, he could no longer wander around the place, tootling from the house to the paddock or the shed, fixing things. Mum was still reasonably mobile.

About 90 minutes later, my phone rang. The caller ID showed it was my older sister, Estelle, who lives up at Wagga. I thought, *Beauty, looking forward to having a chat with Stell.*

She was distraught, but somehow managed to let me know that Dad had died.

The news smacked me in the face. I just slumped in my chair. I looked across at a photo of Dad on the bookshelf and wept and wept.

There had been an accident and the ute had ended up in the dam. My father had spent his whole life fretting about rain and irrigation and now, in the middle of a drought, he had drowned in the only decent drink of water to be found on the farm.

As I sat there wiping at the tears, I remembered a conversation we'd had during one of my visits. I'd asked if he and Mum could ever live anywhere else in their twilight years. 'I'll never move away, boy,' he had chuckled. 'I was born here, and I'll die here. Hopefully with my boots on.'

If we live long enough, genuine grief visits us all. With adversity we can find a way to move on, but with utter grief we never totally get over it, we just move forward.

With Dad, the disbelief was not so much that he died at the age of 90, but more at the way he had died. There was no anger or blame or bargaining around his death, but the desolation of his loss was felt deeply. It was raw and, in a way, I had trouble accepting that he was not still alive. There are moments that instinctively trigger a thought to tell Dad something – a mention of grain shortages, a footy result, a family achievement or a news item about new farming techniques – but they just as quickly deliver a sharp reminder that there will be no more chatting to the old man.

The first step in acceptance was the finality of attending his funeral. But I don't feel I will ever fully let the grief go for the rest of my days – I just hope that, in time, it will express itself less through sadness and more through the warmth and fondness of memories.

★

I've talked about the five stages in the cycle of grief: denial, anger, bargaining, depression and, finally, acceptance. This model was put forward by psychiatrist Elisabeth Kübler-Ross in 1969 and became a popular way to understand bereavement and other forms of acute grief. More recently, it has been accepted that there is variation to how we grieve, and different schools of thought have emerged about whether we should wait for grief to shift on its own or do something to initiate the process.

All forms of grief are heartfelt, but some are more heartfelt than others.

It doesn't work to tell people to snap out of it – people need to deal with anguish at their own pace. A 15-year-old girl will grieve after being dumped by her boyfriend and, in that moment, her anguish may be felt every bit as acutely as is that felt by a 21-year-old footballer facing his second knee reconstruction. She needs time and support to move through the cycle in her own way, and hopefully her character and attitude allow her to bounce back fairly swiftly.

As a father, when my kids went through tough times, I resisted the urge to try to solve their problems for them. Parents need to strike a balance between being supportive and being overprotective, and sometimes we need to accept that heart-ache is part of the bigger picture of life and helps our children learn and grow.

When we were dealing with the death of our beloved 14-year-old family dog, there wasn't a lot of disbelief, because Tully was old and struggling to go for her daily walk. The blame didn't go any further than, *Why didn't I give her a big cuddle before I went off to work this morning?* A loss like this is not going to take as long to work through the stages as it would the unexpected loss of a close relative. That's not to say there won't be genuine sadness, but any anxiety or depression might not be as enduring.

How grief is handled also depends on the personalities of the people involved. Some can catastrophise a situation and find disaster in even minor stumbling blocks, like hosting a dinner party where the chocolate mousse didn't work. Others find it difficult to ever release their hold on grief and allow it to fester and take on other forms, such as bitterness and revenge. Theirs is a life-lasting grieving process, and it's not healthy. There's the ripple effect to consider too: it's not only your behaviours and actions that cause your own suffering to continue, but it goes beyond you. It can ripple for generations.

Then there is the grief around failure. The irrefutable truth is that if we seek to accomplish things in life, there will be times when we fall short, and sometimes it will be through no particular fault of our own.

Some people rebound from failure more quickly than others because they are prepared to regard failure as a learning opportunity, whereas others see failure as irrevocable and grieve over it. This is where it comes back to attitude. It is up to *you* whether you're open to new opportunities after your plans go wrong, knowing you might fall on your face again. If you fall over while having a crack, hopefully you learn from that, and have another crack down the road.

It's not a question of *if* there will be tough times, it's just when and how often. Real sorrow will exist at some stage in all our lives. Failure and loss are on the other side of the coin from happiness and success. Sure, hard work, talent, resilience and courage are key ingredients to making a good life, but you still need a bit of luck to go your way.

In that regard, all you can do is barrack for the coin to land on heads most of the time, not tails.

★

I felt personal loss keenly when Essendon was knocked out of the 1982 finals by North Melbourne, the Bombers' third elimination-final loss in four years. I was glad to have the distraction of my studies at RMIT, which was probably healthier for me than constantly thinking about my knee rehabilitation program.

After that 1982 season, Sheeds called Terry aside. 'You're the new captain,' he said. Terry maintains that he told Sheedy to 'go and get someone else, I'm just trying to get a kick. Get Madden'. Sheedy replied, 'You're the captain.' When Terry asked his coach what was expected of him in the role, Sheedy said, 'Just be yourself.' And what if media wanted to talk to him, Terry asked. 'Don't worry, I'll tell you what to say,' Sheeds replied.

Terry took on the captaincy in 1983. He was a good leader, a good nurturer and people followed him because of it. I'm not sure they would have followed me. Never leading the Bombers onto the field as skipper didn't bother me, I was more perturbed by missing out on opportunities to play well and show on-field leadership in finals. When Terry took on the role, I put to him a proposition: he would help lighten me up a bit and I would prod him to be 'just a little bit serious'. He said, 'Mate, I'll do it my way.'

In that 1983 season, with the Bombers entrenched in the top five, I began to step up my running and training loads, hoping to return in time for finals. But my knee became swollen and sore and the decision was made to defer any comeback until 1984.

I was at the MCG to watch as the team, captained by Terry, made it through to the 1983 Grand Final against Hawthorn. I wasn't the only Essendon player unlucky to miss the match, and was sitting it out alongside guys like Bill Duckworth, Ron Andrews, Paul Salmon and Frank Dunnell. It was difficult to stomach the then record 83-point loss.

Kevin Sheedy was filthy afterwards. Speaking at that evening's function at the Southern Cross ballroom, he didn't hold back, describing the loss as probably his most disappointing day in football. 'Look, if it doesn't hurt tonight then Essendon will never win another premiership.' He told the team that if he saw anyone smiling, they would not be at the club in 1984. 'I don't want you to enjoy tonight.' There was no danger of that. I was terribly low that evening, knowing that the club was hurting and that I had not been able to make any contribution.

Up at Ungarie that Christmas, I did my running on the more forgiving freshly ploughed paddocks while Terry and Anthony, who was now playing for the Sydney Swans, pounded the dirt roads. Part of my training was learning to jump off my left leg because the right one had no power, no spring. When we returned to Windy Hill, I joined in the kicking and marking drills straight away, but I wasn't able to start back on the competitive work until just before the 1984 practice matches.

Finally, the time arrived to test my knee out in a game – I was scheduled to take the field for one half of a reserves practice match against the Swans at Lake Oval in early March. Afterwards, a few journalists asked how I went. 'I was nervous as hell, but all I wanted to do was to be able to walk off the ground,' I told them. The season proper began with me playing a reserves match against St Kilda at Moorabbin, and as the game unfolded, I could sense that the joint was a bit proppy. Test results revealed cartilage damage and came with advice to have minor surgery and spend another few months on the sidelines.

I was beginning to wonder whether a return to VFL football was just not meant to be.

The Sterling Cup grand final of 1984 in July was the first of the season, and saw Essendon take on the Sydney Swans in the decider of the night series at Waverley Park. Terry lined up for the Bombers and Anthony for the Swans, and they both featured in peculiar incidents at either end of the match.

At the opening bounce, Terry gave away a free kick for clouting Swans rover Jamie Siddons, who would later become better known for his 16-year first-class cricket career. Then, at the 30-minute mark of the final quarter, with Essendon leading by 51 points, Anthony had a free kick at centre-half-forward when many of the 30,000 fans decided to swarm on to the oval. After the masses were eventually cleared, with the help of mounted police, the game only went for about another minute with no change to the scores. As captain, Terry accepted the night premiership trophy – unusually, presented on a podium in the changing rooms – and must have put it down somewhere. The Sterling Cup was stolen and never returned.

Four days later I made another comeback, this time in a reserves match against Footscray at Western Oval. Sheeds reckoned I had a smile as big as Luna Park when I walked off unscathed at the final siren. Three more reserves matches followed and by the time I was named best afield in a reserves match against St Kilda at Windy Hill in round 20, a VFL return was on the cards. But with the top-of-the-ladder senior team heading to the Sydney Cricket Ground to play the Swans that Sunday, the club didn't want to risk the interstate flight so I played in another reserves match on the Saturday at Lake Oval.

In the second quarter, I went to spoil in a marking contest and one of the Swans players came across my body, dislocating my shoulder. Our doctor, Bruce Reid, tried to put the shoulder back in, but my muscles, tense with the extreme pain, wouldn't allow the joint to slip back into place. The medicos even lay me facedown on the rubdown table and tried pulling on my arm as it dangled over the edge, but to no avail. Eventually I had to get it done under a local anaesthetic at the Alfred Hospital. My season was over. When Terry drove me home from hospital that evening, I looked out the car window and thought, *Bugger this, I don't know if I can come up again.*

Essendon was flying and heading to finals again and it burned inside knowing that once again I wasn't going to be there.

At the age of 22, I did not have the life experience, let alone the wisdom, to realise that what I was experiencing was the tribulations of adversity, which build character and in time can bring us to hope.

Here's what I know now. I learnt in my early twenties what other people work out at 45. They go, 'I've worked all my life on my career, is this it? Is this all there is?' Or they get retrenched at 50, and suddenly realise they've given their life to something that is an illusion. They wonder, *Have I wasted my life?*

I was lucky, I got the lesson early. Shit happens, so deal with it as best you can. And don't forget to count your blessings.

10

It's often in the darkest skies we see the brightest stars

There were several things I enjoyed when visiting new friends' homes as a young teenager. One was checking out whether my mate's mum was as good a cook as my mum and the other was checking out what was hanging on the back of their toilet door. I know what you're thinking . . . *He's a bit of a weirdo!* Think of it this way: the quotes and aphorisms now posted on Instagram used to hang on the dunny door where you couldn't avoid noticing them.

The popular ones I remember from the 70s were Rudyard Kipling's 'If' and Theodore Roosevelt's 'It is not the critic who counts'. Another was the Serenity Prayer:

> God, grant me the serenity to accept the things I cannot change,
> The courage to change the things I can,
> And the wisdom to know the difference.

This prayer by American theologian Reinhold Niebuhr didn't win a place in our bathroom because Niebuhr was Protestant rather than Catholic, but the sentiment slotted in comfortably alongside my parents' values. For me, the second line is where to focus.

Whenever we are mired in despair, the crucial point comes when we reach a level of acceptance about the situation – 'it is what it is' – and we courageously decide to move forward, looking to commence what I have come to call the 'cycle of hope'. Our steps towards hope will be a gradual ascent, but at least we are looking ahead, which allows us to uncover opportunities. We might have to look hard to find that opportunity, but once we do, our trajectory rises sharply.

We all know it's much easier to destroy than it is to construct. I'm a big believer that most of the bad things in life – the ones that plunge us into despair – invariably happen suddenly, while the good things in life take time, often a long, long time. You don't wake up one day and start thriving. However, the first sign you are heading in this direction is when you are open to the idea that opportunity might be out there, somewhere.

Once you identify an opportunity, you can work towards it with an optimistic and positive attitude. You can then call on the characteristics of resilience and persistence to turn your hope into something, rather than giving up when you hit a hurdle. Hope is about the future.

Whether you think there's opportunity or you think there's none, either way you'll be right.

★

On 29 September 1984, I sat in the stand on grand final day at the MCG, watching Essendon take on a Hawthorn team that had trounced them the previous year.

There was no despair for me that day, just the euphoria of watching the Essendon boys show incredible grit, physicality and character to come from behind and power to the 1984 flag with nine goals in the final quarter. They had trailed by four goals at three-quarter time, but this was now a team that believed it could win, coached by a man who would never concede defeat. And Kevin Sheedy's optimism and open-mindedness were definitive that day: his approach allowed him to have the courage at half-time to unexpectedly shift defenders into attack and forwards into the backline, in an era when such flexibility within the team was relatively uncommon.

There is a sense of remoteness from the premiership experience for injured players, and I was no exception, but overriding that was elation over the long-awaited triumph – the first since 1965 – and also a feeling of relief that the players and staff now had a well-deserved reward for their years of toil and commitment. Watching TD, as Terry was universally known, lift that 1984 premiership cup on the dais after the match is a highlight of my time at Windy Hill. There he was, my easygoing 'she'll be right' brother – the one I kicked the footy with in the paddocks, dreaming one day we might both get to play on the MCG – actually holding up the premiership cup. I was thinking, *You've come along way, mate, and I'm bloody proud of you. Well done, brother.*

That evening at the Southern Cross ballroom, the players witnessed a vastly different Kevin Sheedy to the angry man who had spoken at the same function 12 months earlier. He directed all of the credit and praise towards the playing group. And during his speech, he threw in a line about how he 'hoped and prayed to see Neale Daniher back playing football for Essendon again soon'.

And so the door swung open on the opportunity for another cautious comeback from injury. I knew it would be a long and testing trek back, but that acceptance was the start of coming back up the curve and paved the way to choosing the cycle of hope.

★

There was no time for 'poor bugger me' thinking that summer: Jan and I were preparing for our wedding, to be held on the Australia Day weekend of 1985.

Six months earlier, when Jan was teaching art at Trafalgar High School in Gippsland, I had taken her out for dinner in Essendon during the midyear school holidays. In my mind, I had gone to a lot of effort. I had booked a table at an Italian restaurant – one of those candlelit jobs that Dad had warned me against – and I had spruced myself up, put on a nice shirt. Jan's enduring memory of the night is of my very matter-of-fact proposal: 'Do you want to get married?' She replied, 'Yes, of course', and so we were engaged. I hadn't even brought along a ring, because I didn't know if she'd say yes. Jan's other lasting recollection is of the couple sitting at the table next to us having a massive barney that ended with the woman sobbing loudly. Jan later told me that she thought to herself, *Oh dear, is that what marriage is all about?*

When it came to planning our wedding, the logistics of the ceremony itself were complicated. With Jan's family heavily involved in the Uniting Church and my family staunchly Catholic, we knew some diplomacy would be required. Reading this today, my grandkids would be thinking, *What's the big deal here, Pops?* But the Catholic versus Protestant mistrust is centuries old and was felt more acutely in my grandparents' day. My grandfather still hadn't forgiven Oliver Cromwell! That bad feeling spilled over into my parents' generation, and I think if Mum had any say in it, she would have preferred all of us to marry Catholics. But that wasn't happening. I was marrying the granddaughter of a mix of English-Irish-Protestant stock.

Out of respect to both our parents, we tried to find a middle ground. The choice of venue and celebrant was going to be tricky, so we decided to involve both a priest and a minister in the service. Our wedding ceremony was held at a fairly sterile non-denominational chapel at Monash University. In trying to avoid offending anyone, we pleased no one. Fortunately, everyone had a cracking time at our wedding reception in Elsternwick.

It wasn't until I walked my youngest daughter, Bec, down the aisle to marry Drew at a rowing club on the banks of the Yarra in 2017 that anyone from the Daniher family was married outside a church.

My view was, 'Darling, you get married wherever you want to.'

★

Essendon's 1985 pre-season training was as gruelling as anything the players had experienced, driven by Sheeds' determination to put the 1984 flag behind us and focus on the next challenge. The club medicos were careful to ensure I didn't push my body too hard, and it was evident that I was going to have my work cut out for me forcing my way into the league's most powerful team. I had never been a particularly quick player but had an ability to create space for myself on the field. Now, with a banged-up knee, I found that my athleticism had dropped away and so had my confidence in jumping for the ball. I felt as though I was only 70 per cent of the footballer I had been in 1981.

For the first two months of 1985, I rebuilt my game in the reserves. Although I was named as one of five players in contention for the two interchange spots in the senior team to play Melbourne in round 9, I didn't attend the Thursday evening team meeting, assuming I was not in the 20. The next day, Sheeds invited me in for a cup of tea and confirmed that I would be playing – my first senior game in three years and eight months.

I was nervous on the day. I had become accustomed to the earlier timeslot of the curtain-raiser games, so I woke up early and had to just sit around. I told *The Sun*'s Lou Richards: 'It was like waiting for the executioner.'

That Saturday afternoon, the Windy Hill crowd – comfortable in the knowledge Essendon was trouncing the Demons – took great pleasure in cheering every time I laid my hands on the ball. It was a wonderful relief to be back.

Now my aspirations had shifted, and my primary focus had become retaining a place in a team that looked capable of winning another premiership. In an interview with broadcaster Tim Lane, I conceded: 'With the body the way it is you can't make too many long-term goals. In the back of your mind, you just can't help but feeling sometimes, *Is this the last time that I'm going to run onto the ground?* In a way that's good, because you play that little bit harder, whereas other players, who are 22 or 23, think they can play forever. And that was the case when I was 22. I used to think, *Isn't this game great, we can go out and play footy and I'll be back on next week.* But that isn't the case now, if I don't walk off tomorrow, it could be all over.'

Over the next month I held my own as Essendon recorded four more comfortable victories. Next up was a midweek Foster's Cup quarter-final against Norwood in Adelaide. Coming off a win over Fitzroy on the boggy Windy Hill ground, I ran out onto Football Park a few days later wearing boots with long screw-in stops to make sure I kept my feet, but the surface was much firmer and I should really have been wearing moulded-sole boots. A couple of minutes into the match, I went to leap at a marking contest and my left foot planted while the rest of my body lurched in the opposite direction. My leg twisted and I fell to the ground clutching my left knee, the good one.

Knowing I had done some sort of damage, I put my hand up to signal to the interchange bench and limped off, straight down the race into the changing rooms. I flumped onto the concrete floor, my back propped up against a bench, a blue towel swaddling an icepack against my knee. The broadcasters cut to that image while the game continued and back in Melbourne, Jan, who had invited a girlfriend over for dinner, burnt the meal while she sat glued to the TV watching on in dismay. In the living room up at Ungarie, Mum's heart sank too; she said she just wanted to reach through the screen and give me a hug.

I was thinking, *Well, this is it. I'm stuffed.*

A couple of days later, when the specialists confirmed that I would require a third knee reconstruction, the cold truth began to sink in.

Once I acknowledged the fact that my football dream had now slipped away, the decision to retire became relatively simple. After so many months of not running out with the team, of not having a game to look forward to each week, the reality was that as much as the club had tried to include me, I no longer felt a part of it. I was cooked.

It took several months but eventually I found peace of mind with the decision. I knew I couldn't just sit back and mourn my dodgy knees for the rest of my life. Staying stuck in despondency wasn't going to help anyone: not me, not my family and not Essendon. It was time to move on from playing football.

★

Fortunately, as I dealt with the disappointment of an aborted football career in the winter of 1985, there was enough going on in my life to provide an impetus to turn towards hope. Ideally in tough times we can gain momentum by identifying a strong purpose, and if you're in survival mode, it may be enough to just have a reason to get out of bed every morning and catch the tram to go to work.

Back in 1985, being a VFL footballer was still a part-time commitment and my full-time job was working as a computer programmer. After finishing my RMIT course in 1983, I had spotted a newspaper advertisement for a job at Canon Australia's office in Hawthorn and sent off my resumé. Much to my surprise, I landed an interview – which made me worry they would discover that the young graduate was actually way out of his depth. But to my even greater surprise, I landed the job.

My hunch in 1979 that this was a burgeoning industry was proving to be right. The role involved maintaining accounting software to ensure that Canon's ledgers and payroll services ran smoothly. I had very little idea what I was doing, and technical snags cropped up so constantly that it often felt like I was playing that arcade game, *Whac-A-Mole*. Fortunately, there were good people to guide me and I learnt more in six months on the job than I did in four years at university.

After two enjoyable years at Canon (where my boss, Wolfgang, confessed to having no interest in Australian football), I took on a position as a programmer at Bongiorno Financial Services on St Kilda Road. The guys at Bongiorno's were big Essendon fans and ironically my time starting with them pretty much coincided with hanging up the boots at the Bombers. The company's expertise was in offering financial advice and although there was a backroom of about 15 staff, only two of us were writing the software. I threw myself into the IT work and within a couple of years was pretty much running the backroom processing show.

I have a lot of empathy for modern AFL footballers who walk straight from high school exams into 10 or 15 years of devoting their daily lives to the game. They can emerge out the other end ill-prepared for a career in the decades beyond football. In a way, the eulogising of retiring players – tributes such as laps of the MCG, elaborate video homages and commemorative merchandise – perpetuates the notion that elite athletes die twice, the first time being when their sporting career ends.

As much as I had another career to turn to in the absence of football, what most helped me turn towards hope at the end of 1985 was that Jan and I were newlyweds, looking to set out on a new, shared journey. The love was there and, if anything, would now only have more room to flourish in the absence of the requisite selfishness that comes with pursuing a career as a professional sportsperson.

Primarily, turning towards hope required a recalibration in my reasoning. To that point, hope for me had largely revolved around football concepts such as becoming a respected 200-game player, a proven finals performer or a member of a team that won the grand final (which Essendon would go on to do again in 1985). Now I had to accept that those aspirations had vanished – I had to stop feeling sorry for myself and to understand that there were ample avenues to find opportunity elsewhere. It might take time and involve a few setbacks, but you can't allow your hope to become a balloon that is popped at the first sign of adversity.

Three knee reconstructions in four years might have cruelled my football career, but those years proved to be an important phase in my evolution as a person. I learned lessons in resilience and perseverance, but also in finding hope among the ashes of despair. I learnt about not taking setbacks personally, and that they are generally not as severe as you first think and that the grief is temporary. Those knee injuries made me stronger, primarily because they helped me realise the folly of relying on your meaning of life coming from something that is completely selfish – that sets you up for an all-or-nothing existence. It has to be more than that.

I was 24 years old, a healthy young man safe in the knowledge that I had great people in my life who were loving and supportive. I had a good job in a growing industry, a bit of a profile and a few connections and scope to move into the non-playing areas of football if that appealed. What reason was there to be anything but abundantly hopeful?

Only a matter of days after watching Essendon win the 1985 premiership, Jan and I watched on as a scan confirmed she was pregnant. The birth of our first child, Lauren, in April 1986 was a light-bulb moment, a reminder that life's not just about you, mate. You have every reason to embrace hope and you have a new responsibility like no other. Don't mope around thinking about your crook knees and having to pull the pin on your football career. You've got this little bundle of joy over here relying on you now.

Keep both hands on the wheel

In this era that elevates the importance of high self-esteem, many people want to tell us that we're fine just the way we are. If only it were that easy – just keep patting yourself on the back and away you go, having a great life! But being human means we have flaws. We will never be perfect, but my view is that we have a responsibility to keep trying to be better, to become the best version of ourselves. I hasten to add that a good dose of liking yourself and wanting to keep getting better are not incompatible.

On a very basic level, we all understand responsibilities when they're neatly outlined in our job descriptions at work. However, you don't get the luxury of a detailed job description for life, although you'll find plenty of people along the way who are willing to give you one if you let them. The better option is to work it out for yourself, and this starts with taking responsibility for the kind of person you can become.

At 18, living in the moment and having a good time, you might not care about your future self, but at 28 you might be married with kids. What if you are suddenly compromised by something stupid you did a decade ago?

And that 28-year-old has a responsibility to your 38-year-old self, and your children. You certainly don't want your 58-year-old self asking your 38-year-old self, *What the hell were you thinking?*

Taking responsibility for tomorrow might seem like my father planning for the worst up on the farm, but it extends beyond that. I'm talking about wearing the consequences of some life-changing poor decisions. When a heightened sense of self leads us to choose instant gratification and we give our character flaws free rein, we might get away with bad behaviour in the moment. But not only are we hurting others, our future self also pays the price.

Life throws up complex problems which is why you need to be in the driver's seat, mapping out your own journey. While the solutions are often complex too, one thing is simple. As Muhammad Ali put it: 'The person who views the world at 50 the same as they did at 20 has wasted 30 years of their life.' Life experiences change you, so when you hit a pothole along the way and collect a few bruises, take time to reflect on who you are and who you could be, and accept that life isn't as easy as you hoped it might be.

Taking on responsibility to becoming a better you is a foundation of living a good life. You will consciously bend towards the better side of your nature, so that you're not only helping yourself, you'll find that you're being a better person to and for others. And this comes with its own wonderful rewards.

★

With the birth of Lauren, it began to dawn on me that my personal responsibilities were much broader than striving to be an elite athlete. I was starting to understand that it included new responsibilities to my wife, my child, friends, colleagues and community. And what use would I be to any of them if I could not take responsibility for myself, for developing the better side of my own character?

Throughout childhood it was always drilled into us that we had responsibilities. That might be doing farm chores, or it might be upholding the family's values or protecting Assumption College's football reputation. As a young boy on the farm, if I ever questioned why we were expected to do a particular thing, my parents would answer, but if my questions persisted, their rationale was usually along the lines of, 'Yours is not to reason why, yours is but to do or die'. Never mind that this was a conviction that had sprung from a Tennyson poem about the Light Brigade charging into the valley of death!

As a footballer, I understood that I had a responsibility to the team, to be the best player I could be in the quest for premiership glory. It was simple: if I didn't measure up, I wouldn't be included. At work, I understood my responsibilities to Bongiorno: there were clear things I had to do in exchange for my salary.

Becoming a father changed things. As parents, Jan and I had full responsibility for guiding our innocent little baby into the world. Our baby helped to give my days a wider context and took my focus away from self and the idea that it took egocentric pursuits to find meaning in life.

Had I still been playing VFL football, the self-serving might have been merely dulled a bit, but because I had retired, the perspective came to the fore more readily. It was well and truly time to consider how blessed I was to have such a fortunate life beyond football. Knowing that we could have children was important to us, because we both saw our future life being centred around family. For some couples, that cherished prospect is not so uncomplicated.

The previous year we had bought a little house in Levien Street, Essendon, and my job at Bongiorno's meant that we could keep chiselling away at the mortgage. In a cot inside that house we had a happy and healthy girl, a real little ray of sunshine.

We were also surrounded by the love and support of our first families, the ones with whom we had grown up. I get on well with all of my 10 siblings and we've had more fun times together in adulthood than we did even as a bunch of free spirits, finding ways to make our own amusement and mischief on an isolated farm and in the streets of Ungarie in the backblocks of Australia. We will always share a bond forged in knowing exactly where we all came from.

Looking back, my marriage and parenthood created a great opportunity to begin thriving in this new world. However, let's be clear. At the tender age of 25, I had no grand vision for my life, other than we would live it as a family.

★

When I talk about contemplating my responsibilities, I wasn't having a St Paul moment, converting on the road to Damascus. Rather, parenthood provided even more reason to adjust my mindset and reinforce that life wasn't just about me, it was about *us* – we were a family.

At the centre of all of this was Jan, and raising our daughter together gave me a new appreciation for the warm-hearted and strong woman by my side, sharing this new responsibility for another human being with me. I had married the Queen of Hearts and there was space for our relationship to flourish.

Jan and I were closely aligned in our beliefs and values as parents. Looking down the track, we both thought our kids would do better with their mum around full-time, especially early on, and alongside that, we began to consider how we would influence the way our little girl thought and behaved as she grew up. Therefore, we had a responsibility to question what belief systems we wanted to operate under as parents.

I saw it as an obligation to examine the Catholic principles under which I had been raised. This was not a matter of rebelling against my faith, more an acknowledgement that it was the foundation of my values system. What underpinned it and did it hold up to the flame of the Bunsen burner? I had spent my life riding on the Catholic bus, now I wanted to look under the hood.

I enrolled to study theology one night a week at Melbourne University. Again, you're probably thinking: *What a weirdo!* The lecturer was an old Jesuit with white hair and a beard so flowing that he could easily have featured in one of those old Hollywood epics, most likely cast in the role of Moses. We studied the Old Testament earnestly and although I had previously read great slabs of its labyrinthine pages, I was still taken aback by many of the barbaric passages: there was destruction and genocide, human sacrifices and plagues, stonings and retribution. While that theology course didn't turn me away from Catholicism, it did make me think, *Hang on, is this the benevolent God I've grown up worshipping?* Surely the Old Testament couldn't be interpreted literally! I have to admit I came away with more questions than answers.

More importantly, studying provided a platform for a period of self-reflection and examination of many philosophies and belief systems that I thought was beneficial. Even back then I believed, as the ancient Greek philosopher Socrates put it, 'the unexamined life is not worth living'. I guess I was at an age where I thought, *Mine is to question why . . . not just do or die.*

Thinking about how to raise a child made me acutely aware of my own personal strengths and weaknesses. I think it was the first time I experienced a willingness to look into how I could improve, outside of a football environment. I was used to looking at how I could improve my skills, but I wasn't so used to examining my temperament, my personality and character off the field and how this might impact the bigger game called life.

Knowing who you are is a crucial step in working on becoming a better person, one who will provide well for your future self and those you love.

These days, character development is seen as an old-fashioned outdated practice. Too often, style is valued over substance, with a high societal value put on how you present yourself outwardly – how you answer the 'what do you do?' question, your fancy job title, smart clothes, new car, renovated home. We all strive to build up achievements and skills – 'resumé virtues' – to impress others and enhance our career prospects.

However, developing character is about working on the internal aspects of our selves, what's hard for others to see – 'eulogy virtues'. We are defined by our character – the combination of morals and beliefs that dictate how we treat other people and the planet, and how we take responsibility for our actions.

To seek an understanding of how and why we behave in certain ways is to dive into some pretty complex territory. Our behaviour is a combination of our personality, biases, prejudices, ignorance, emotions, impulses and beliefs – and that's before we consider the cultural setting or the situation that we find ourselves in. The thing is, no matter what drives our behaviour, we must ultimately own it. By taking on this responsibility, you begin to build self-awareness of not only what brings forth your better side, but also of the darker side of your nature.

Understanding your personality, which is somewhat fixed, is a part of that, because it allows you to know when traits work for you and when they don't. But more important is the process of character-building, especially moral character, which is more malleable and involves not just strengths, but identifying weaknesses and working on them.

Let's start with my personality. The Myers-Briggs test I did 30 years ago suggested I was an ISTJ type: Introversion (I), Sensing (S), Thinking (T), Judgment (J). Probably a fair call. These days, I prefer the CANOE model, which defines our five main personality traits as: Conscientiousness, Agreeableness, Neuroticism, Openness and Extroversion.

This how I assess my 'big five' traits.

Conscientiousness: High on the scale. Give me a project I feel strongly about and I'm like a dog at a bone. If I'm unenthused by the project, I'll just do what I have to (farm work and schoolwork felt a bit like that). However, once I'm in, I'm 100 per cent in, often to the extent of driving other less committed team members to total distraction.

Agreeableness: I'm not that agreeable and at times that can get me into trouble. I tend to be a bit judgmental and impatient and have never been too concerned about what other people might think of me (outside my inner circle), which is a strength at times, a weakness at others. I can call bullshit when I see it and that can upset people. As I've aged, I have improved in this area.

Neuroticism: Not an issue. Always felt able to deal with anxiety and fear. My way of dealing with stress was to exercise or to allow music to take my mind away. When I was coaching, match-day stress could lead to angry outbursts in the coaches' box, but once I'd vented I could more or less let it go, without carrying the anger forward.

Openness: Over the years I've been more closed than open. As a younger man, I definitely tended to have a more black-and-white view of the world. Even though I've always been open to learning, I was more interested in the answers than the questions. I wish I'd been more curious and a better listener. I wish I'd asked better questions. As I've become older, this is something I've worked on.

Extroversion: I'm naturally an introvert, which could be interpreted sometimes as being buried in my own thoughts, not listening, being a rude bastard. I can be an extrovert at certain times (noting that leadership responsibilities require this trait), but to recharge, I need my own 'quiet time'.

Needless to say, all these personality traits weren't totally self-evident to a younger 25-year-old Neale. Looking back, it's a great reminder that life experiences do change you.

Back then, I knew I had to get my act together, but what did that mean? Fortunately, I had been given some strong signposts by my upbringing. I had a clear understanding of what was right and what was wrong. I was taught the better side of my nature would emerge by being less self-centred, showing compassion, learning that being open and honest creates trust, that tolerance and acceptance of others is a way of showing respect, to seek fair outcomes, that life isn't easy and persistence and resilience are prerequisites for getting anything good done.

Yes, I learnt all these, but knowing about them and putting them into practice are not the same thing. To be human is to err – we all fall short at times and that's often when our darker side emerges.

Getting my act together involved becoming more aware of what made up my character. And with that awareness, I could take ownership and responsibility to commit to the difficult lifelong task of trying to become a better version of myself.

If a long car drive is a metaphor for life, I was beginning to understand why Dad always said, 'Keep both hands on the wheel' when he was teaching us to drive the ute.

★

On the surface, all this talk of self can seem a bit self-indulgent. But I like the oxygen mask theory when it comes to taking responsibility for being your best self. On a plane, we're all familiar with being told that in the event of an emergency, you put your own mask on first before coming to the assistance of others. It sounds selfish but think about this: if you don't put your own mask on, you are going to be useless to the people who depend on you, and who you care about. You probably won't even survive.

You owe it to your future self and those you love to get your act together. Capitalise on your strengths and work on your weaknesses – it will stand you in good stead for the long haul.

Taking responsibility for the person you are and who you can be is not an end, it's a means to an end. If you do it well, not only you but the ones you love will be the beneficiaries.

Life's great rewards are hidden in humanity's messy glory

A veteran football coach, when contemplating his imminent retirement, joked that he would be happy to go and sit at the top of a lighthouse forever. I know where he was coming from – he was looking forward to escaping the turmoil, the public scrutiny and the constant noise that comes with the job.

We'd all like to head up to the lighthouse from time to time when people drive us mad: when relationships get strained, when we're let down, when promises are broken, when we feel hurt. I'm sure you sometimes find yourself thinking, *Relationships, yeah, I'm all for them but do they have to come with people?*

But here's the thing. If you want to live a good life – one where you take responsibility for becoming your best self – then other people are major players in your journey. They're not your passengers, they're fellow travellers and they have roles as protagonists and antagonists in how your journey unfolds.

If the man in the lighthouse was the only person living on this planet, there would be no need for a moral or ethical code. He could enjoy the views in splendid isolation and do whatever he liked, because he couldn't harm anybody. But once you accept that other people are part of life's deal, you realise that relationships define your life and are a constant testing ground of your values and beliefs. They also provide the opportunity to build the better side of your character. Caring about other people takes you outside your own ego, to find a greater purpose and meaning beyond yourself. This is all part of learning to thrive and, eventually, to arrive.

Relationships test your courage to be vulnerable because there's an element of personal risk. We're never so vulnerable as when we trust someone, but paradoxically, if we cannot trust, neither can we find love nor joy. You might be hurt, disappointed, feel like you've wasted both time and energy . . . but there's also an even-money chance you might feel enriched, fulfilled and loved.

You can't choose your family, but you can have a say in who your friends are. Therefore, choose wisely: look for people with whom you can form positive relationships, whether we're talking about colleagues, friends, teammates or a partner.

There's a big difference between periods of solitude – which can be good for the soul – and isolating yourself out of fear of rejection. The sweeping views from the remote heights of the lighthouse might be appealing sometimes but remember this: to love and be loved are key ingredients in living a good life – they're the rewards of engaging with humanity in all its messy glory.

★

In 2009, during my time as general manager of football operations with the West Coast Eagles, I headed off to Singapore to undertake an advanced management course. In one session focusing on personal growth, the lecturer asked the group a simple question: 'How many friends do you have? Raise your hands if you think you have 10? 20? 30?' Some hands were still going up at 40, a few at 50, the final hand went up at 80.

The lecturer then explained how easily we delude ourselves about who our friends are. He asked what criteria we used to decide on our number. He let us dwell on that for several minutes. He then proposed what he considered to be the criteria for people to classify as friends. Do these people make time for you? Do they know where your life is at? Would they come to your aid in a stressful situation? Would they answer your call late at night?

Against that criteria, most of us realised that the number of people who belonged in that true friendship category was probably in single figures. That was the first time I had stopped to reflect on the levels of my relationships with people and the significant investment required to be a true friend. It also reinforced the idea that there are two fluid tiers: friendship and mateship.

Mateship is highly valued in Australia – so highly that in 1999, then Prime Minister John Howard wanted to include it in the preamble to our *Constitution*. We don't need to go that far, and we also need to shake off some of the blokey connotations – my wife, daughters and sisters all have mates – but mateship at heart is an admirable trait if we're talking about generosity of spirit, ability to take a ribbing and a good sense of humour.

For me, the friends versus mates thing is not about sorting the wheat from the chaff – while true friendship is at the top of the pyramid, mateship is still important and good for the soul. Nor do I wish to separate my friends and mates into two lists. Rather, the message I took away from that exercise is that it's worth thinking about who is in your inner circle, whether you are making time for those people and whether you should make your circle bigger. Instead of looking at what they offer you in a transactional way, turn the questions around. Do you make time to catch up with them? Do you know what's going on in their lives? Would you be there in their time of need? Would you instantly pick up their late-night call?

Those authentic friendships are, along with family relationships, the gold nuggets in our lives. They make you feel loved and valued, and also push you to be the best version of yourself. They're in for the long haul and they're worth holding on to – who better to share the thrills and spills of life with?

It's impossible to encapsulate in words how good friends can enrich your life. Often, it's as simple as the fact that they're there and you know they have your back. They understand you, they forgive your shortcomings and, at times, challenge you because they want the best for you. You love their company and you'd like to think you mean the same to them.

Everything that is important in life is connected to someone else. We often need a reminder of that, because we can too easily put friends, partners and family on the backburner as we strive for the elusive satisfaction of success. We're effectively putting our relationships on hold, saying, 'I'll catch up with you later.' We've all done it – I'm guilty as charged.

I'm certainly not going to be on my deathbed saying, 'I wish I'd strived a bit harder', and I don't want to be wishing I'd spent more time with the people I care about – I've deliberately tried to address this in the last five years. As I've faced my mortality, I've come to appreciate the relationships in my life more and more. I was dealt a very good hand of family cards and I've been lucky to have great mates and friends, some dating as far back as primary school and Assumption College, some emerging from football clubs, and some through connections with our kids and the neighbourhood.

It's a common imbalance – and it often slips by unnoticed – that we can unintentionally devote more of our precious time to dysfunctional relationships than to looking after the good ones. Just think about how much time people spend talking about their annoying work colleagues, the uncaring boss (or coach!) or their obnoxious teammate or that parent who forgot it was their turn to drive the kids to Auskick.

You don't want to wake up late in life and realise that your marriage has failed, you've pissed off everyone who's been close to you and you're no longer talking to your kids or close mates. You might blame the other parties and try to delude yourself that life's great by staying on the treadmill of striving and telling yourself you've got a great job and a nice house. But what does that amount to if you're surrounded by broken relationships? Remember, you have a responsibility to be the best possible version of yourself. Blaming others to justify why your inner circle is really small or – worse – why you have retreated to the lighthouse will never allow you to develop towards your better self.

Sure, in life you may feel that people have let you down, hurt you deeply, betrayed you. By being burnt there is some justification in thinking, *I'm not putting myself out there again.* You're going to be more guarded, less trusting, even cynical, keeping people outside your inner circle so you won't get hurt again. This might feel safe for a while, but in the end it's a self-defeating path as it leads to isolation and to loneliness. Instead, reflect on your role in the relationship breakdown, think about whether there have there been times where even your absence has let others down. Reflect on what you learned from the experience. Maintain the courage not to retreat from life. Become a better judge of people and continue to engage, even when it gets messy – a lot of life's goodness is to be found there.

It's worth pausing to acknowledge that it is *people* who are at the centre of our move towards thriving – that's when we start to look beyond our own self-centred pursuits and towards what we might bring to someone else's life.

Don't wear your busyness as a badge of honour and let it get in the way of spending quality time with the people you care about. Tell your ego to take a back seat and shut down that voice telling you that you've got important things to do, that you don't have time to waste idly connecting with other people.

When I catch up with my friends, it's the banter, the camaraderie and the laughter that connects us and makes us feel alive. It might sound like we're talking crap and taking the mickey out of each other, but we're all sharing that moment, we're present in body *and* spirit. Enjoying a barbecue with a few glasses of red and some great music with my family and friends – that's as good as it gets.

★

No one is going to listen to advice from me about matters of the heart – the most complex relationships of all. I wouldn't expect them to – it's not like I have a magic formula for choosing your perfect life partner. All I know with absolute certainty is that common bedrock values are even more important in the most intimate relationships: you need to be trustworthy and honest in order to be trusted with someone else's love. No core relationship is going to be smooth sailing all the way, so you have to work at it.

Jan and I have been married for 34 years. I'll use a cricket analogy, as Jan loves her cricket: we make a good opening pair because even though we have different styles, we complement each other very well. Early on, I sensed that we shared similar values, and this has proven true over time. We both prioritise family, we work hard, we're determined and resilient and we like a challenge – if we take something on, we give it our best shot. We work through problems together.

In some ways we are the yin to each other's yang: I like order, Jan is more flexible, happy to go with the flow. Jan is friendlier and more social than I am and has a great ability to make other people feel welcome and important, whereas I can be impatient and am a huge fan of a quick goodbye at all social outings. Jan challenges my opinions, bringing a level-headedness when I stray towards stubbornness. I believe the candour in our relationship plays a big part in maintaining our closeness and bolsters us when the chips are down. There's no pretence.

Jan has always been a very giving and patient person — a woman who brings out love in other people. Why did Jan gravitate to me? I have no bloody idea. She says she was drawn to the fact that I was honest and down to earth and had a strength about me, a resolve. And there I was thinking it was because I was such a funny, witty guy.

We've raised four kids and we've had big adventures, relocating to the other side of Australia a couple of times. We've done a lot of miles together, with some challenging times to come. Already, I've had to confront the reality that I can no longer put my hands on the wheel — I have had to relinquish control of some parts of my life. But I trust that Jan and I are in this together — with the support of family and good friends — and that's more reassuring and comforting than any material possession or job title.

We're also fortunate that we slotted into each other's families well, despite the fact that my family is Irish-Catholic blood and Jan's are Methodist non-drinkers. The saying goes that the apple doesn't fall far from the tree, so if you want to get an insight into your future partner, take a good look at the tree. The bigger issue for me was how accepting Bruce and Margie

McCorkell would be of their daughter's choice of partner. It didn't take me long to test them out.

★

Picture this: a hot summer night, pre-season, I'm 22 and I've been out with the boys. We've had a big night. It's around one o'clock in the morning, and since I'm coming back Jan's way, I decide it would be a great idea to drop in and say hello.

I'd been to her home before, but in the dark of night everything seems a bit unfamiliar. Not wishing to wake the whole house, I think, *I'll just knock on her window.* I bravely take a guess . . .

Tap, tap, tap . . .

To my horror, Jan's father appears on the other side of the glass. Oops, wrong window.

When Bruce came out, I didn't know what to expect – I felt very foolish. But before I had time to apologise, he said, 'Hi mate, come on in.' To my great surprise, he was good-natured about it. He could probably tell I was a bit partied out. We had a bit of a chat – I don't remember about what exactly – and Jan came out to say hello. Anyway, Bruce and Marg were very gracious, and I suggest they behaved much better than I would if this same scenario ever unfolded with my own daughter.

It's fair to say that my relationship with my father-in-law could have gone really pear-shaped after I stood all over his newly planted azaleas. It's a testament to what wonderful people Bruce and Margie McCorkell are that I wasn't banned for life. In fact, over the decades I've known them, they've continued to ignore my bad traits and have loved me like a son. Most importantly, I believe their tolerance has helped bring out the best in me.

My children are the product of both the Danihers and the McCorkells so it's only fair I share a little of the history of the other side of the family.

As I frequently tell her, Margie is my favourite mother-in-law. Her father, Ernest, was born in London and by the time he was 12, he'd lost his father to World War I. Margie's grandfather, Private William Henry Kidd of the 14th Battalion, Highland Light Infantry, died at the Somme on the Western Front in 1916. Ernest stepped up and took on responsibility for his family. He came to Australia when he was 20 and spent a bit of time in the bush, working on the land. He married Priscilla and had two kids, Margie and Edward. They had a strict but loving Protestant upbringing and were regulars at the same church in Camberwell as Bruce's family. In fact, Margie first met Bruce at that church when they were three years old.

Margie trained as a teacher and ended up at Rossbourne School in Hawthorn, working with students who had encountered problems with mainstream education.

Bruce was born out Blackburn way, the boy in between two sisters. His mother moved away from the family when he was around 12, and as a consequence, Bruce had a distant relationship with her. His father, Edwin, raised Bruce. His childhood wasn't easy, but he never complained or was bitter. He finished school at 15, and later went off to RMIT to study business and management part-time. He started work with RP Scherer pharmaceuticals and rose through the ranks of management and procurement. Everyone loved him, and he loved work — throughout his whole tenure, he only ever took one-and-a-half sick days. And that was for a workplace accident that resulted in him losing the top of an index finger.

Bruce and Margie got married and Jan was their firstborn, then came Sandra, then Ross. Their life revolved around family, community, sport, work and the East Burwood Uniting Church.

In his 37th year with RP Scherer, a new general manager arrived. If we needed any further proof that life doesn't promise to be fair, once the new GM had milked Bruce's knowledge, he was shown the door. These days, we're used to the ruthlessness of the work environment and we change jobs every five years or so. Back then, it came completely out of the blue. But Bruce was soon snapped up by Heinz, where he worked for another decade.

You'll see a pattern emerging when I tell you that Margie set up East Burwood Netball Club in 1972 which, at its peak, had 30 teams. The club lasted nearly 40 years, with Margie tapping out the weekly newsletter on her typewriter. Bruce's sporting passion was cricket and during the winter he was a football field umpire. When he could no longer do that, he became a goal umpire and, eventually, a coach to the goal umpires. He finally retired from that role when he was 81!

Bruce and Margie are endlessly giving and optimistic people. But my father-in-law, in particular, was genuinely worried when an Irish-Catholic Aussie Rules footballer looked like running off with his oldest daughter. Bruce remembers that we talked about it and I turned him around by saying, 'Brucey, at the end of the day we all worship the same God.' Luckily, it did the trick. Our similarities have ended up being far greater than our differences.

We grow up, mature, get wiser and realise that the people who come to mean the most to us over the journey – our inner circle – might well be those who we appeared to have little in common with at the start.

★

That great modern poet Mick Jagger reminded us that we can't always get what we want. I will take it one step further and say that we eventually realise that we don't always *know* what we want, especially when we are young and immature.

Sometimes this continues into later life when what we thought we wanted comes at the expense of what we truly need, that is, strong, supportive, loving relationships with family and friends. In life, it's important to work out what we truly value and give it the attention it deserves. Too often, we give our attention to things that don't really matter. Things like comparisons, envy, regret, anxiety, outrage, victimhood, getting even. Take time to reflect on and assess what you believe is truly valuable and pay attention to it, and you might find that you get what you need.

Wanting – striving – is all about 'me', whereas living a good life – thriving – is all about 'us'. If you want to talk about 'us', you need to put a bit of work into the relationships that matter.

There are two things to think about when you consider the value people bring to your life. Who are the people in your inner circle? Look after those people. And think of friendship as a two-way street. As Zig Ziglar said, 'If you go looking for a friend, you will find them very scarce, but if you go out to be a friend, you will find them everywhere.'

Stuff it, do it anyway

Life is a maze of the decisions we make, yet we're often paralysed by indecision, waiting for the right path to reveal itself, for the perfect time to make a move.

We fear taking a risk because there is no certainty on the other side of our decision, even if we really want to make a change or try something new. Instead we often make no decision and by default settle for the familiarity of staying still, even if the situation has become mundane, unfulfilling and possibly a bit dismaying. We let fear get the better of us.

You can wait forever for that elusive perfect timing, justifying inaction with a thousand reasons: you don't have enough money, you don't really have time right now, your plan might backfire. Waiting for certainty consigns you to a holding pattern, whereas mustering up the courage to make a decision and work through the consequences is what living is all about.

Of course, there are risks you shouldn't take – those that are ill considered or against the law, that will have a negative effect on yourself and other people and are guaranteed to cause harm.

You are less likely to regret a decision that involves having a crack at something even if you come up short. You're more likely to regret not having had a go at all, ending up on a treadmill of what-ifs.

If there is something that you really want to do, something that's nagging away at you, but fear is nipping at your ankles, maybe you need to ask yourself what's the worst thing that can happen. Then take a deep breath and say to yourself, *Stuff it, let's do it anyway.*

Often the worst thing that can happen is . . . status quo. You stay stuck because you made no decision at all.

★

By 1986, for the first time in a decade, I wasn't immersed in football. It was an exhilarating time for Essendon, in the wake of consecutive premierships, and I still had an interest in the progress of former teammates and in the fortunes of my two brothers – Terry at Essendon and Anthony at Sydney – but there was no hovering over the sports pages in the newspaper, no flicking over the TV channel to watch the footy replay or the match of the round, no desire to engage in analysis of the previous or upcoming round of matches.

In that first year out of football, I was confident I had strengths and abilities that would somehow lead me to flourish:

as a family man for a start, and also perhaps I had a future as a computer guru. On one level, it felt as though I had made a clean and easy break from my life as a footballer. But often the shrouded truth emerges to grab hold of you in the most unexpected of ways.

On the weekends, Jan and I would potter around in the backyard of our little house in Levien Street, and when conditions were still or there was a breeze from the north, the unmistakable sounds of a home game at Windy Hill would float the kilometre or so to our garden and hang wistfully in the air. I thought I was on top of it, but the call of the siren lured me back in.

As those faint blasts of the siren drifted into our yard, my mind would drift to melancholic thoughts of what might have been. I would wonder how the past few years might have unfolded had I not been injured. Like any footballer I would have loved the chance to have tested myself out in September. I had only played in one final, a loss, in my first season. How would I have performed given a chance in those past three grand finals? Would I have made a significant contribution on the big stage? The sinister scars on my knees were an enduring reminder that any aspiration to return to playing was nothing more than a fantasy, but there remained a hole that had once been filled by competitive sport.

Kevin Sheedy would occasionally touch base and as the year progressed, he tossed an idea into the air. 'With the way you think about football, when are you going to come back to the club to get involved in coaching?' he asked. 'There's an office waiting for you when you want to return and even if there wasn't, I'd make one for you.' My inclination was to bat away the prospect, but Sheeds knew I had to digest an idea and consider its implications before I could come around to it. He knew the offer of an off-field football role would simmer in my mind.

Towards the end of 1986, I asked Jan what she thought. She knew I missed the camaraderie, being part of the club that my brothers and close mates were all still involved with. She simply replied, 'Why not give it a go?', and with that, I accepted Sheedy's offer to take on a part-time role as Essendon's skills coach in 1987.

I found a way to bring my two working worlds together. Drawing on the computer expertise I'd gained from working at Canon and Bongiorno's, I initiated the club's pioneering use of video analysis as a coaching aid. We filmed all of our games and I would then use the VHS tapes (no digital stuff in 1987!) to edit highlights and passages of play that helped to educate individual players.

This foray into coaching opened my mind, at age 26, to the notion that it was possible to gain purpose from football beyond playing the game. I was involved at the highest level, enjoying it and playing to my strengths, and through helping others gained an appreciation of how to thrive in a football environment.

★

I suspect that, subconsciously, there was another dimension to Kevin Sheedy's effort to coax me back to Windy Hill. During the backslapping after Essendon's 1985 flag, he had encountered our mother, Edna, amid the smiling faces that evening. Wasn't it marvellous that Terry had captained another premiership? he'd asked. 'Oh yes, it's wonderful,' Mum had agreed, before softly musing aloud whether the coach thought it possible that one day all four of her sons might play in the same team at Essendon.

Sheeds is drawn to the sentimental possibilities of football; in some ways, he is an old romantic. 'Graeme Richmond and Alan Schwab were two exceptional administrators at Tigerland, and they taught me that when you hear an original song like that, it's music to your ears,' he would tell me later. 'The seed of a possibility like that would stick in their minds and they would then go and move heaven and earth to get a player to their club to make it happen.'

As 1986 drew to a close, Sheeds managed to find a way to get all four of us to Essendon, with Terry as captain, me as an assistant coach and the recruitment of our younger brothers Anthony – squeezed out of Sydney by the Swans' salary-cap struggles – and 20-year-old Chris, who relocated from Ungarie to have a crack at the VFL. That 1987 season was the first time the four of us had been involved in the same team and we cherished the experience.

By 1988, there was even the occasional chance for us to get out on the oval and have a kick together. It was great to be around my three brothers on a daily basis. Ants was just coming into the prime of his career. His transition into defence was working well for him and he was great company, the most easygoing of us boys. Chris – our little fox terrier brother – had grown up emulating TD. He worked hard, laughed a lot, didn't overthink things (unlike me!) and let life unfold.

At that stage, I was taking a more active role in the coaching set-up and training sessions and late in the season I trusted my knees enough to join in on the drills. If I needed to demonstrate where a kick was meant to go or if we were one player short for a drill, I would get involved rather than telling players from the side. One Thursday evening, as Sheeds and I discussed how a few of the younger players were progressing, he distractedly chewed on his lip. 'You know, I reckon you're ready to play again,' he said. 'And don't think you can't because you're training as well as anyone here.'

Sheeds says I responded by looking at him as though he was half mad. All I could do was let out a little snort to scoff at his evaluation.

'No, you're up to it,' he said. 'Listen, you've only got one more chance to play VFL football. And this might be the only chance you'll ever get to play alongside your brothers. You'll get plenty of chances to coach.'

In typical Sheedy fashion, he didn't mention the prospect of the comeback again. He just left the hook dangling in the water, waiting patiently for his fish to get on the line. For weeks I contemplated his proposition, knowing I would have to make a decision before the club lodged its playing list in late November. Essendon could afford me the opportunity, a gamble that would cost them almost nothing.

What did I have to lose? There were increased responsibilities on the home front – we had welcomed our son Luke to our little family in July – but Jan was supportive, probably sensing a certain restlessness in me. The knowledge that I had only played five games in seven years and had not completed a full season since 1980 created lingering doubts. There's no question I knew how to persevere, but the belief that I might only be capable of playing at something like 60 or 70 per cent of my ability made me question the point of perseverance in this instance.

In the end, I arrived at the conclusion that the only thing holding me back was a fear of failure. Egos aren't overly keen on 'setting out without any guarantee of success'. I had come to the VFL as an 18-year-old with my ego in strive mode, channelling the stereotypical American mantra of 'be the biggest and the best or go home', whereas at age 27 I was looking more to the Australian bush ideal of 'having a go'.

Being prepared to have a go suggests taking a risk, so you need to be courageous. It takes a spirit or will or attitude to move forward in pursuit of an ideal that is more important to us than our doubts and fears. What was the worst that could happen in my case? Sustain another injury and it would all be over again? Or have someone in the stands form an opinion that I wasn't the player I had been? So what?

I weighed up my options and thought chancing a potential injury or some harsh commentary was a fair trade-off for the opportunity to look back on my VFL career without any regrets. I decided to give playing one last crack, to find out definitively whether I still had some petrol in the tank. If I was on empty and failed, I felt I could live with that.

I managed to complete a solid pre-season and my knees were pain-free heading into 1989. With Anthony now wearing the Number 6 Essendon jumper, the club handed me the Number 36 that I had worn during my years at Assumption College; I saw it as a good omen, joking that I'd never missed games through injury while wearing 36. As I strung together a block of reserves games, I felt my skills were still at the level required to play VFL football, but my movement wasn't great, and the game had become significantly quicker. My brain was quick enough, but my body wasn't.

Sheeds would have liked to achieve his goal of selecting all four Danihers when Terry reached his 250-game milestone against St Kilda at Windy Hill in round 5, but I didn't merit inclusion in the team alongside the other three. Instead the club began to play me as a ruck-rover in the reserves in an effort to improve my fitness and conditioning. That season I managed four senior games. And while I struggled to have an impact at the elite level, I stood out at the tier below.

At the end of 1989, Sheeds told me that the Bombers were going to delist me, with a view to picking me up again in the pre-season draft. 'If we delist some of the others on the fringe, other clubs might snap them up,' he explained. 'But nobody's going to take a punt on 28-year-old who's done three knees.' I couldn't fault his logic and actually really appreciated his candour. I like hearing things straight. The club duly recommitted to me with pick 46.

Mum's dream of watching all of her sons run out for Essendon looked like becoming a reality in 1990, but the stars just weren't aligning. I managed half a dozen games, but they coincided with injuries to either Anthony or Chris. We would often have three brothers in the 20, which was a strong outfit that finished second on the ladder in 1989 and first in 1990.

In May there was reason to celebrate when all four of us were picked to play AFL State of Origin for New South Wales against Victoria, with Terry as captain. On a sodden night at the SCG, the locals sprang a huge upset, defeating the all-powerful Big V by 10 points. My father was generally an unemotional man, but he rated that win as one of his favourite football moments. Of course, he was enormously proud that his sons had helped New South Wales, which was often viewed as a second-class citizen in Australian football, get bragging rights over the state that liked to think it owned the game. For twenty years, he'd watched New South Wales get flogged by the Big V, so let's just say this win had a positive effect on his mood. Dad was on the boundary in the rain after the match, clapping Victorian figurehead and chairman of selectors Ted Whitten off the ground.

When we returned to Windy Hill, however, the prospect of another historic Daniher on-field reunion diminished by the day. Chris suffered a compound fracture of his finger – it still juts out at a right angle to this day – and Anthony a broken jaw. Yes, it's a tough game! I found myself adopting a slightly different mentality when I played. My concentration – which I had always proudly considered one of my strengths – was waning during games and there were brief moments where I found myself looking around the crowd, soaking in the atmosphere. I sensed that this would be my last season playing AFL at this level, and I became less intense about football and started to find enjoyment in the experience of simply playing. In a sporting sense, maybe I was in arrival mode, simply enjoying those moments – and never more so than in the final match of the home-and-away season.

With top spot on the ladder assured, Sheeds took the opportunity to make my mother's dream come true. He decided to rest a few senior players ahead of the finals and selected us four brothers in the same team – a VFL/AFL record. The round 22 match against St Kilda would be my first senior game in five weeks and Chris's first in three months.

Mum and Dad, busy on the farm with crop spraying and sheep shearing, hastily organised to head down to Melbourne, driving out of Ungarie before 4 am to catch a 6.45 am flight from Wagga Wagga. The whole clan was at the ground when we ran through the banner that read 'History In The Making' and to our respective positions on the boggy Moorabbin ground. Terry was at fullback, Anthony on a wing and Chris in the centre, while I started at full-forward.

All seven of my kicks that day were scoring shots, and I finished with a score of 3.4. A few people mentioned afterwards that it was a shame I didn't kick straighter and thereby press my case to hold my spot in the team. 'It was at bloody Moorabbin,' I replied. 'There was mud and pools of water all over the ground and every time I went back to take a shot, I had to move three feet to find a run up.' In reality, I'd jagged a couple of soft goals and simply wasn't good enough to be in the team.

There was an inkling that it would be my final game when I ran into the chairman of selectors Brian Donohoe in the rooms after the game. Cheekily I nudged him. 'Three goals, Brian, not bad, eh?' I had spent a fair bit of time with Brian on the match committee in 1988, and he raised his eyebrows and looked across at me with just the faintest hint of a smile as if to say, *We both know, Neale.*

I trained with the team through September, really just as a case of 'break glass in case of an emergency'. My three brothers played in that year's grand final without me, which we lost to Collingwood by eight goals.

★

Whenever I see him now, Sheeds often says wistfully, 'We really should have played you in that finals series.' But I knew deep down that footy had passed me by at the home-and-away level, let alone at finals. Coming out of retirement had only resulted in another 11 senior games and 150 more chances to take possession of the ball. But it created priceless memories of playing for Essendon alongside my brothers and gave me peace of mind about how my career finished.

I'm sure Sheeds would have had the courage to make the decision to cut me at the end of that season, in the best interests of the team cause, but I made it easy and told him I was done.

A long time ago I read something – probably on the back of a dunny door – that said it's better to attempt something great and fail, than attempt nothing and succeed. It resonated with me straight away and has become my personal mantra. It's stayed with me for life.

When it's your turn to go, you've got to go

We throw the word 'courage' around in a range of contexts, from warzones to sporting fields and everything in between. But what is courage? I agree with the definition from German writer Johann Wolfgang von Goethe, who described it as 'the commitment to begin without any guarantee of success'.

If you know what you believe in, there's a certain confidence that comes with that. This is the 'courage of your convictions' and it's what guides your life journey. It's the courage that kicks in when you're under pressure, giving you the confidence to do what you know is right, even though other people might not agree or approve.

Courage can be found in the unlikeliest of places. I admire the courage of ordinary people in their everyday lives. People like my great-grandfather, who set out into the uncharted and unforgiving Australian outback to start a new life as a farmer.

While they were breaking their backs clearing the bush, they probably didn't consider themselves courageous, they just thought they didn't have many choices. Carving out a living in brutal isolation may have been the best option they had, so they had to make a go of it. But not many of us would have the courage to press on and make it happen.

If you can face adversity armed with the courage of your convictions, you will find there's something extra inside you, the better side of you will emerge. Over time, as you encounter more roadblocks, you will respond to crises and hardship with less fear and more courage.

I like the way former British Prime Minister Winston Churchill summed it up: 'Fear is a reaction, courage is a decision.'

★

In the realm of football, when talk turns to courage it usually revolves around observations about physical courage – putting your body on the line.

There are many footballers whose courage is admired. Who knows whether they feared for their safety as they charged back into packs? Maybe they did, but to them the fear of being seen to be dishonourable or weak was probably far greater than the fear of getting hurt. That attitude, that spirit within them, that determination to not lose face in the eyes of their teammates, was a more powerful motivator than the fear of breaking a rib or being knocked unconscious.

This 'badge of honour' form of courage is most visible when a player fails to produce it. The worst scenario for any AFL player is when the Sherrin floats just over their head and they are caught in a no-win situation. There are definitely times when players think, *I really hope that kick just goes a fraction further so that it's out of my reach and I don't have to go and get crunched.*

I always felt that physical courage was a non-negotiable in football. As a coach, I was prepared to accept that it wasn't every player's forte and that maybe the slighter and smaller players were better off playing to their strengths, rather than trying to reinvent themselves as warrior footballers – for example, they might discover their strength is in endurance running through-out the game. Just so long as when it was their time to show physical courage for the team, they delivered. And then you would just marvel at it, you would admire it.

It's not easy to show that physical courage on a sporting field, but at times it has to be done. In professional football, it comes with the guernsey to a degree. The slogan often used is: when it's your turn to go, you've got to go.

How do you know, though, when it's your time to go in everyday life? The answer might require you to stare down the fear of personal consequences to stand by your beliefs and convictions and do what you believe is the right thing to do. The two key things here are firstly, ensuring you have firm beliefs and values to direct you and secondly, having the courage to face the consequences, if they eventuate.

At some stage all of us will need to find courage to conquer the little doubts and fears in our lives. I'm not talking about the extreme courage needed to scramble out of a trench and charge the enemy's machinegun nest. Sometimes it's simply staying the line with a long-term vision or having the courage to admit your mistakes and to set about rectifying them. Sometimes we need to summon courage when we are feeling stuck in life, whether that's in an unfulfilling job, a loveless relationship or a miserable living environment. In making a decision, even if it's the wrong one, at least we are looking for a way to improve the situation. And if it's not there, then keep looking. It will be somewhere else.

★

To my mind, the most exemplary form of courage is moral courage. When a person looks at a situation, weighs it against their values and decides that they have, in fact, 'got to go', despite the risk of adverse consequences. That is the sort of courage that is most worthy of admiration.

It's the kind of moral courage exemplified by Martin Luther King Jr and Mahatma Gandhi, who risked their lives to stand up for causes they believed in. It is the courage of the unknown man who stood in front of the tanks at Tiananmen Square when the Chinese government sent in the military to forcibly suppress protestors in 1989. It is the courage to risk being shot or imprisoned by standing up to a despot's cruelty and corruption. It is far more consequential than risking injury on a sporting field or taking a chance on starting up a new business.

My admiration of moral courage is the reason I love what Ron Barassi did on New Year's Day 2009. 'Barass', a former champion player and coach, was sitting at an outdoor table at

My first grandchild, Cooper, was born in February 2019 and I'm so glad I got to meet him. We have this great telepathic thing happening where we can talk to each other about life!

Dad (Jim) on the left, and his brothers, Jack and Leo, played footy for Ungarie for decades. Love of the game is in our blood – this is me, below, at the age of six, with my brothers Terry (right) and Anthony (left).

Our youngest seven siblings called us the 'top four': Estelle, Anthony, me and Terry.

With ten siblings, you quickly learn how to cooperate and compete.
L–R: Chris, Terry, Colleen, Fiona (foreground), Angela (behind Colleen),
Julie, Anthony, Estelle, Nerolee, me, Dorothy, Mum and Dad.

I was proud of Terry (right) as captain, and thrilled for Kevin Sheedy (left) and the boys when they won back-to-back flags in 1984–85. I had other things going on: Jan and I got married in January 1985.

Coming out of retirement created priceless memories and gave me peace of mind about how my career finished. Anthony, Terry, myself and Chris played one game together for the Bombers in 1990.

Driven, intense and uncompromising – just a few of the words that describe me as coach of Melbourne.

In time I would come to appreciate how much I'd learnt from the wild ups and downs of coaching. I like the rollercoaster. You get more out of it than the merry-go-round.

This is the Big Freeze 3, 2017, with my FightMND co-founders, Pat Cunningham (left) and the late Dr Ian Davis (right), a fellow MND sufferer. Bill Guest, below, is our current chairman.

Daniher's Drive

The annual Daniher's Drive has become a rolling party through regional centres – a wonderful chance to spend quality time with family and friends and meet some unsung heroes who do amazing work in the fight against MND.

The Big Freeze

The Big Freeze at the MCG is our annual Queen's Birthday weekend fundraiser. Well-known people dress up (or down) and slide into a bath of ice in front of a huge AFL crowd. We raise millions of dollars.

2015: Tim Watson.

2015: Mick Molloy.

2016: with Joe Daniher (left) and Kevin Sheedy (right).

2017: Lleyton Hewitt.

FIGHT
ND
S PEOPLE

2018: Chris Fagan as 'The Reverend' (me!).

2019: Nick Riewoldt as Freddie Mercury.

Fundraising is only possible through family and community support. All ten of my siblings were part of Daniher's Drive in 2017. L–R: Anthony, Nerolee, Colleen, Terry, Dorothy, Fiona, Julie, Chris, Estelle, me and Angela. I got right into the rock'n'roll theme. Bec and Lauren (above) took Woodstock by storm in 2018.

Surrounded by the FightMND army on the Walk to the G, 2017.

Jan and our children are the most precious jewels in my world. Thank you Ben, Lauren, Jan, Luke and Bec – for everything.

a St Kilda restaurant late that evening when he saw a young man punch a woman in the face. The woman stumbled to the ground next to Ron and the young man turned on his heel and took off up the street. Most people would have viewed the altercation as morally wrong but none of their business, and maybe expressed their disgust and checked to see if the woman was all right. But Ron was incensed that a man would hit a woman, and at age 72 he went after the young man and confronted him. For his trouble, he was also set upon by the man and his friends, kicked while he was down and ended up with bruised ribs and arms and a swollen face.

If I had been in Ron's shoes, I'm not sure I would have had the courage to act as he did. How many of us, if we were out late and saw some drug-fuelled thug attacking an innocent person, would intervene? We would have no doubt about our moral position on the incident but would be thinking about the consequences of becoming involved. *People can get beaten or stabbed when they step in. I've got a wife and kids, do I want to risk my life by intervening?* All we can do is rely on our belief system to direct us towards the right course of action, to give us an answer when we wonder, *What's the right thing to do?* One person's idea of courage will be another person's idea of foolishness. And in some situations, we don't get to choose whether it's the right time to act, we just have to go with our instinct in the moment. That is why I admire Ron for instinctively deciding to act upon the courage of his convictions.

Courage is not something that's necessarily front of mind; it's often an informed intuition based on strong beliefs that force your decision to act. When it comes to our values and beliefs, all we can hope is that we don't let ourselves down in the moment. No doubt we have all let ourselves down somewhere along the line when it comes to the crunch. We didn't speak up when we should have or didn't go to someone's aid.

When I was 14, I witnessed a burly rugby-playing kid – a big bully who scared the crap out of everyone – giving a fellow schoolmate hell. I knew the bully, he was an angry lump who had been expelled from our school and who I had played alongside in representative cricket teams, so I piped up and said, 'Hey, ease up, mate.' Well, the bully turned his attention from my mate – who was smart enough to seize the moment and race off – towards this new voice and ended up belting me. That intervention didn't feel like a particularly courageous act in the moment, it was just my values and beliefs coming to the forefront, telling me that what I was seeing just wasn't right. I guess it helped that I didn't realise the bully was going to whack me, though, or I might not have been so quick to get involved.

One of the first and most significant challenges around moral courage inevitably involves our peer group when we are teenagers. It comes when a group of mates put pressure on you to act in a way that we suspect or know is the wrong thing to do. We all fall into that one because we're tribal creatures and we all want to fit in and not be outsiders. Our ego wants us to be accepted by the coolest kids and we get dragged along in the direction they choose. But it might mean falling in with a crew who think it's cool to devote their spare time to drugs or graffiti or petty crime. Luckily, as kids in Ungarie we fell into football clubs, which were a more constructive environment.

But even within good environments, there are choices to be made based on our beliefs and values. As much as parents or leadership figures try to guide kids, teenagers need to learn and understand that there will be times when they are floating along on the current of a river and they have to decide whether they are happy going with the flow or whether it's time to swim over to the riverbank, get out and walk back the other way. Subconsciously teenagers have a belief system to guide them, but it can be the hardest thing in the world to bring those forward and question what they are doing.

It takes real courage to speak up against what we perceive to be an injustice, and an even greater test of our character is to then act upon that injustice. It is about having the nerve to stand up and say something, it's about having the nerve to *do* something.

★

At times, courage is required to effect change in a broader land-scape than the situation directly before us. Moral codes shift with the times and often change agents have few supporters, which can make it more difficult to take on.

After I returned from Perth to Melbourne in 2014, I learned that old Demons great Noel McMahen was living in an aged care facility not far from our home in the eastern suburbs. Noel played 175 games for Melbourne including three premierships in the club's golden era after World War II. He became the

VFL's first full-time coach when South Melbourne appointed him in 1962 and was among the most supportive former players during my time as coach of Melbourne.

I dropped in from time to time to visit Noel and he would call over another of the residents, former Carlton captain and coach Ken Hands. We'd chat about football back in their day. You could not meet two finer gentlemen. They believed in good manners and respect but recalled how it was normal when they played football for players to belt the hell out of each other. There was one umpire, no video reviews and a greater acceptance of hits and square-ups. As Captain Blood, Richmond great Jack Dyer, once said about those days: 'You retaliate first!'

As an 18-year-old centre-half-forward, Ken played in the infamous 1945 'bloodbath' grand final against South Melbourne, in which 10 players were reported for 16 offences, resulting in suspensions totalling 69 matches. He was clobbered off the ball late in the first half. For their grandkids, it would be hard to fathom that footballers used to regularly belt each other on the field, and that the standards of the time deemed it an acceptable norm.

In 1990, Essendon and Collingwood players became involved in a brawl at quarter-time of the grand final. Numerous players and officials received lengthy bans as a result, and Terry was suspended for 12 matches on two striking charges. He was just doing what was expected in those days, standing by his teammates. The AFL decided to make an example of those involved in the hope of getting the message through that such melees would no longer be tolerated, a stance that was long overdue.

To some extent, it would have been easy for the league to continue to say, 'This is how we do things.' Over time the decision-makers have had the courage to implement changes – some of them unpopular at the time – that have all but eradicated blatant thuggery from our game. It has stopped giving good men reasons for doing bad things, and that's got to be considered good governance anywhere.

Through vision and legislation, it is possible to lead societal change. I mean, can you imagine a time when people thought slavery was acceptable? Not only did many people think it acceptable, they genuinely believed they were entitled to have slaves. Thankfully there were other people who understood that the concept was fundamentally flawed, cruel and abhorrent and had the courage to act and effect change. And to wear the short-term consequences of doing so. It might take years, generations, but attitudes can evolve when people have the courage of their convictions.

★

The Big Freeze is well and truly established as the main annual fundraiser for FightMND, the foundation I co-founded to create awareness of the disease and to fund much-needed research. The main attraction takes place at the MCG before the Queen's Birthday match between Melbourne and Collingwood football clubs, and involves well-known people going down a slide into a bath of ice in front of a huge crowd – up to 90,000 people.

In the lead-up to the first Big Freeze in 2015, I went on Fox Footy's *AFL 360* talk show to promote the event. Journalist Mark 'Robbo' Robinson asked me an important question.

'How did you overcome your fears? To know your body's dying on you, your mind's sharp, to take this to the public . . . to show people "This is who I am, this is what's happening to me." Was that a tough decision?'

'I'd prefer not to do it, Robbo,' I said. 'I'd prefer to be on the other side of that camera looking at someone else's challenge, but there's a saying in football, when it's your turn to go, you've got to go. This is my time to go.'

I knew I couldn't expect people to fight for the cause if I didn't take up the fight myself. It was simple for me: while I still had a voice, I had to step up to the plate.

Passion might ignite the flame, but purpose keeps it burning

Mark Twain wrote: 'The two most important days in your life are the day you are born and the day you find out why.' I'm pretty happy about that first day – I wouldn't have missed it for quids! However, finding out why – finding my purpose – has been a lifelong quest.

These days, there's plenty of advice that says that to find true meaning you should just follow your passion. If only it was that simple.

You may well have passions and dreams for your life that you believe are tied to meaning and purpose, but then you discover that life doesn't always go according to plan. What if you're no good at the thing you're passionate about? What if you really want to be a pro golfer, but you simply don't have the talent? I say stick with golf – it's good exercise and a great way to spend time with your mates – but don't confuse enjoyable pastimes with your purpose.

Very few of us find a calling – a passion that crosses with a vocation – let alone one that lasts a lifetime. As John Lennon reminded us, life is what happens when we're busy making other plans. Instead we are driven at various times by different passions, starting with childhood dreams of being a firefighter or an astronaut and (hopefully!) fine-tuning them along the way.

Don't get me wrong: working out your unique strengths and talents is one of the greatest things about life. There's nothing like having a real crack at doing what you love; you have a consuming interest that gives you a reason to keep learning and working toward mastery. This is what striving is about.

The wisdom here is in where you draw the line between feeding your ego and finding your purpose.

Obsessive passion can be dangerous. If you put all your eggs in one basket and trip up, there's not much left when all the eggs break. If you're driven purely by 'I want to be a star' but don't possess the requisite talent and work ethic, you are delusional, and destined for disappointment when it all comes crashing down.

I was lucky – I got the wake-up call in my early twenties when injury forced me to look at real life, rather than on my narrow self-centred plans. In order to build the better side of our character and become the best version of ourselves, I believe we need to look at who we serve outside ourselves. When you look beyond your own selfish motivations, and towards something honourable you will discover your purpose and begin thriving.

I know this for sure. You might hit several dead ends before the right path emerges and you begin to thrive, but once you find that path, make a note of the date. It's a very important day.

★

Those final two years wearing the Bombers jumper had reignited my enjoyment of the game and reminded me why I fell in love with footy in the first place.

I remembered being a little kid and taking in the liniment smell before a game and wondering why the adults were so fired up – I figured the game must be important.

I remembered the smell of a new Sherrin footy.

I rediscovered the sheer joy of jumping, marking, spinning, avoiding the opposition and kicking a footy – being totally in the moment, in a state of flow.

I had renewed appreciation for the freedom the game provides, being able to run anywhere with no offside rule, and that you get to kick, mark, bounce and handball as well as chase, block and tackle.

I remembered how much I loved that every player gets to handle the football – unlike rugby.

There is an intrinsic team spirit about footy. As much as I love cricket, it is a team game played by individuals: and as an opening batsman, once you are dismissed, you spend the rest of the day sitting on the boundary unable to contribute. In football, however, if I dropped a mark, I could still try to win back the footy when it hit the ground. If I wasn't in a position to kick a crucial goal, I could still find a way to help a teammate do it.

Having retired from the elite level at age 30, I found I wasn't quite ready to give up the energy that comes with being part of a football team and the joy of running around trying to get a kick. The challenge of testing myself in the next tier down, the Victorian Football Association (VFA), really appealed and several clubs were interested in signing me up. In the end I chose Werribee for a variety of reasons, not least because they had several quality people in leadership positions.

The coach, former Fitzroy rover Leon Harris, was a down-to-earth fella from country Victoria and a good mate, and one of his support crew, Bernie Sheehy, was a former Essendon reserves coach I had been close to for years. Bernie was an unconventional guy, a bit of a maverick and never short of an opinion. He had a sharp football brain and had a successful coaching career in his own right in the VFA and the amateur competitions. But he also had interesting views on a broad range of life issues – some quite left of centre – and we spent many an evening sitting around talking over a few beers.

Nearly everything turned out perfectly that season. The environment at Werribee was closer to the country football vibe I had grown up with in Ungarie. They warmly embraced players and their families at their Chirnside Park home ground, and Jan still rates it as her favourite football season. She had never been to the footy until we started going out together and, even then, her devotion to playing and coaching netball on Saturdays meant that she never actually saw me play in a senior match for Essendon. VFA games were played on Sundays. Now she had the chance to bring our three young kids along – Bec was born in August 1990 – and immerse herself in an authentic community football experience. Mind you, in between keeping a sharp eye on three youngsters and chatting with girlfriends, I'm not convinced Jan ever actually watched me play!

Everything clicked for the team on the field that year. Playing as a key forward, I appreciated the less frenetic pace yet physical nature of VFA football and an injury-free season allowed me to chip in with 44 goals as the Tigers finished on top of the ladder. In the second semifinal I managed to jag six in what was the club's first finals win since it had joined the VFA in 1965.

We were confident going into the grand final at Princes Park, even more so when we were leading by 30 points early in the third quarter. But in the end, we were edged out by nine points by a pretty handy Dandenong outfit. My contribution was less than I had hoped.

That season was as enjoyable as any in my career. The players were a ripping bunch of blokes and I continued to catch up with them regularly for decades afterwards. At 31, there was scope to play on for another season and with the team having come within a couple of kicks of their first premiership, I felt an obligation to go around again. However, Kevin Sheedy had other plans.

Sheeds had just had his contract extended as Essendon coach, and was in my ear about coming back to the Bombers as an assistant coach in a revamped football department. A few weeks after that VFA grand final, he ramped up the pressure by writing in a newspaper column that his first priority was to get me back into the Essendon fold. Knowing that my future in football was now in non-playing roles, I accepted the offer of a part-time coaching position.

Returning to Windy Hill as an assistant coach and selector presented its challenges. My three brothers were still playing at the club, and halfway through 1992 Sheeds decided that he wanted to give some of the younger footballers more games in the senior team. There were some young forwards coming through, such as James Hird, Todd Ridley, Michael Werner and a kid in the reserves, Daniel Winkel, and Terry who at 34 was the oldest player in the league was under pressure to retain his spot in the team.

Sheeds had marked my brother's card, dropped him back for his first ever Essendon reserves match in round 12 and probably half-hoped the old fella would retire. It was tricky, because Terry was an absolute club legend, an ultra-competitive beast, as fit as any 34-year-old and he still wanted his spot in the senior team. As a selector, I was caught in the middle. When I spoke to Terry, he stubbornly maintained that he'd done the hard yards and was going to play out the season, even if that meant playing in the finals series with the reserves. *That's fair enough*, I thought. Denis Pagan, who had been appointed Essendon's reserves coach that year, was delighted to have Terry and another fading club legend, Simon Madden, in his team to bolster his young group of emerging players. He was even more rapt when Terry – who had cracked his shoulderblade playing a farewell seniors match against Geelong in the final round – declared himself available for the reserves grand final and booted six goals to help the Bombers win the premiership.

I doubt that there's ever been a footballer with more passion for playing the game than Terry. The next season he saddled up as captain–coach of the Wagga Tigers, leading them to five premierships out of six grand finals, and he was still running around chasing a kick in the bush in his fifties. He even fronted up to play in a FightMND charity match in Ungarie at the age of 61.

★

Returning to Essendon as an assistant coach made me examine my career vision and to start weighing up where I saw the most scope to flourish. In fact, every aspect of my life was going swimmingly. The sun was shining for Jan and I and our three children. We had moved into a larger house in Essendon, Lauren was starting primary school and Luke was at preschool.

With much of my IT work in the finance sector, I had studied part-time from 1987 to 1989 to complete a Diploma in Applied Finance and Investment at the Australian Stock Exchange. This gave me confidence that I could branch out from in-house employment and work as a consultant with a small firm in Brunswick called MicroHelp. I enjoyed the new challenge of creating revenue for a business, rather than just assisting internal processes. The role involved putting on the suit each day and going to meetings to convince people to take on our firm for substantial projects. One of our biggest clients was Vic Roads, where we spent 14 months rolling out a new software platform across the state, educating staff on how to install and use it. It was challenging but rewarding work.

I had a good annual income, with about 80 per cent of it coming from the IT work and 20 per cent from the part-time coaching role. And yet I kept finding myself drawn back to how much I enjoyed the hours spent in football. Again, it was the call of the siren.

Working as an assistant under Sheedy not only provided some useful lessons and satisfying moments, it could also bring a bit of fun and enthusiasm and it certainly ignited in me a passion for coaching. One of my favourite memories from the time came at the start of 1993, a year in which I took on the role of reserves coach after Denis Pagan accepted the job of senior coach at North Melbourne. Sheeds and I were interviewing some of the young Bombers ahead of a practice match in Adelaide before the 1993 season. In walked Mark Mercuri, a precocious talent who had turned 19 a few days earlier. After a while Sheeds asked, 'Where do you think we should play you?' and motioned to a whiteboard with a football oval on it. Mark grabbed the magnet with his surname printed on it and slapped it bang in the middle of the oval. Sheeds began to explain the issue with putting a kid with three games of AFL experience in the midfield. Mark cut him off. 'No, I'll be fine in there,' he said.

After Mark left, we looked at each other and I laughed, saying, 'I hope he's half as good as he thinks he is.' He was. Mark Mercuri would go on to play more than 200 games for the Bombers, including two premierships, and was selected in an All Australian team in 1999.

★

Kevin Sheedy was the perfect man to do a coaching apprentice-ship under. Apart from learning from his deep football knowledge, all of us deputies benefited because he was prepared to empower us, to hand over some control, listen to ideas and give us some specific responsibilities. He used to say, 'If one of your coaches is good at something, leave him to play with that toy.'

That young 1993 Essendon team, the 'Baby Bombers', finished the season on top of the ladder. Ahead of the AFL finals series, alongside my role as reserves coach, Sheeds charged me with employing my video analysis prowess to dissect what was happening at the centre bounce in matches. That was the coach giving me a toy to play with. The timing was perfect: for the first time, we were starting to get footage from broadcaster Channel 7 that showed vision from behind the goals.

In the qualifying final, our injury-weakened team lost by two points to Carlton, who had finished second on the ladder, equal with us on points. The vision of the centre bounces was instructive. Carlton often gained an edge through its exceptional 206-centimetre tall ruckman, Justin Madden, tapping the ball down to Greg Williams and Craig Bradley, two of the greatest midfielders to play the game, as well as a strong supporting cast of Brett Ratten, Fraser Brown and Adrian Gleeson. They had a damaging system that involved blocking to create space for each other, and the more I studied it, the more I detected the system of their clearance work.

We beat West Coast in a semifinal, then Adelaide in the preliminary final. We'd made it to the grand final and so had our arch rival, Carlton.

Based on my analysis, I wrote up a detailed five-page report with diagrams on how to counter Carlton at centre bounces and faxed it from the MicroHelp office to Sheeds and the key coaching staff. The problem was that I got caught in a conversation and momentarily left the document on the fax machine. To my horror I discovered that one of the office assistants had accidentally hit a button that faxed the report to one of our nearby suppliers. I made a few panicked phone calls, emphasising the classified nature of the report. Our office was in Lygon Street, the epicentre of Carlton FC heartland, and the supplier who received the fax was a massive Blues fan and a club sponsor. In Melbourne, club loyalty trumps most things and therefore the report was forwarded to the Carlton Football Club. Fortunately, Carlton was probably getting mail and faxes from hundreds of supporters with great ideas about what they should do in the grand final and nobody in the Blues' inner sanctum laid eyes on my report until after the game. Carlton's coach at the time, David Parkin, tells the story of his astonishment at coming across the report when he was clearing his in-tray, just days after losing the grand final!

That 1993 flag – the only one I was directly involved in during my time at Essendon – gave me a real sense of joy and pride.

In the grand final, Essendon managed to counter Carlton at centre bounces and was 37 points up at half-time. It was enormously satisfying when, just before three-quarter time, our David Calthorpe sharked a Madden tap and his teammates cleared space for him to have two bounces and kick a 50-metre goal on the run.

Anthony was stiff to miss out on selection. In the qualifying final, he had played on Carlton skipper Stephen 'Sticks' Kernahan, who'd kicked six. Sheeds then made a brave decision to go with talented teenage defender Dustin Fletcher in his place. Kernahan kicked another six in the grand final, but that didn't do Fletch's career any harm. He went on to be a Bombers legend, playing 400 games, the fourth most on record at VFL/AFL level.

I was disappointed for Ants, but was thrilled that my youngest brother, Chris, had become an AFL premiership player. CD was not a superstar, but people tended to underestimate how handy he was as a footballer. An enduring memory from that match is the moment, not long after he came on to the ground, when he crumpled to the turf after receiving a whack in the guts from Kernahan. In that era, the coaches' boxes at the MCG were two covered adjoining rows of seats in the Members Stand, separated only by a perspex shield.

When he saw Chris stumble, Sheeds, no doubt fuelled by his memories of the physical stoushes against Carlton in his days as a Richmond player, scrambled over me and started banging on the perspex, yelling at the Carlton brains trust that he wasn't going to cop any of their thuggery. As the bewildered Blues coach, David Parkin, and his steadfast lieutenant Adrian Gallagher contemplated their response, I grabbed at Sheeds' sleeve to pull him away. 'Look, he's milking it. Chrissy's just milking it for a free kick.' His jaw jutting out and his eyes still fixed on the Carlton camp, Sheedy slowly settled back into his seat, muttering about how he still wasn't going to put up with any rubbish from the other mob.

The biggest thrill for me that afternoon came in the third quarter when Chris charged onto a loose ball, produced a Dustin Martin-like fend-off to break a tackle from Blues defender Matthew Hogg, and ran into an open goal. I got a bit emotional watching him celebrate that goal.

In the aftermath of that grand final, Sheeds was very gracious in talking up my contribution, but I was just one of many cogs that helped set Essendon in motion for that win.

Sheeds was keen for me to further the use of video analysis to pick apart the way the game was played. That was the beauty of Kevin Sheedy's open mind. He used to throw a lot of darts and it was impossible to predict which ones were going to hit the dartboard, let alone score a triple 20. Occasionally he would say, 'Neale, are you following that up?', and that's when I would say, 'I'm onto it', and start to give his idea some genuine time and consideration. At the third mention, I'd tell myself, *OK, he wants it, I better go and complete it.*

At one point in 1994, he suggested studying basketball defences to see whether there was anything worth implementing in an AFL game plan. At first glance I considered the merits of a forward press and setting up a defensive zone, but there was also a concern that it was too risky at that time and that if it didn't come off, a team could get ripped apart. Let's just say the idea was parked, but it's a great example of Sheeds looking for innovation.

Sheeds was ahead of the curve. About a decade later, other AFL coaches began to implement some of those basketball strategies and they were rewarded with team success.

★

Subconsciously, I was starting to lean towards a view that football coaching was where I wanted to hitch my wagon. As promising as it was, the prospect of a secure future in the fast-growing and potentially lucrative computer industry didn't stir me as much as the idea of throwing myself back into the adrenaline-fuelled domain of the AFL. I really enjoyed my work as a project leader at MicroHelp, and even though I was part of a group of people who worked well together, it was a fair way from the closely bonded team mentality that kept luring me back to football. The AFL culture centred around 'team', a brothers-in-arms mentality, and contributing to something with real clarity that was bigger than yourself – at their best, that's what great football clubs are all about.

Over the years I've met various intellectuals who turn up their noses at football, scoffing at what a fairly basic and oafish endeavour it is. I simply nod and inquire what they do for a living. They might tell me they're in the law, adjudicating in property disputes or writing a thesis at university, and it would make me wonder what made them feel so entitled, what gave them such a sense of superiority. *Each to their own*, I'd think. Don't get me wrong, there are many honourable vocations more important than coaching. Many more. I know that finding better ways to get a pigskin between two posts is not saving the world, but for me it was about working with people to realise their potential. Helping young people follow their dreams, steering them towards understanding more about themselves and growing to become better people. That's where there is meaning to be found in coaching beyond the simple aim of leading young men to kick more goals and win more games.

We all spend a great deal of time at work, made easier if we can find a way to enjoy what we do. I understand not everybody finds themselves in that situation, and it can be difficult to find meaning in a job you don't like, that you're doing just to put money in the bank. You can also waste a lot of time striving to find the job you're passionate about, when some interests are best left as recreational pursuits. Like my golf game.

There is a little fable I like to share that helps explain the importance of attitude in everyday life and how that helps us in the search for purpose.

It is about a medieval traveller, who is wandering across the countryside and stumbles upon a group of workers chipping away at huge chunks of granite with their hammers and chisels. Curious about their work, the traveller asks the first tradesman what he is doing.

The man is surly, barely looking up at the stranger before replying, 'I'm cutting stones.'

The traveller asks the second man what he's doing. He is a bit more friendly and replies, 'I'm a stonemason. We're carving out blocks to build walls. It's back-breaking work but it puts food on the table for my family.'

The traveller thanks him and moves on to the third worker, who is absorbed in carefully chipping away at the stone. When the traveller asks him what he's doing, the stonemason runs his hand across the smooth surface, looks to the sky and says proudly, 'I'm a stonemason and I'm building a magnificent cathedral.'

Three men, all doing the same task, but with three different attitudes about the meaning and purpose of their work.

So all I would say is that if you're just surviving at work, you *can* do better, and it's all about attitude and the way you view your role. If you can find even a small thing that brings meaning to your work, you'll be more engaged. Even if you can't make a living doing something you absolutely love, you'll benefit if you spend time finding meaning beyond yourself in what you are doing. If you can't, maybe you should try something else. Life's too short to get stuck.

Think back to that Ungarie farmer who found meaning in believing he was helping to feed the nation. It's a state of mind that beats watching the clock until knock-off time.

★

At the end of 1993, the AFL announced that a new team would be based in Fremantle, competing from the start of the 1995 season. As the media focused on the potential nickname, colours and likely player signings over the months that followed, behind the scenes the club was looking to assemble its football department around inaugural coach Gerard Neesham. The Western Australian club's new president, Ross Kelly, sought advice from his former West Perth teammate, Essendon president Ron Evans, about potential assistant coaches with solid AFL-experience in the league's Victorian heartland. My name was put forward. Soon, Fremantle offered me a role as an assistant coach.

Of course the position appealed to me – it was an opportunity to work full-time in football. Did I throw myself into the less-predictable vagaries of a football coaching existence, or stick with the safe option of the booming and well-paid IT industry? From a purpose-with-passion perspective, the decision to choose football was clear-cut. But there was a more important consideration: this time it wasn't just about me, it was about *us*. The job involved uprooting my family to live in Perth.

This was a fork-in-the-road moment.

The move didn't bother me – this is where leaving home at age 11 really pays off! On the other hand, Jan grew up in the eastern suburb of Blackburn and it had been hard enough for her to shift house to the other side of Melbourne, let alone to the other side of the continent. I broached the subject and could sense her hesitation, but as with all of the major decisions in our life together, she was prepared to consider it with a positive and open mind. She didn't dismiss the notion out of hand.

We made up a list of pros and cons. My list had about a dozen pros, while the cons largely hinged on moving away from family and friends and concerns about diminished job security. Jan's list had a dozen reasons against and the only advantages listed were: Neale's career, better climate, nice beaches and 'getting rid of the old couch'. Over the past year our family had also grown to six, with baby Ben joining Bec (four), Luke (six) and Lauren (eight). We felt the kids were at an age where they would adapt readily enough to a move, but there was the issue of a dimin-ished support network around our young family. We tried to rationalise the factors surrounding the decision, but in the end, it needed both unemotional reason and intuition. Somehow Jan's gut feeling was that a move to Perth was worth a crack, so we packed up our young family and headed off.

We rented in Winthrop in the first year then we bought a house in Bicton, alongside the Swan River, and the family revelled in the light and open coastal lifestyle. With Fremantle being a start-up operation, all of the coaches, staff and players were new to club, so they were welcoming to their colleagues and brought a freshness and enthusiasm to their work. Some of us had moved to Perth for the job, which accelerated friendships and support networks. Within six months Jan loved the place so much that she never wanted to move back.

The decision to seize the opportunity resulted in a great adventure that was fun for the whole family, and effectively launched me in the direction of a working life in football. Our family has been the beneficiary of support and nourishment through my association with coaching that I suspect we would not have found had I opted for a safer life working with computer screens.

On a personal front, I was thriving: I loved the work and I was secure in the knowledge that Jan and the kids were settled and happy.

Being outside our comfort zone gave me an opportunity to view our marriage in a different light and fully appreciate that I had a life partner who would give anything a go, and who kept me grounded. We were forming a pretty formidable partnership which would stand us in good stead for the challenges that lay ahead.

In my three years at Fremantle, if anyone had asked me, 'What are you doing?', I know what my answer would have been. I would have told them proudly that I was building a brand-new football club. One that, like a cathedral, would be around for hundreds of years.

Don't be too hard-arsed

The older you get, the more you realise that everyone sees the world differently. Two people can have the same experience and yet have very different versions of what happened. This is because our core beliefs give us the lens through which we interpret our experiences.

In an unexamined life, we take on foundational beliefs about ourselves, other people and the world we live in without question, then we rationalise or justify them post adoption. We all are suckers for our own confirmation bias. However, in an *examined* life, there comes a time where we should hold those beliefs to the Bunsen burner – that's how we can see which beliefs are helping us through life, and which are hindering us.

It's not easy to change a core belief, especially if it's served you well earlier in your life. It helps to have an appreciation of how applying our beliefs looks from an outside perspective, and to understand that what works in one situation might not be appropriate in another. This is where challenging our beliefs can become a delicate balancing act, because sometimes we are determined to stay the course with an undying conviction that others will eventually come around to our perspective. Changing with the wind is certainly not the answer and nor, at the other end of the scale, is pig-headedness.

In my mid-thirties, changing with the wind was unlikely to be an issue; my challenges were more likely to be around stubbornness . . . in other words, being a hard-arse.

If an aspect of your life is not working, it's worth reflecting and examining the reality, not just your vision. If possible, listen to what trusted confidants have to say on the matter. If the evidence points to the need to change or adapt your behaviour, summon the courage to do that.

There are many qualities that contribute to us becoming the best version of ourselves, and one of these is a willingness to put ourselves in another's shoes and see from their perspective, feel with their heart.

If we are not prepared to challenge our beliefs *and* our method, even our strengths can become weaknesses.

★

In hindsight, it's easy and enjoyable being an assistant coach. You have some responsibility, but it's not your head on the chopping block and, from a pure coaching perspective, you have fewer interruptions. Eight years working in various assistant coaching roles provided me with great insight into the tussles that can exist between collective and individual priorities.

When I was considering a return to Essendon at the end of 1991, I remember telling the team manager Kevin Egan that there was no way known I could become a senior coach because I couldn't imagine having to tell footballers that the club had cut them or that their AFL careers were over.

Every year a coach has to make the call on ending six or eight young men's dreams – on the other hand, they get to tell a similar number of young men that they now have a chance to realise their dream, so there are two different ways of looking at it. Given that I was still playing footy that season and had only been delisted by an AFL club 12 months earlier, it was not difficult for me to put myself in a footballer's boots and see the situation through his eyes. Again, I was young and yet to really understand that leadership does not come without certain burdens.

In the environment of an elite sporting club, leadership is incredibly difficult and often demands tough and, at times, ruthless decisions. While it was important to be aware of other people's emotions, if a coach avoided honesty or confrontation because he didn't want to hurt someone's feelings, his ability to lead people towards a shared goal could be compromised. In recent years, we have seen some AFL coaches – such as Collingwood's Nathan Buckley – benefit from revealing a more vulnerable side of their personality to their players, but a good coach will always show leadership that favours the team cause over the hurt feelings of an individual player. A coach might keenly feel a player's disappointment or despondency but has to keep his eye on the greater good.

The three years I spent at Fremantle really invigorated me; the club was new and bright and innovative and, being at a fledgling organisation, brought the coaching staff and their families close together. Gerard Neesham was a vastly different senior coach, tactically and methodically, to Kevin Sheedy, and that experience, paired with our robust discussions about football, provided me with a fresh perspective on the game. And that was exactly what I needed to round out my experience, after spending nearly 13 years at the one club, under one coach.

In the background, there was a sense that other AFL clubs were keeping an eye on my development as a coach. Back in 1988, after I had first retired as a player, both Geelong and Richmond had reached out for informal chats about coaching opportunities that had arisen through the departures of John Devine and Tommy Hafey respectively. Towards the end of 1994, Geelong interviewed me after the departure of Malcolm Blight, but I was nowhere near ready to step up as senior coach. After a year at Fremantle, however, I began to feel that perhaps the timing was right to take the helm at an AFL club. Looking back, it was probably too soon.

Towards the close of 1995, the Richmond coaching job came up and the Tigers included me on their short list of candidates to succeed John Northey. The speculation was that they were going to give the job to Brisbane Bears mentor Robert Walls. The word was that it was a done deal, but I duly presented my credentials in an interview at a hotel room in Melbourne. The Richmond coaching subcommittee included former Tigers premiership player and coach Tony 'TJ' Jewell, who was now the club's chairman of selectors.

I went straight onto the front foot. 'Realistically, TJ, am I any sort of chance? The word on the street is that you've already promised the job to Robert Walls.'

Well, his nostrils flared, and he took a deep breath, looked me in the eye and growled, 'While I'm at Tigerland, no Carlton %@# will ever coach our club.'

Three days later, Richmond appointed Walls. Presumably there were others at the club who did not have such a vehement aversion to anyone who had played for the Tigers' arch enemy, and they overruled TJ. But whenever I ever bumped into TJ in later years, I always had a little chuckle on the inside.

The opportunity to coach an AFL club came two years later, in 1997, when Melbourne was looking for a candidate to take over from Neil Balme. The Demons put me through what they believed to be the most comprehensive interview process ever for an AFL coach, with psychological profiling, personality and abstract thinking tests.

There were some whispers coming out of Essendon from people who doubted my ability to do the job: he's too intense, he's too forthright, he probably won't be a good media performer. To some degree, they were probably right – I was quite earnest and driven. Mr Negative emerged and whispered to me, 'Maybe you aren't ready', before I banished him. But I believed I was capable of being a good AFL coach and that I'd served a good apprenticeship.

The coaching subcommittee, led by CEO Cameron Schwab and vice-president Bill Guest, arranged for me to be interviewed by the Melbourne president, Joseph Gutnick, who had been elected in the wake of the club's failed merger with Hawthorn 12 months earlier. The interview with Gutnick was the final step in the long process.

I was aware Gutnick wasn't a conventional AFL type – for a start, he was a wealthy Jewish diamond mining magnate. I also knew that he'd wanted to publicly depose Neil Balme as coach mid-game, when he wasn't happy with the team's losing streak. As the next candidate for the job, it's fair to say I was a bit wary.

In his luxurious St Kilda Road office, Joe Gutnick sounded me out with a series of questions directed from his seat at the far end of the timber boardroom table. He ended the interview with a hypothetical scenario: 'What will you do if you get the job and the team loses its first six games and the media starts to come after you?'

I leaned forward and fixed him in my gaze. 'Don't worry about me, Joseph, I think the question is, "What will *you* do?"' A broad smile broke through Gutnick's thick beard. A few days later, the Demons offered me a two-year contract.

As always, I had Jan's support, but had I missed out I'm sure she wouldn't have been too perturbed. Our family had grown to love the Perth lifestyle and people, the weather, the Swan River, nippers at Leighton Beach, crabbing at Cockburn Sound and netball at St Christopher's. We even added one new member to the family, a Labrador pup named Freo. But an opportunity had arisen, and it was time to pack up and head back to Melbourne where another new adventure awaited.

★

There is an intoxicating energy that comes with being appointed coach of an AFL club. You realise that there is an opportunity to share with a willing new group of players what you understand to be the immutable truths about the game of football, buoyant with hope that they will become a better outfit as a result. You are not just offering your football wisdom and experience; you are putting forward a belief system for the group to embrace.

Back in 1987, my motivation for dipping a toe into the coaching pool had been as simple as: 'I love footy, but I can't play anymore, so what can I do to stay involved?' If playing AFL football was 10 out of 10, coaching was the next best option, but it seemed like an 8 out of 10: I wouldn't do it if I could still be playing. Maybe part of the attraction was that I was unfulfilled as a player and was looking for fulfilment as a coach. Being involved in the 1993 premiership as an Essendon assistant coach had provided joy and a degree of satisfaction, but I thought it would be one tenth as gratifying as playing in a premiership (and I would love to be in a position to make that comparison).

Over time, I grew to understand why some coaches said they savoured coaching a flag more than playing in one: it's because they felt they had a more overarching influence on the outcome as a coach than they had as a player. Through coaching there was scope to thrive by being central to the group cause and scope to be involved in all aspects of a team sport.

★

Walking through the doors of the Melbourne Football Club, I expected the greatest challenge to be taking on a team that had ended the previous season four games clear on the bottom of the ladder. Rather, what I found to be the most enduring obstacle was that Melbourne was a somewhat dysfunctional club.

The Demons were still carrying the scars of the failed 1996 merger attempt with Hawthorn, which was only avoided when Hawks fans had rejected it. The board was split between those who were pro- and anti-merger. The relationship with the Melbourne Cricket Club was strained, and Gutnick wasn't making any friends at the AFL. There was a sense that the Melbourne hierarchy's primary objective was survival, just keeping the doors open. Their focus was necessarily on that aim as they realised Gutnick's cash injection would not solve Melbourne's off-field financial issues.

There I was, oblivious to these issues, heading up a football department that I wanted to steer in the direction of becoming an elite team. OK, we had some challenges but, somewhat naively, I believed we could overcome them, even though the two parts of the football club were not even under the same roof. The brains trust was based in the shadows of the MCG at Jolimont Terrace, while the football department was five kilometres away at Junction Oval in St Kilda, and the rooms, gymnasium and other facilities were underwhelming. Worse still, access to our training base during the off-season was limited because the ground was given over to cricketers in summer. If the St Kilda Cricket Club made the finals – which it seemed to most seasons – we would get access to the venue at best the week before the AFL season started. That meant we trained in a council parkland across the road that the players had come to affectionately call 'The Slope'.

I was determined that neither I nor the playing group would ever use these 'challenges' as excuses. At least we weren't flying across the continent every second week like the Perth-based teams.

My assessment of the playing list was that, despite finishing last the previous season (much to do with a bad run of injuries), we actually had a fair bit of talent, although the core group was ageing and tired. We were bolstered by the off-season signings of former number 1 draft pick Jeff White from Fremantle and grand final fullback Jamie Shanahan from St Kilda, and we'd picked up a gifted teenager Travis Johnstone with the first selection in the national draft. The players joked one part of the locker room belonged to Hollywood Boulevard.

I swept in there determined to make it clearly known what was needed for improvement – the standards and values that could not be compromised – probably influenced by the way Kevin Sheedy had arrived at Essendon in 1981. The playing group was up for it. They were ready for change.

Many of the senior players had invested in $3000 bicycles to use for cross-training over the pre-season. I told them they wouldn't be needing the bikes: they were going to be doing a lot of running instead. My belief was that football was a running endurance game – we had to learn to gut run, because minds, not bodies, give up first.

For a month we based ourselves at Caulfield Grammar School, with the days starting at 6.45 am and running through until about 4 pm, the time split between training and theory. Football university, we called it. At the time, we were mocked by certain sections of the media: *How bad were Melbourne if they had to go back to the classroom?* However, I believed that every player and coach needed to understand what we were doing. The players were taught the game plan and how I wanted them to play, with the idea that we would reinforce that style throughout the season, and there would be plans A, B, C and D depending on opposition and specific game situations.

I wanted to coach a direct and attacking game style. I am not a fan of what football would become in the mid-2000s: defence first, low scoring, boundary hugging, locking the ball in, constant stoppages. Give me a free-flowing game where the ball is in constant play, and two teams attack each other back and forth through the middle of the ground. That's the essence of Australian Rules football to me.

The point is that I cared about the look of the game. I also cared about the club – it is the oldest football club in Australia, and I didn't want it going under on my watch. I cared deeply about the team – each team has a personality and I wanted any team I coached to know that the betterment of the group was more important than any individual. Notwithstanding all this, I cared about the individual: you must know the individual to coach the individual.

★

By all reports, Melbourne's previous senior coach, former Richmond hard man Neil Balme, had a fairly relaxed, affable coaching style. It didn't take long for everyone at the club – myself included – to realise that I would register on the opposite end of the scale come game day.

My first match at the helm was a 1998 Ansett Cup game played in Wellington, New Zealand. This was the pre-season competition and we were playing the Sydney Swans, who had been grand finalists in 1996. After arriving at the ground, I took the opportunity to clamber up to the coaches' box and just sat there with my good mate, match-day assistant Darrell Fenton, taking in the majestic, mountainous backdrop. Neither of us could quite believe that the first act of this new adventure was about to play out on such an unimaginable stage, off Australian shores.

I looked out across the lush Basin Reserve turf and thought to myself, *Now don't get too worked up today, don't be too intense. It's only game one and this group were wooden spooners last year. There's a lot to do and a long road ahead. We are playing the Swans . . . I know you want it all to happen straight away, but just understand it's going to take a while.* And I actually reassured myself, *Yes, Neale, I'll behave.*

Some of the guys who played that day still rib me about what happened next. At half-time, the Demons were nine points down. The scoreline wasn't the issue; I had outlined some expected standards and I wanted the players to be very clear that I wouldn't accept what they were dishing up. I marched into the rooms and went off my rocker, tearing strips off senior players David Neitz, Todd Viney and Jeff 'The Wizard' Farmer.

'Neita, any danger of helping out your teammates by hanging onto a mark? And you, Toddy, no wonder he's not taking his marks with the way you're kicking it to him.'

And Farmer's blast was little more than, 'Wizard, Wizard, WIZARD!', accompanied by a withering look and a shake of my head in dismay.

By three-quarter time, my voice was so raspy that assistant coach Greg Hutchison had to address the huddle and deliver most of the instructions. Although we went on to defeat the Swans by two goals, the greater gain from that match was a personal reminder that there was no point simply yelling at the players until I became hoarse. Intensity had its place, but it needed to be accompanied by clarity – specific reinforcement of the way we wanted to play and the non-negotiable aspects of our game plan. Those technical elements had been drilled into the players ever since the Caulfield Grammar sessions. But that day, let's just say that I learnt my feedback around the 'what and how' of our game needed a major rethink.

Although I was quite methodical as a coach, I did like to try to touch the players' hearts by telling an occasional yarn with an underlying message that I thought might lodge in their psyche. That summer we watched some footage from a wildlife documentary that showed a pride of lions hunting in Africa. The lions ambushed a wildebeest, which gave up the ghost immediately, rolled over and succumbed. In another scene, the lions attacked a water buffalo, which threw around its horns, fought them off and survived. The footage ended with the water buffalo standing there defiantly, flared nostrils snorting as the lions retreated.

'Boys,' I said. 'What do you want to be, the wildebeest or the water buffalo? You choose.' Of course they chose the latter. 'OK, that means we need to commit to running straight for the footy at every contest and never giving up.' The water buffalo yarn resonated with the players and would become a recurring theme among the group during the season.

That group of Demons desperately wanted to regain respect as a competitive football team. Some of the players were in their football infancy; some had been hobbled by injury in recent seasons; and some had been discarded or overlooked by other clubs, but they all responded when told they had something to prove to the rest of the competition. The playing group went into the season with plenty of belief, cohesion and trust, and they started to enjoy playing football again. We were not yet kings of the jungle, but we believed we could be water buffaloes.

That 1998 season had a bit of everything. The first win came in round 2 against a seasoned North Melbourne team that contained some stellar players at the peak of their careers, such as Wayne Carey, Mick Martyn, Glenn Archer and Anthony Stevens. Victory against such a powerful and proven outfit built on the Melbourne players' conviction that they could match it with the best. We won five consecutive matches, struggled to overcome injuries to several key players, lost consecutive mid-season matches by 95 and 85 points, and then surged home to finish the home-and-away season in fourth position. We carried our momentum into September, winning our first two finals against the previous year's grand finalists, Adelaide and St Kilda, before going down to flag favourite North Melbourne in the preliminary final.

Getting so close to a crack at a premiership felt like a real missed opportunity, but we did take encouragement from having risen 12 rungs up the ladder – at the time, it was a record for the biggest climb from one season to the next.

★

Even though we had several influential ageing champs retire at the end of 1998, there was considerable optimism about Melbourne's prospects heading into 1999. Once again, we put the team through four weeks of 'football university' during the pre-season. But the summer also featured some off-field disruptions that slowed the club's momentum.

An investigation into player payments revealed salary-cap breaches (pre-dating my time at the club) that would eventually lead to the club being fined $350,000 and stripped of selections in the 1999 and 2000 national player drafts. Chief executive Cameron Schwab and president Joseph Gutnick were not on the same page over several issues and factions began to develop among the club's powerbrokers. The friction became so acrimonious that Schwab stood aside in the second half of the season. When Gutnick eventually left the club in May 2001, Melbourne was once again struggling financially, devoting all of its energy into how to survive, rather than on how to become a great club.

While all of the off-field turmoil was distracting, it did not excuse the on-field drop-off. In the end, we won four of our first seven games before finishing the season poorly, losing our last nine in a row. We were back to fourteenth on the ladder and had to find a way to revitalise a playing list that was now losing some experienced top-end talent. The departure of Brownlow Medallist Jim Stynes at the end of 1998 was followed by the retirement of former captain Garry Lyon, as well as our 1999 captain Todd Viney and vice-captain Glenn Lovett, who had both struggled with persistent hamstring injuries. And the salary-cap breaches meant we would go to the national draft stripped of our first-round selection.

Reflecting at the end of 1999, there was no point just sheeting home the blame for a disappointing season to administrators, the board and the playing list. I needed to reflect and examine what the evidence was telling me about how I was tracking as a coach. When I challenged my football beliefs – a structured and attacking game style consolidated by values such as putting team first, being honest, working hard and never giving up – I felt that they stood up.

But how was my coaching *method* being received and did it need recalibrating?

As an immature Essendon captain, my beliefs about the way the team needed to improve were appropriate, but the way I acted upon those beliefs and expressed the message was not received particularly well and therefore lacked cut-through. Was I about to make the same mistake again?

I viewed the game as a relentlessly demanding sport. My mantra to my players was that we would be judged by our actions, not our words. I wanted them to tell me what they were going to do, and then back it up with actions to the best of their abilities.

Lurking in the back of my mind was the knowledge that AFL football is difficult enough for the players, without them having any doubts about my leadership. I thought that they needed me to provide firm direction, particularly in those early days, so I defaulted to providing the players with clarity about the team vision and how we would enact it. My approach might have been too harsh at times, and probably had an impact on the performance of some players who simply needed their coach to throw an arm around them more often and ask them how they were going. I'm sure when I was too hard on those sorts of players, they were thinking, *Get stuffed.* I had assumed that the players understood where I was coming from: that I had a responsibility to the club and to the team, and that the collective cause was paramount. This is a reminder that it's not what you say that's important, it's what they hear.

Of course I knew that the players, like all people, are a tapestry of emotions: they might be arguing with their girlfriend or upset over what somebody said about them or missing their family in another state. But I also knew that once a player crossed that white line, nobody gave a stuff about those feelings. That's why I was hellbent on getting the message across about what the players needed to do, when it was their turn to go.

This time, when I could sense I was losing traction with the players, I sought advice from trusted confidants such as assistant coaches Chris Fagan and Greg Hutchison, and several senior players. For me, delivering honest feedback has never been a problem and I would like to think the same could be said of receiving it. In the coaches' box I would say, 'Don't tell me that the opposition has kicked the past three goals, or that their star is cutting loose. Give me a suggestion about how to turn it around. I know the problem, what's the solution?' I made it clear that any suggestions would go into the mix because we wanted the best idea to emerge. It was not about whether my idea or their idea was better.

But outside the coaches' box, I needed a more nuanced approach.

Hutchison, who had been Melbourne's caretaker coach in the latter part of 1997 and had previous coaching experience guiding Prahran to a VFA premiership, had some sage advice. 'Mate, you've got to take a deep breath and slow down,' he suggested.

I was too driven and at times too reluctant to delegate any responsibility. My manner towards the players was uncompromising and extended to micro-managing matters such as their pre-game preparation. The workload that I had created for myself was enormous, driven by the old maxim 'the harder you work, the luckier you get'. And because that method had produced results in my first year, I felt it was vindicated and the appropriate way to operate. But it was not a sustainable approach to coaching an AFL club.

However, we had a very small coaching team at Melbourne, so it was hard to know who to delegate to. Fagan and I discussed the fact that most of the directions and feedback delivered to the players came from me, and while hearing one voice had been necessary in 1998 to ensure clarity of direction and to avoid mixed messaging, that needed to change. Now I should have confidence that others knew the vision and could help realise it. There was scope to be more inclusive with the players and to give them more ownership of the team and responsibility for performance. Listening to this counsel helped me to see the situation through others' eyes and provided impetus for a change in method.

Going into season 2000, the belief system remained but there would be a subtle change in method. It would no longer be all about, *I'm the leader, you follow.* It would be about how we could share the vision and the responsibility, and about building an environment where the players owned it and the senior coach was the facilitator.

Now it would just be a matter of implementing those changes, and what remained to be seen was whether they would work.

As I evolved as a coach, I understood that there are many layers involved when it comes to giving personal feedback around how an individual needs to change. There needs be candour about what the issues are, as well as thoughts on how to address them. What worked best for me – hearing it straight, undiluted – didn't necessarily bring out the best in other people.

And unless the person receiving the feedback is convinced there is a need for change, then change won't happen.

I knew change was necessary and I felt ready to change. I was up for the challenge of being the best leader I could be.

The seed is in the dirt, it just hasn't shot yet

Leadership is hard, and it's not for everyone.

Leadership is all about influence: if you can't influence outcomes, you can't lead. Leaders rally people towards a better future, which involves change, and change is often resisted. It requires clarity of message. It's about clearly explaining the current reality of the situation and setting out why we want to build towards an improved reality. If people don't understand the 'why', they will be reluctant to put their heart and soul into helping everyone get there.

To be a good leader, in any given situation you need to continually sell your vision of this better future to your constituents and how great it will look and feel once you're all there. You need to show them the road you're going to take. You will be called on to make decisions when there is uncertainty and you need to be prepared to be unpopular at times. You need to accept that you might piss people off when you make hard calls, and that sometimes you'll get things wrong. You need to be both patient and resolute in sticking to your guns, which means you need to have great self-awareness and a strong sense of purpose. You need to be accountable for the outcomes even though others in your team will have an influence on those outcomes.

The best leaders are very clear about who they serve. They are not driven by servicing their own ego.

Leadership (why and where) initiates management (what and how). Without credible and reliable management, leaders can lose all authority. If leadership is not supported by strong management, the 'what and how' becomes ineffective when put into practice. This can disillusion the team who will say, 'I understand the *why*, but *what* we are doing and *how* we're doing it isn't taking us forward. You don't have any credibility here.'

Positive momentum starts with good leadership. Great leadership is required at all stages of any challenge, but no more so than at the start to drive the initial change or the start-up endeavour.

As a leader, you need full and informed confidence in the vision – the why – and the courage to stay the course. The ultimate measure of a leader is not where he stands in moments of comfort and convenience, but where he stands at times of challenge.

Often the most challenging period for a leader is when there's still nothing to see after lengthy preparation and everyone's patience is wearing thin. It's the most testing time, but don't give up. Sometimes it's just before the grain shoots.

★

Melbourne was widely predicted to finish near the bottom in 2000. People outside the club, and even a few inside it, were casting doubts about the quality of our playing list. I felt our top-end talent was there, but realistically 2000 shaped up as a season of development for the group, aspiring for some solid progress up the ladder and continuing to rally our people towards a better future.

There was good reason to predict growth among some of the younger footballers who had come to the club either through late draft picks or the rookie system, guys such as Daniel Ward, Guy Rigoni, Nathan Brown, Brent Grgic and Peter Walsh, while the potential of first-year players Brad Green, Matthew Whelan, Cameron Bruce, Troy Broadbridge and Paul Wheatley was an unknown quantity.

When the critics are doing their best to undermine trust in your vision, leadership is a tough gig. There will be times when you doubt yourself and your methods. You might even wonder whether you should abandon what you're doing altogether. It might be that you are the only person truly convinced of the direction you're heading in. People might tell you, 'It's not working.'

You find out what you're made of when the going gets tough, especially when you're under scrutiny as a leader. Real leadership is needed when people are questioning whether the leader is credible and whether they're worth a heart-and-soul effort.

The American author John C. Maxwell suggests that there are five levels of leadership. The first level is when we attain a leadership position, a title that suggests certain power and control, but does not guarantee the hearts and minds of our followers. We are yet to earn that. The next level is reached through relationship building, by establishing rapport and trust with our people. With that belief in each other comes extra effort. At level three, a leader has the group working well together, being productive and getting results. Level four involves the leader delegating responsibility and developing and stimulating other leaders within the group. By level five, the leader is helping the emerging leaders get to level four and creating an environment that benefits everyone.

Simple, isn't it!

Leaders generally need a certain amount of healthy ego, but at times it is important to put that ego to one side and realise that no one has all the answers. Staying true to our vision is one thing, but it can be counterproductive when we are too stubborn about process, and tell ourselves, *Come on, I'm good enough, I can do it all.* We can still accept that our 'why' is right, but our 'how' needs adjusting, and that's when we need to be open to listening to feedback along the way.

That's not to say we should treat our leadership as a popularity contest. Political leaders fall away because they worry about opinion polls and where the votes are coming from. That's not leadership, that's about staying in power. Their 'why' might be nothing more than clinging to their nominal title of 'leader', with the pretence of doing what's best for the electorate. By putting off hard decisions or avoiding them because they don't want any negative feedback, they are no longer leading.

While I was a senior coach, I learnt some valuable lessons about receiving honest feedback and, in particular, about who to listen to. At a football club, there's plenty of free advice on offer, especially from disgruntled fans.

When you are a manager, coach or leader, if you don't have a keen sense of what your employees, players or followers are thinking, you can easily become ineffective. You need to listen to candid feedback and be open to act on what you think is relevant and true. As a coach, I tiered feedback into three distinct areas: outer sanctum, inner sanctum and inner circle.

The outer sanctum is the largest, most emotional and noisiest group: fans, print and broadcast media, social media, football commentary. You need to be aware of this group, and careful not to react to their noise. When taking in feedback from this group, it's wise to remember: it's never as good, or as bad as they say.

The inner sanctum refers to those in the know: people inside the club (players, staff, management, the board) and a few trusted outsiders who offer their perspective and wisdom. This feedback is vital and you should encourage differing viewpoints.

Then you have the inner circle: a small group of confidantes whose judgement you totally trust. Ignore these people at your peril.

Within this circle, it's important that you don't create an echo chamber and seek feedback from people you know will agree with you. You need a spread throughout the club to ensure you get a broad perspective, which is why you might include a trusted outsider. Once decisions are made, it's important that your inner circle knows they have been listened to, even if their advice isn't always followed.

In my case at Melbourne, our captain, David Neitz, was inner circle, as well as coaching and key fitness staff and the general manager of football. The CEO and chairman should have been, but with the regular rotations in those positions, it didn't always happen that way.

There's one thing you need to be very mindful of as a leader and you see this happen in all walks of life. When the pressure builds, sometimes leaders stop listening. Then the inner circle shrinks to just you, and if you fall for that, you are a dead man walking.

★

Ahead of the 2000 season at Melbourne, the feedback from trusted confidants had helped me realise that I needed to delegate more responsibility to the assistant coaches and nurture more leadership among the players. I had absolute faith in Chris Fagan, a very positive man I could dependably lean on. He was a really strong sounding board. I could always ask, 'How are we going there, mate?' or 'What should we do about this?', and he could give me a plain-spoken view and one that might be quite a contrast to what I was thinking.

When I was first appointed Melbourne coach, the club was keen to have a good Demons man as reserves coach. Several former players held enormous sway and they had earmarked a former Melbourne defender for the job. He was a good fella, but I wanted to interview candidates for the role.

At the time Chris Fagan was a bit of an unknown, a former premiership player in Tasmania who was coaching the under-18 Tassie Mariners. I was impressed during the interview by his character, outlook and credentials. I also liked the idea that he would owe no one at Melbourne anything (except me, for giving him the job!), so a few days later I rang him. He answered his mobile phone while riding on the Ferris wheel at the Royal Hobart Show. 'You better have a talk to Ursula,' I said. 'There's a fair chance the job's yours if you're prepared to get across here.' His appointment proved to be one of best calls I made during my time as coach of Melbourne.

Unfortunately, though, at the end of 1999 I lost the services of both Matty Rendell and Greg Hutchison, the latter accepting a senior assistant coaching role at Richmond. Realising that I needed to share the coaching load was an important step, but other than Chris Fagan, who could I turn towards to help share the load? In a meeting with the club's general manager of football, Danny Corcoran, I appealed for the club to loosen up its threadbare purse strings. Former Bulldogs champion Brian Royal came on board to replace Hutchison, and we identified that recently retired Demons greats, Garry Lyon, Jim Stynes and Todd Viney might be interested in returning to the club as part-time line coaches. All three understood the vision for the future and could promote the team values, while also adding nuances from their own wisdom and experiences during their time at Melbourne.

All of this created a great dynamic, allowing the playing group to hear the messaging from an array of speakers, rather than have it continually drilled into them by the lone voice of the senior coach.

In my first year at Melbourne, the knowledge that a trio of club stalwarts was nearing the end of their playing careers had created an acute awareness that we needed the middle tier of footballers to step up and fill the void. During the 1998 season, we had sent a group of ten players to the Victoria Police Academy for a seven-week leadership course, where they had been addressed by the likes of union boss Bill Kelty, four-time premiership coach Allan Jeans and Victorian treasurer Alan Stockdale. Going into 2000, Fagan suggested putting in place a two-tiered leadership group, with one group consisting of captain David Neitz, vice-captain David Schwarz and their deputies Andrew Leoncelli and Shane Woewodin, being supported by another eight players in a secondary tier.

One evening before the opening game of the 2000 season against Richmond, we gathered the entire club staff on the field of the MCG. We placed the club's 1964 premiership cup — their most recent — in the middle of the group and on the two massive scoreboard screens we showed footage of that grand final victory, spliced together with vision of the current players in action. The players' leadership group presented the new vision statement they had developed. Our 'why' was now truly shared and our 'how' had been tweaked, and with it came fresh energy and hope.

★

It might seem easy for me to talk about leadership in the context of sport, where results are measurable and public, but many leadership learnings actually apply to getting any group of people to work towards a common goal. In elite team sport, there are many attributes that contribute to successful leadership, but three that I rate as critical are character, competence and clarity. A good leader needs to rate highly in all three areas.

A good leader needs character-based traits, such as honesty and integrity, so that followers can believe in the person behind the vision. But you can't just have character without competence – a leader also needs an understanding of how to move the group from the current circumstance to a better future. Followers expect a leader to know the 'how'; the leader might not have the whole blueprint but must have confidence that the right people are on board to help reach their common goal.

And in every aspect of leadership, the most crucial requirement is clarity. If people know exactly what actions are expected and which targets are the priority, they are more likely to work their hearts out to strive for the better future that has been defined. Clarity engenders confidence, persistence and resilience.

If you have the required level of competence, and you're a character of great integrity, without the ability to clearly communicate your vision for the shared better future, you're probably not going to make a great leader.

When I took on the Melbourne coaching role, part of that job was establishing clarity in management: how I wanted the team to play. We drilled the new game style into the players, but it was also about clarity in outlining the expected attitude. I felt that before the team could learn to succeed, the players had to embrace an approach where they were prepared to fight and scrap like hell whenever they were challenged.

Underscoring all of this was clarity around the vision for any player pulling on a Melbourne Football Club jumper.

My focus was on the team vision, on where we wanted to get to and what was required, and I knew I needed good people around me. Jack Gibson, the great rugby league coach, believed the primary role of the coach is 'to keep quality in the joint'. That strikes a chord with me. 'Quality' includes players, staff and volunteers. Quality people help identify when someone might benefit from a little individual attention. In my case, one of the assistant coaches, often Chris Fagan, would say, 'Mate, I think you should sit down and have a chat with that bloke.'

In the AFL now there are vastly bigger football staffs and there are also development coaches who can monitor more aspects of how a player is going and be across what is happening in their life outside of football. In the end, though, the players still want support from the senior coach.

As a coach who strongly believed in team above individual, it was difficult for me to use up too much energy on a footballer whose pride was a little bruised by having his own expectations pushed behind those of the collective cause. That was a leadership choice made against the backdrop of my core beliefs and mixed in with some influence from my DNA.

At times, when I'm being impatient or judgemental or critical, Jan has been known to say, 'You're just like your father'. And when someone says that to you, it's rarely offered as a compliment.

'Don't bring my father into this,' I'd laugh, trying to ward off a broadside.

She was hinting that my father was an old-school farmer, one who had to shoot distressed sheep or cut chickens' throats without allowing himself to get caught up in the emotion of it all. He was always prepared to take on the tough jobs that nobody else wanted to do, because he knew they had to be done. It's a harsh life on the farm and aspects of it are hard to fathom for someone who has grown up in the suburbs. Farming was not the life I chose to pursue, but I do have a similarly stoic outlook. In a way, Jan was right: at times I am a lot like my father. Luckily, he was a great bloke!

Getting people to buy in and follow us is a crucial element of leadership. In a sporting context, players are either going to follow their leader or they are not. Some teams really try, some just look like they're trying, and some teams think, *Stuff the coach, I've had enough of him*, and they only half-try. In my time as Melbourne coach, I experienced all three scenarios.

You might find yourself promoted to a leadership position, but unless people follow you, you're a leader in title only. It's fine to set out strategies and to guide people through process, but leaders also have to understand what will make their followers buy in and stay motivated to give effort and perform. You need to know the individual, and also to know your mob. If a leader loses touch with their followers, they become ineffective.

Across my decade as coach of Melbourne, I would like to think that I did show care for player development, both as individuals and as a group. However, when I'm around Melbourne footballers from that era now, I'm half-waiting for them to say that I was too tough on them. And I'm surprised when it doesn't come – maybe they are just more forgiving than you'd think.

I never tried to be friends with the players I coached. It's not that I sought to be unfriendly, but first and foremost I saw my job as setting out the vision and expectations and helping them understand how they could get the best out of themselves. Sometimes that required a bit of love, sometimes a bit of tough love, and the latter was a clear priority above gaining their affection.

As it turns out, some players have now become mates and one of my former captains, David Neitz, is now a close friend. And I still see many players from that era pretty regularly. They have an informal running group that I would get along to maybe three or four times a year. Recently we organised to catch up and I said that after they had dragged themselves around The Tan running track, I would shout them breakfast. Usually only eight or 10 of them front up a run, but on this day about 40 strolled through the cafe door. I think it was a record . . . and I had a great laugh with the lads. It was a monumental stitch-up.

*

Despite the recalibration towards a more collective responsibility, Melbourne's first half of the 2000 season was unremarkable:

we won half of our opening 12 matches and then suffered an embarrassing 16-goal loss to Carlton that left us clinging to a spot in the top eight.

But over the next eight-game stretch, our only loss was to reigning premiers North Melbourne – by one point. We went into the finals with momentum, on the back of a five-match winning streak that saw us at third spot on the ladder.

A telling example of that momentum came in the first final against Carlton, when we were down by 21 points at three-quarter time. We'd been outplayed and our likeliest match-winning threats – David Neitz, Jeff Farmer and David Schwarz – were struggling to have an impact. During the huddle before the last quarter, we told the players they had no option but to go on the attack, and explained we planned to isolate a couple of first-year players, Brad Green and Cameron Bruce, up forward. In the final term the team persistently pumped the ball forward and the young fellas kicked three and two goals respectively to sneak us home by nine points.

A fortnight later we lined up on a Friday night against North Melbourne, playing in their seventh consecutive preliminary final, and the subsequent 50-point win meant we'd made it to the grand final – the Demons' first grand final appearance in 12 years. Our opponent would be a powerful team that had lost just one match for the season: Essendon. Coached by Kevin Sheedy.

★

As a coach, I liked to tell the playing squad stories. During 1999, a tough year, we were talking about how there might be times in life when we're slogging away and doing all of the right things but not seeing any signs of success. We all go through lean patches, doing the work with very little to show for it.

I shared my 'Secret Garden' story with them: told them how Mum had a garden back up on the farm that she'd nurtured in that barren land in the middle of nowhere, spending countless hours tending the roses, flowers, fruit trees and lawn. She didn't do it to present to the world, she wanted to create something beautiful for the family.

When my mother arrived at Hillview as a newlywed in the late 50s, my Uncle Leo's parting words were, 'Good luck growing anything there!', as he moved up the road to his new farm. But Mum was not deterred. She knew all good things take time. It was tough soil, but she soldiered on through decades of droughts and locust and mice plagues, and our footballs landing in her rose bushes.

Dad used to plough the hell out of the area surrounding it. Mum would push out the garden boundaries; it was her occupied territory. He would say, 'Don't go beyond that plough line – anything beyond that line is fair game for the plough.' He was supportive of Mum's endeavours up to a point. I guess the bigger picture was that he was concerned about her working herself to the bone and there was always the issue of the water levels in the dam.

After many decades, Mum's garden surrounded the whole house. It was magnificent, this little green oasis in the red dust, and gave everyone great pleasure.

Sometimes I queried her vision, saying, 'Mum, looks pretty bare over there in that patch, what's going on?' She would reply, 'Oh Neale, that will be my shining glory, just wait. The seed is in the dirt, it just hasn't shot yet.'

The point is that my mother had a vision. She was passionate about that garden and totally devoted to it. There were times when she did the hard work, and nothing came of it.

Anything worthwhile in life is like that. It takes time. When I was coaching, sometimes I'd hear Mr Negative chipping away, a bit like Uncle Leo: 'Good luck growing anything there, mate. Can't see anything for all that effort you're putting in.' Particularly when you're a leader, if your plans don't come to fruition straight away, don't just give up. It's about maintaining belief in what you're doing and putting in the work.

When we persist, even a beautiful garden in the wilderness is possible, but it's worth remembering that the real work is done when there is no result yet to see.

One finger can't lift a pebble

Two very important events occurred in 1961. John F. Kennedy announced his vision to put man on the moon by the end of the decade, and I was born. On the latter, I might be biased but I know my mum agrees with me! On the former, this vision inspired a nation and became a rallying call towards an emboldened future. As JFK stated, they chose that audacious goal because 'that challenge is one that we are willing to accept, one we are unwilling to postpone, and one which we intend to win'.

Just selling the vision wasn't going to deliver a giant lunar step for humankind. To get that job done required precise strategy, management and execution, and a committed, high-performing team.

Leaders understand the single most powerful motivation for teams is a clear and compelling performance challenge. However, that is only the beginning. Getting the job done isn't just about the lion's roar, it's equally about the silence of ants working patiently, persistently and never giving up.

Individuals become teams through disciplined and spirited action. The discipline is enacted when individuals commit to shaping a common purpose, agree on performance goals, define and buy into a game plan, develop complementary skills and hold themselves mutually accountable for delivering results. But here's the secret. I believe that for any team to be truly high performing, this disciplined action needs to be overlaid with a 'spirit'. It's a less measurable ingredient that all great teams develop, and unfortunately you can't buy it off the shelf.

Spirit emerges through time spent together, which allows all team members to build a high level of trust and respect. It happens when each member is there for the right purpose: the agreed team purpose. This level of trust allows members to manage conflict and resolve issues that emerge in all teams, because there is a genuine commitment to find the right answers and make team-first decisions. If the spirit is there, all issues are dealt with in an open, respectful manner and commitment to the common cause is built upon, not eroded. When the team commits to decisions and standards of performance, the members have no issue in holding one another accountable. The development of trust, respect, commitment, resilience, hope and faith engenders a spirit within a team that eventually leads to love, a genuine care, concern and compassion for the welfare of all team members.

Building a high-performing spirited team is a means to an end, it's not the end. Delivering on the performance challenge is the end but getting the job done – getting a man on the moon – should always remain the focus.

Where the spirit is willing you will find a thousand ways; where there is no spirit, you will find a thousand excuses.

★

I worked with groups of people in the IT industry, and even though this was enjoyable, what was required of those teams never equalled the requirements of high-performing sports teams.

In how many other professions do we unreservedly demand that the individual always parks self-interest for the betterment of the group? The non-negotiables for the members of elite sporting teams are extreme: I'm talking about the demands of mutual accountability, preparation, execution and attitude – where the requirements of their profession permeate their private lives.

However, there are many common things required by any group of people working towards a common goal.

Every team has a collective personality, as well as a mix of individual personalities. When an AFL club brings together 40-odd footballers, the mix can be extremely diverse, because the main thing these people have in common is their ability to play football. The group might include a knockabout from Hobart, a Melbourne private school captain, a kid from the Tiwi Islands, a lad from Kalgoorlie, Dublin or Texas . . . even a farmer's son from Ungarie. There are fresh-faced teenagers and fathers of three alongside each other, silent types and blokes who fancy they would make a ripping game-show host.

The common denominator with all of these young men is simply their level of talent and ability, their love of football and their desire to be part of the team.

Not all players have to like each other; it is more important that they respect each other and respect what they can bring to the team. But it does help if team members do like each other, and it's essential that enough members of the team do, otherwise you can never build collective trust.

A couple of years after the Chicago Bulls had won three consecutive National Basketball Association championships, they brought in forward Dennis Rodman – he was unconventional, at times controversial and not everyone's cup of tea, and he had antagonised the Bulls when he was playing for their arch rival, the Detroit Pistons. But he could contribute to Chicago's cause with excellent rebounding, physicality and defensive hustle. He made the team better and they won another three titles in a row, but that doesn't necessarily mean all of his teammates wanted to hang out with him socially. Strong teams have an engagement and flexibility about them that can usually accommodate eccentricity better than poor teams.

I go back to Kevin Sheedy's assertion during his time as Essendon coach that 'you have to have some cowboys in your team'. It was his way of saying that a lot of the match-winning players are 'cowboys', a bit wild, and the challenge of coaching is knowing how to deal with them. Sheeds dealt with Paul Vander Haar, Merv Neagle, Ron Andrews and Terry in the one team. All great blokes, just stubborn and not easily tamed. They walked their own paths.

Coaches need to be careful – they can have an unconscious bias towards selecting a team full of players whose personalities are similar to their own. Subliminally, coaches think, *I know that guy, I get where he's coming from.* Sheeds, who revelled in having his own coach, Tommy Hafey, describe him as a 'bloody back pocket plumber' – even though he was also a crafty Richmond premiership ruck-rover – was probably hardest on the more complex and thoughtful players, such as Simon Madden, Tim Watson and Garry Foulds. He used to call them 'the schoolteachers'.

If a coach has no cowboy in his own personality, he might have less empathy for and understanding of them. I had players at Melbourne who would fall into Sheeds' definition of cowboys, and they were always the players I found trickiest to coach. But if a coach altogether discounts players of the personality types he struggles to relate to, all he is doing is reducing the talent pool. It's far better to keep them in the fold and establish a way to get the best out of them.

A team needs complementary skills, but it also needs complementary personalities. They all add to the mix. A lot of team sport is about the locker-room banter, and the extroverts make it a lot of fun. They can take it too far now and then, but they add some flavour to the cake mix, otherwise a coach might bake a beautiful-looking cake, but it's a bit bland.

To create a team that works well together, coaches need some flexibility and tolerance, as well as clarity about when to tell players to pull their heads in. You need to be very clear about the non-negotiable demands for those unconventional personalities: you turn up, you work hard and you play by the agreed team rules. Without that, coaches and teams are accepting varying standards, and the group will become dysfunctional, with people pulling in different directions.

★

The Melbourne squad of 2000 had a nice blend of rookies, established performers, introverts and extroverts. The team's personality struck me as eager, hardworking, ambitious and willing to sacrifice for the greater good.

When it came to assessing their individual personalities, I like the profiling model set out by performance psychologist Phil Jauncey, who was the Brisbane Lions' mental skills coach between 1994 and 2008 and also worked with many other groups, including the Australian cricket team. In examining people's different personalities and how they impact on approaches to life and interactions with others, Phil's model suggests that our personality types fall into four brackets: the enforcers, the thinkers, the mozzies and the feelers. Each personality type tends to have a dominant type and a mix of the other three.

The enforcers, guys like our captain David Neitz, just want to know which hill we're taking, our method and his role. He's thinking, *OK, let's go*. The enforcers don't need to be smothered in love, they need respect and strong direction and then they're easy.

The thinkers need absolute clarity and a plan. They're the players who take a coach's information on board and want to consider whether there's a better way. They're the list makers, the people who write things down in the team meeting. Sometimes they need a coach to go through his reasoning and explain why the team would be better off with them starting on a back flank this week, rather than as a forward. They're the guys who say, 'Four weeks ago you said this, but now you're saying that. Why the change? I'm sensing a bit of mixed messaging here, coach.' Thinkers are conscientious and they quite often have an alternative take on the situation.

I was a bit of a thinker as a player. Kevin Sheedy reckoned he could sense me thinking about the question I knew he was about to ask. Sheeds found it interesting that my brother Terry and I were somewhat different in style. 'Terry would always expect the sun to come up again tomorrow morning,' he once said. 'You would look at the sun coming up in the morning and wonder why.' So I understood the thinkers in my team, guys like Cameron Bruce. I got them.

The mozzies are the raging extroverts who buzz around the place. They can be flighty and do all manner of stupid stuff and at times can drive me crazy. However, they can spark the team. Their approach is, 'fire, aim, ready'. But they are also the life of the party and crucial to the group dynamic. Travis Johnstone, Paul Hopgood and Jeff Farmer were among the mozzies at Melbourne, and so was our big forward David Schwarz, even though he also had enforcer characteristics.

Mozzies are usually very passionate about their footy, but the coach has to keep reinforcing the message with them, because they might have a tendency to forget what was said to them

20 seconds ago. They would reason, 'I'm instinctive, coach, don't box me in, just let me play.' And I'd respond, 'That's fine, but you've actually got to play with your teammates.' And they'd reluctantly accept that was a fair point. 'Aw, yeah, I guess that makes a bit of sense. Hang on, the phone's ringing.' And four minutes later they'd be back, saying, 'Now what were we talking about, again?'

Mozzies need patience and affirmation, because any praise is never enough and if we criticise them or don't give them enough love, they want to know why the coach is picking on them. They're caught up in what's happening with themselves and what feels good in the moment. They are either brimming with confidence and high-fiving their teammates on the way to pulling out match-winning performances, or they're down in the dumps thinking, *The world's against me, the coach doesn't rate me, my teammates aren't kicking it to me.* A coach needs to very patient with mozzies and to accept them for who they are while reminding them that team rules are meant for them as well.

The feelers often have the capacity to be the best team-oriented players, it's just that they need a lot of love and empathy. They are often the glue that keeps the team together. All the feelers want to know is whether the coach really cares about them because if they trust that, they'll work their arse off for you. They're the ones who don't care how much you know until they know how much you care. We had a lot of feelers in that Melbourne squad – guys like Nathan Brown and Jeff White – and I'm sure AFL clubs now have even more of them. The feelers were probably the players who I didn't give enough to: they needed to be reassured that I knew they were bringing something to the team, they wanted me to put my arm around them, pick them up and dust them off when things didn't go so well. Don't ever harshly criticise feelers or give them any reason to feel they have been berated or shamed.

As a player I wasn't a feeler — I didn't need that sort of attention. I wanted to know that my coach valued and respected what I did, but the odd pat on the back or a nod from him was enough. That meant that fulfilling a player's need to get the occasional cuddle was not a natural extension of my approach towards coaching. Feelers need more than just coherence and honesty from their coach. I found it trickiest to bring the best out in the feelers and the mozzies.

It is only in hindsight that I realise some of the players were possibly looking for their coach to be a bit of a father figure for them as well. The all-consuming nature of the job made that challenging at times. At 39, with four young kids at home, it was a juggling act trying to deal with all my responsibilities, which included those of husband and father.

The players, most of them caught up in striving to make it as an AFL player, had no concept that I probably had a lot of balls in the air at the time. But life experiences change our view of the world, and I suspect that now they have kids of their own, and a whole range of other responsibilities, they would look back on that time with a bit more empathy for everyone involved, just as I do.

There's a great story from 2000 that shows what it's like to coach the kind of player who was least like me in terms of personality. Jeff Farmer – the Wizard, or 'Wiz' – was a classic mozzie.

Halfway through the year in 2000, we were only just going. In round 14, coming off a round 13 thrashing by Carlton, we were playing Collingwood at the MCG in our annual Queen's Birthday game. I remember this as the day the Wizard kicked nine goals in the second half.

Before the game, I could sense he wasn't on. At half-time we were three points up, but Wiz had one kick and one handball to his name, and I was very annoyed with him. Everyone can have an off day, but I always wanted 100 per cent effort from the players.

We have magnetic boards where all the players' names are lined up against those of the opposition. At half-time, on the way down to the rooms, I was so pissed off that I grabbed Jeff Farmer's label and threw it over my shoulder, thinking, *Well, I won't be needing that today.*

During the half-time break, I pulled Wiz aside and let it be known very clearly that he was letting himself down and, more importantly, he was letting his teammates down. The latter message would have stung – one of our team values was, 'Don't dud your teammates'!

At the start of the third quarter, I sent Wiz to the bench – by this stage, it's fair to say he was as annoyed with me as I was with him. I put Ben Beams on the ground. He'd had little opportunity and now it was his turn to go.

Five minutes into the quarter, Beams broke his wrist. *Fuck it,* I thought, *I'll have to put the Wizard back on.* Wiz trudged on, shooting a quick glance at the coaches' box which said, *Stuff you, coach . . . I'll show you who cares.*

Within five minutes, he'd kicked three goals.

I leant over to Chris Fagan in the coaches' box. 'Fages, we might need that Jeff Farmer magnet. I think it slipped off the board on the way down at half-time. Can you retrace our steps and find it?'

I didn't want to go to the huddle at three-quarter time without the Wizard's name on that board. To my enormous relief, Chris came back with the label. He quietly slipped it into my hand, and the Wiz was back on the board. He then went on to bag another six. The Wiz was back!

Jeff Farmer kicked nine goals in the second half of that game, and we won by 65 points. That win turned our form around.

That's the thing with mozzies – they're unpredictable, they can make you batty but when they're on, they can be matchwinners. You need them in your team.

★

Sometimes when momentum arrives, you're not sure how it happened. When you've got it, though, don't tinker with it, just ride it. When a team is playing with that magical essence known as 'spirit', being involved as a player or coach is pure pleasure.

One of the principal reasons Melbourne made it through to the 2000 Grand Final was that during that season all of those personalities came together seamlessly, the teamwork gelled, and the players fully devoted themselves to the team cause.

To succeed, a football team still needs a reasonable contingent of players with sheer class and ability, but it also needs players with complementary skills, and that 2000 Melbourne team had those qualities.

There is also the teamwork of the football department support staff and foremost among them are the assistant coaches, who become like a band of brothers. I had a rule in the coaches' box: there's only one lunatic and that's me. The rest of them had to stay cool, calm and collected. I explained that I was prone to getting annoyed and angry – especially if a player invented his own team rules – but that once I got the frustration out in the open, I was better. It'd be a quick burst and then I'd say, 'Right, I'm good now boys.' And I would be. After the game, I'd apologise to anyone who copped it in the heat of the moment. Venting allowed me to regain composure and a clear perspective. It was in stark contrast to my approach as a player, where I could remain composed and channel any anger or frustration into energy to put towards the next contest.

More often than not Chris Fagan was the assistant coach who could identify when my blood was boiling and could calm me right down. Years later, when Chris was appointed coach of the Brisbane Lions, I took a perverse pleasure in seeing a seasoned and rational 55-year-old lose the plot in the coaches' box. I remember laughing at the TV, 'That's it! There you go, Fages, this coaching caper gets us all in the end. Even you.'

Maybe I needed to be sitting next to him, telling him to settle down.

★

One of the most important issues for our coaches to wrestle with heading into the 2000 Grand Final involved the team dynamic. Essendon had been a powerhouse all season, with their only loss coming in round 21 when the Western Bulldogs had narrowly edged them by flooding players into the backline.

Early in the week we discussed the possibility of revamping our approach, but we knew our team was playing well, had got to within a couple of goals of Essendon during the season, and had momentum. In the end, we were conscious of disrupting our players' cohesion and messing with their confidence by having the coach make a change that might suggest he didn't believe they were good enough to win on their own merits. Had we changed our style and lost by seven goals, I would have had to live with our players wondering why the coach didn't back them in and just let them play. The other truth was that I knew we were going to struggle to introduce a new system over a couple of days of training. We decided to roll the dice.

Grand final week was a bit of a blur. It began brightly on the Sunday when our second-tier team, Sandringham, won the premiership in the revamped VFL competition, followed the next evening by our young midfielder, Shane Woewodin, being awarded the Brownlow Medal as the AFL's fairest and best footballer.

The fact that I would be coaching against my old mentor Kevin Sheedy aroused curiosity among the journalists but was of no extra significance to me in the moment, other than knowing the experienced campaigner would have his team well prepared for the big match. I also knew that Sheeds was not averse to a few mind games, so it was probably best to ignore any comments from the Essendon camp. It was just more noise in a noisy week.

In Essendon's previous five grand finals, there had been at least one Daniher listed on the team sheet, but this time our family's involvement extended to Terry's role as part of the Bombers' coaching set-up. At age 41, he had finally hung the boots up as playing coach of the Wagga Tigers and, in 1999, he had returned to Essendon as the reserves coach, guiding them to a premiership (his seventh in eight seasons). When we crossed paths that week after the grand final parade, our chat about the next day's game centred mainly around which members of the family were planning to attend, tickets and a bit of banter about how Mum had backed Melbourne to win in the local Ungarie paper, because 'Essendon have had their turn over the years'. Mum and Dad drove down from the farm to be at the game, where they were surrounded by many of their dozens of children and grandchildren.

My kids were excited about their father's involvement in the AFL's biggest week: at school they made a book about the upcoming game, and my youngest son, Ben, who was seven, was chuffed at getting to sit beside me in a convertible during the grand final parade. He was proudly decked out in a Demons jumper and beanie and even managed the odd wave to the crowd.

On match day I tried to normalise the build-up for our young team. Steven Febey was the only player who had experienced playing a grand final in his AFL career, and eight members of the team had played fewer than 50 senior matches.

Once the ball was bounced, we started brightly but didn't take our opportunities. After quarter-time, the game started to slip away. Essendon was a juggernaut, one of the great teams of the modern era, and they exposed the gap between themselves and the rest of us, winning by 10 goals.

Overall, our Melbourne team's performance that season was superb. Sometimes a team can simply have great teamwork; the players are young and they're trying to be a great team, they're doing a great job helping each other out, but they're just not ready to go all the way. Ultimately, though, success in team sport is measured by premierships, and even though that developing team may have produced exceptional teamwork, they got little credit that season. There's one premiership team and the rest are duds. The losing grand finalist sometimes gets painted as the biggest dud, while people tend to gloss over the teams that lost the week before and finished third or fourth. But that's football; teams are measured on wins and losses, it's black and white. They don't hand out a cup for having the best teamwork.

Team unity can be really challenged in defeat. Strong teams do not fall for the pain and blame that wants to surface after a heartfelt loss. I was proud of what that Melbourne group achieved in 2000, disappointed that they were denied a premiership by an experienced and phenomenal opponent, but also wary of whether we could maintain the momentum, spirit and collective buy-in of that phenomenal season.

★

Regardless of the sort of team we find ourselves in, I would like to think that some of the same principles of teamwork apply. We are best served by creating an environment where the sum of the parts is much greater than the total of the individual pieces: an environment that builds trust and moves people towards being selfless rather than selfish; one that has people who have enough emotional intelligence to have honest conversations and to get through them without crushing anyone.

For that to happen we need to start with the nuts and bolts – the right method, selecting the right people, developing their skills so that they can deliver. These are the bricks, but within all that is the mortar: trust, care and empathy. We need people to trust that the team outcome is driving everyone, to care about that goal ahead of being rewarded for individual effort and to have empathy for the demands on the other members of the team. If we can get these segments aligned, we can build a team spirit, one that is resilient enough to keep our eyes true north. Whatever the level, teamwork is a spiritual journey, and without spirit a team is like an eagle that can't fly.

If we only have the bricks and no mortar, the whole thing might fall over when the first tremble hits.

Save the little white lies for Grandma's cake

I consider honesty to be a bedrock value. At its most basic level, being honest is as simple as not lying, not cheating and not stealing. Essentially, honesty comes down to a congruency in your beliefs, words and actions. If you're a dishonest person, you're not worthy of trust and that flows through to everything you do and has a huge bearing on whether you can maintain enduring relationships.

I grew up understanding that there's a kind of honesty which is embedded in Australian culture. We like to proclaim ourselves as straight talkers, and to give our word as our bond. That's all very well, but I have grown to realise that the true test of honesty is whether you are honest with yourself.

Self-honesty means acknowledging how you truly feel, understanding why you do what you do, admitting to yourself when you're wrong or have made a mistake, when you're acting foolishly or selfishly, recognising when your ego is out of control, what your true desires and motivations are, how certain people or situations make you feel and owning your strengths and weak-nesses. If you see the splinter in someone else's eye, but can't see the log in your own, you suffer from self-delusion.

We all wear masks in our day-to-day lives to some extent, for many reasons, both good and bad. We wear them to hide our identity or to become someone else for a little while. The more masks we wear, the more epic the performance. The feeling that you need to be someone else can be a huge drain on our minds and bodies. Part of being honest with yourself is being aware of these masks: understanding why we wear them and slowly resisting the need to have them at all. Being honest with yourself is learning to accept and find comfort in what Oscar Wilde said: 'Be yourself; everyone else is taken.'

Honesty with others can lead to confrontation: something some people avoid like the plague. Whether in a one-on-one relationship or a team environment, the courage to give and receive honest feedback is critical: it can prevent a mistake from turning into a failure.

If you have integrity, you are entitled to reciprocated honesty. Candour is about not playing games or being frank, but it doesn't entitle you to say whatever you like. Honesty needs to be balanced, because one person's honesty is another person's rudeness. The wisdom is in learning to think before you speak and being aware of the effect of your words on other people – knowing how and when to best deliver the truth.

Honesty, with yourself and others, is a core virtue. That awareness is the gateway to becoming your best self. However, if I'm ever lucky enough to have my grandkids draw a picture for me, I'm not going to tell them that it's not much chop. I'll tell them it's the best drawing ever.

★

Candour is part of my fabric. Look back at my Myers–Briggs profile and J for 'judgement', and the CANOE model for 'agreeableness'.

I have never been afraid to say what I think. For me, it has always been a matter of trying to find equilibrium, to make a considered call on what to say, how much to say and when to say it. That tendency to dwell at the end of the scale that favoured frankness over tactfulness could reveal itself in diverse situations, and it was never more evident than during one European holiday during my time as a young Essendon player in the 1980s.

The playing group had opted for a more elaborate end-of-season trip than was the norm in those days (Bali or the Gold Coast). While relaxing in Germany we inevitably ended up at a beer-hall in Munich. Less predictably, a couple of days earlier we had been on a haunting visit to the Dachau concentration camp, where tens of thousands of inmates were killed by the Nazis. On that evening at the beer-hall, with its steady supply of lager steins and oompah music, our local guide was talking us through the history of Oktoberfest and its significance to the Bavarian tradition. It was all beer and pretzels. There couldn't be a more suitable environment for fun and frivolity.

As our guide enthused about German culture, I decided to challenge him: how could that German culture have given rise to the Nazis? How did the German people reflect on those dark times five decades later? The Essendon boys just groaned as they put their palms up to their eyes and turned their heads away in disbelief. They were more interested in talking Fräuleins than Führers. To his credit, the local man began to give me a few considered, tactful responses before one of the boys cut him off and chipped in with, 'Shit, this German beer is grouse, who's up for another?'

One of the great things about footy clubs is that you're surrounded by mates who keep you grounded.

I was an intense kind of fella, and it used to drive people mad. I'd go and sit on a bench next to a homeless man and ask him what was going on, and the people I was out with would just shake their heads and mutter, 'Here he goes again with his weird cat behaviour.'

Throughout my life there have been many times when I've questioned why I am like that instead of just going along with the others. In accepting that it is just part of who I am, I've also tried to learn that there are times when everyone would be better off if I didn't mention the war.

★

For the Melbourne players to make the 2000 Grand Final was a ripper effort. They had come a long way from bottom of the ladder in 1997. All that stood between the Demons and a premiership was one of the great teams of the AFL era: the Essendon outfit that still holds the record for most wins in a season. But in the hours after the match I wasn't looking at it like that.

That evening, as I mingled with the players behind a curtain waiting to go on stage at the post-match club function, I was disturbed by their attitude. Many of them were up and about, having a few beers and a laugh. It was tricky, because nobody was quite sure whether to be happy about reaching the grand final or sad about losing it. My belief was that this was a sad night and that celebrating their performance that season could come later on. I was thinking, *You blokes don't realise how hard it will be to get another opportunity like this.*

Perhaps I had Kevin Sheedy's flinty speech after Essendon's losing 1983 Grand Final in the back of my mind – the speech that spurred Essendon on to lift the cup the following season. When it was my turn to take the microphone, I had a decent crack at the players, warning them that 'as long as we're happy in defeat we'll never get back here'.

Looking back, the players had every right to let off a bit of steam that night. Many of them had been at Melbourne through the grimmest of times and now they were coming off a cracking few months and an admirable finals campaign. My fear was that deep down they were taking it for granted that they would be back on the big stage the following season. They wanted to relax and enjoy and would have thought, *Come on, ease up, coach.* Instead, the poor buggers copped two clips around the ears that day: one on the field from Essendon and another from me afterwards.

What I was trying to tell not just the players, but the whole club, was that if we were content with the 2000 version of the Melbourne Football Club then we were kidding ourselves. History suggests that my assessment was on the mark: we didn't make the finals the next season and Melbourne has not played in a grand final since that day. But being right doesn't get you anywhere; you have to do something about it. Blunt honesty was one thing, but I'm not sure I did enough to convince the players or the club that without improvement we would regress.

A coach is always seeking the right intersection between support and challenge for their players. Every player wants to know he is supported and acknowledged for their efforts and input. On the other hand, all players need to be challenged and motivated to realise their full potential. Finding that balance is an art form that has to vary from player to player, situation to situation.

That might mean telling two-thirds of the team that they had played well but asking questions of another seven. Some players – in particular, the feelers in the team – might think, *I don't want to hear that, coach, I just want you to pump me up.* If a player isn't on the same page as the coach, the coach needs to find a way to say, 'No, that's not how I saw it', and then go on to have the honest discussion. Players need to be told if they have to do more to keep their position in the team. I believed it was only fair, even if they didn't want to hear it.

At Essendon, Sheeds wasn't always one for telling players when they were out of the team. He would get other people to do it. I decided that should I ever become a senior coach,

I wouldn't leave that job to others. I thought it was my responsibility to let players know when they were being dropped. They had to hear that they needed to work on X, Y and Z to get a recall. Then I would ask an assistant coach to follow up with them and help pick their spirits back up.

It's important to offer honest feedback from the right place and in the right way. Criticism is not helpful if it simply causes resentment, so we need to consider how to deliver it constructively. Don't be like the seagull that flaps around, dumps on someone and then flies off, leaving them wondering what the hell just happened. That kind of seagull criticism doesn't serve any purpose other than making the seagull feel good that they've got some crap out of their system.

Of course we can all tell little white lies in life, but not in that context of a group on a mission. The little white lies should be reserved for Grandma's cake. If she usually makes beautiful cakes and then one day she apologises because she accidentally used the wrong spoon size for an ingredient, why would you point out that your slice of sponge is too dry? Better to say, 'The flavour is lovely.' What purpose does it serve to go straight to honesty?

Brian Donohoe, who was chairman of selectors when I was at Essendon, once advised me: 'If someone else can deliver the bad news, let them. Don't think that you have to do it all yourself, because it does take its toll emotionally.' These proved to be wise words; as my coaching career unfolded, it became emotionally draining being the bearer of bad news around weekly selection.

But that was nothing compared to telling players that I didn't see them as part of our future. That's when honesty felt closest to callousness. The AFL environment demands that clubs have to make changes to the playing group. Coaches have to make calls on players, sometimes courageous calls. Similarly, clubs have to make calls on head coaches!

When a footballer comes into the team and gets handed his jumper, he is thinking how wonderful the world is, he's not thinking about how the coach has had to tap some other poor bastard on the shoulder for him to make his debut. And neither should he. But the reality is that there would be no opportunity unless somebody else was moved aside. A coach feels that acutely when he is making those decisions, and the best he can do is just try to be honest and do what is best for the collective.

When players are told they don't fit into the plan for the future, they don't hear anything after those first few words, and they don't want to hear how much the coach rates them as people or cares about them. They just hear that they're no longer part of it. Most resented being told, some were determined to prove me wrong and a few did.

While I didn't like this part of my coaching responsibility at all, I took some pride in the fact that the players would know that if I called time on their career, it was an honest call, based on what I felt were the best interests of the team.

Probably the toughest call on a player's career I had to make involved Shane Woewodin, a good fella who was invested in the Melbourne cause. He was our vice-captain and a real fan favourite. After he had a belter of a year in 2000, the Demons signed Shane to a lucrative contract extension that made him one of the top earners in the AFL. In hindsight, it was a deal that hurt both Shane and the club. Injuries and a lack of form meant Shane struggled for the next two seasons, while Melbourne had list-management and salary-cap issues at the end of 2002. As Shane fell outside the ranks of our top 10 players, we could not justify him being the highest paid player at the club.

Our general manager of football, Danny Corcoran, brought me into his office and explained the club's dilemma to me. Unless a salary reduction was negotiated, Melbourne would have to sacrifice several better-performing rising youngsters. As the coach, I didn't like this situation at all.

An offer was put to Shane to restructure his terms: less money for the remaining two years of his contract, with an extra season added on. A stand-off developed and ethically Shane had every right to question Melbourne's stance because he was under contract, and in a sense the squeeze was caused by the club's own mismanagement. But the AFL is a ruthless environment and Melbourne told him that something had to give, or he wouldn't have a place at the club.

I met with Shane several times to try to explain the situation, hopeful of the best outcome. It was very tough for Shane and his family and, in the end, we couldn't get it done. Late in the piece, there was a little bit of give from Shane's camp, but list lodgement deadlines determined that it was too late.

The club decided to trade Shane. My final call to him was very tough. When he asked me directly whether I thought he would be at the club in 2003, I could have fudged my answer, but I was up-front and told him that I felt too much water had gone under the bridge, that a trade deal was underway and that there was no turning back. I didn't feel good about it then, and I don't feel good about it now.

Melbourne ended up trading Shane to Collingwood for a first-round pick in a deal that meant we still had to pay a substantial chunk of his wage over the next two seasons. The supporters were dismayed, directing much of their ire towards me, as senior coach. I accepted the responsibility to explain the decision. Having to move players on was challenging enough, let alone ones that we actually wanted to retain, and I vowed to never get caught in a similar situation again. From that point onwards, I made sure I was fully abreast of list management and player contract details.

I've never had any trouble rising to the honesty challenge – it's just been a matter of how best to be honest. I've had to consider how best to deliver the truth without being too blunt, too abrasive and possibly hurtful. But I was never going to fall for the other end of the honesty scale, where I was afraid of confronting an issue, afraid of not being popular, afraid of not going there just because it was too hard. My view was that as a leader of the club, I had a responsibility to stay true to our vision. Sometimes it was not much fun, but if I didn't have the courage to front the hard stuff, then what the hell was I doing there?

The old saying goes that you can please some of the people all of the time, and all of the people some of the time. But if an AFL coach thinks he can please all of the people all of the time, then he is unquestionably in the wrong job.

At Melbourne, I hoped that we were creating an environment where peers could informally challenge a player both on and off the field if they thought he wasn't meeting the agreed team values. I was uncompromising about the team values, and the players knew that the standard they walked past was the standard they were prepared to accept.

Now when I catch up with some of the players I coached, they joke about my no-holds-barred approach: 'One thing's for sure, we were never in any doubt about where we stood with you.' It's a backhanded compliment. These days they see a more lighthearted and relaxed man, and say, 'Geez, I wish you were a bit more like that back then. You were too driven, too intense and uncompromising.'

I tell them, 'Yeah, but it was because I had to coach you bastards!'

★

When I ask myself whether if there are I wish I had been more honest with myself, I want my answer to be no, but I suspect it should be yes. As a younger man, I would like to have handled some situations better, or bitten my tongue, or perhaps realised that people could have worked things out for themselves and didn't need me to jump in and tell them how. But we are too soon old, too late smart. That's how life works.

I would rather know the lie of the land than stumble ahead guessing, and I think most people feel the same, deep down. And it's best to help them put together the most accurate map possible, not gloss over the detail. We don't do anyone, including ourselves, any favours by avoiding hard truths.

Maybe it's easier for me to rationalise things this way, but it's how I operate. As Denis Pagan used to say during his time as coach of North Melbourne, 'Don't piss on my leg and tell me it's raining.'

Trust is the oil that greases the engine to get things done

For all of the importance of leadership, teamwork and honesty in a team environment, they all lack punch in the absence of trust. Quite simply, trust is the oil that greases the engine to get things done.

Trust is at the core of our relationships at a personal, organisational and societal level. With trust comes confidence; without it, there is suspicion, which can destroy momentum in any team environment. When trust exists, things happen, but when there's a lack of trust, pretty soon everything slows down.

We earn trust day by day, week by week and month by month, but we can lose it in an instant. If trust is irretrievably lost, the engine is not just slowing down – there's every chance the car is about to be a write-off.

★

In the seasons following the 2000 Grand Final, life at the Melbourne Football Club was never predictable and the engine rarely hummed along smoothly. We had extremes of low ladder finishes and finals appearances, injury plights and stirring winning streaks, plummeting crowds and membership growth. There was a steady turnover of presidents and CEOs.

We had AFL handouts and financial body blows: a written-off $750,000 pokies venue debt in 2001 and a $1.2 million bill for back taxes in 2003. We signed a five-year deal to play home games in Brisbane, which raised substantial funds but meant that midway through each season we hosted our home games on the powerful Lions' patch. There were salary-cap pressures and there was patchwork recruiting. When we wanted to rookie draft the highly promising Aaron Davey from Port Melbourne at the end of 2003, the club had no budget for rookies, so I had to pass the hat around. We relied on a long-term supporter, Peter Spargo, and some influential coterie group members to raise the funds needed to get Davey in the door. Flagging finances meant severe cuts to the salary cap, the football department was under-staffed and the club had to pass up the chance to relocate its base to the cutting-edge venue on Olympic Boulevard, which then went to Collingwood Football Club.

I had times when I feared getting the sack and times when I signed contract extensions. Life with the Demons reminded me of a scene in the 1980s Steve Martin film, *Parenthood*. Towards the end of the movie, Martin's character, Gil, is complain-ing to his wife about how complicated his life has become. At the end of his whining, Grandma wanders over and recounts the time when she was 19 and her husband convinced her to ride the rollercoaster. 'I always wanted to go again,' she says. 'You know, it was just so interesting to me that a ride could make me so frightened, so scared, so sick, so excited and so thrilled all together. Some didn't like it. They went on the merry-go-round. That just goes around. Nothing. I like the rollercoaster. You get more out of it.'

I'm with Grandma. I could have chosen a career on the computer programming merry-go-round, but I've never regretted opting for the up, down, up, down of the AFL rollercoaster.

But by 2004, the constant turnover of chairmen and CEOs had really started to concern me. Were we ever going to develop a vision for the club that took us beyond survival? It's one thing to have a vision for the team, but it must be aligned with the club vision for change to actually take place.

If even I was starting to lose faith that this was ever going to materialise during my tenure, I knew it would be even harder for Melbourne people to stay true to the red and the blue. The media and the broader football community were whacking the club's board and administration for being rudderless and hopeless, and Carlton president John Elliott took a swing in 2002 by branding us an 'irrelevant' football club. What perturbed me most was that those barbs were often met with silence from Melbourne's off-field hierarchy.

In my nine completed seasons as coach, the Demons reached the finals six times. Among the Victorian clubs, that was second only to Essendon and yet many of the other worse-performing teams seemed to avoid the same level of damning criticism.

And this was before the AFL's Competitive Balance Policy was introduced in 2014 to reduce the financial gap between big and small clubs, so that 'any team can win on any given day'. Cash-strapped Melbourne was matching it with teams that had far greater budgets to spend on their football departments.

I had become so frustrated by the lack of anyone publicly advocating on Melbourne's behalf that I started going to bat for the club. It wasn't a conscious decision to plant the flag and declare a counterattack on behalf of the Demons, I just decided that someone from within needed to voice a strong opinion, so I did it and then kept doing it. Part of it was also a gut-instinct response when I felt the team was being unfairly attacked.

I didn't want our players thinking I was the wildebeest to outside criticism, just rolling over and conceding defeat. Someone had to step forward, and I saw it as a 'my time to go' opportunity. That's how I found myself speaking up not only for my team – which many of the players respected – but also for our maligned club and our supporters.

Whenever external disparagement came, I would push back: 'Sure, we have our issues, but we're working through them. We're a proud club and we're competitive and we're relevant.' More than that, I was selling hope. I was trying to get Melbourne people to trust in the direction we were headed. 'Get on the wagon' was the message. My former Essendon teammate Tim Watson, working in the media, saw it as a form of footy evangelism, and dubbed me 'The Reverend'.

The spruiking wasn't just about protecting the club, it was about making sure the players maintained their trust in what the team was building. I had no real say in overall club direction, but I had a responsibility to the team. When there is trust, everyone keeps moving in the right direction and can focus on the issues that matter; when trust falls away, people don't focus on the important points. Instead they start to doubt and waste energy on the problems they can't control, and things don't get done. Maintaining trust is done through actions, not just words.

★

2007 was a pivotal year in my appreciation of trust. It was my tenth season as Melbourne coach and the likes of David Neitz, Adem Yze and Jeff White were all nearing the end of their careers. We were coming off three consecutive finals campaigns, and I felt that we had one last roll of the dice left with that group of players.

That's the outlook I presented to the board heading into the 2007 season. Sure, a lot of key players had post-season surgeries that would probably impact the start of our season, but with a little luck, I thought we could be very competitive again.

I also felt our game style needed updating, as I was concerned it had become slightly one-dimensional. So we looked to introduce more of a run-and-carry based approach to our old kicking-dependent strategy.

The season began disastrously. We had more than a dozen players sidelined by injury and the new game plan simply wasn't working. We lost the first five games of the season, convincingly. Rounds 6 and 7 were narrow losses, but then we got thrashed in round 8. Then we lost by the narrowest of margins.

We won our next two games, but I was feeling worn out, starting to believe that my message was losing its edge. With a win–loss record of 2–11, it was inevitable that the playing group's trust would start to wobble.

The jungle drums were beating loudly. The media coverage of our miserable season became a blood sport, with newspaper columnists predicting I would be out of a job by the end of every week. The storm clouds were gathering, and everyone could see them.

On radio, prominent presenter and Melbourne fan Neil Mitchell ran a poll: 'Should Neale Daniher be sacked? Hear the results at the end of the hour.' Jan was taking the girls to netball when she heard that one and nearly drove the car off the road. She took the criticism personally, but I just told her she needed to switch channels. Up on the farm in Ungarie, whenever talk on the airwaves turned to the possibility that the Melbourne coach would be sacked, Mum would seek refuge in her garden, watering or weeding.

Even though the media hysteria made me angry, I'd remind myself that I was the one who signed up to be an AFL coach and that a high level of scrutiny came with the territory.

For an AFL coach who is under the pump trying to retain his job, the media coverage is like one of those scenes in a spaghetti western where you see a cowboy trudging through the arid wilderness, parched by the midday sun with only a few drops left in his canteen. He glances up and there is a vulture hovering overhead. He keeps slogging on over the next ridge then looks up to see that there are now four vultures in the sky and another three watching from the branch of a nearby tree.

Sometimes all it takes is for that coach's team to have a stirring win and the vultures disappear over the horizon. If the AFL club is strong, it sees the vultures taking wing and makes an effort to scatter them, but if it's a financially strapped club, they not only fail to hunt the birds off, they invite them down from the sky.

Midway through 2007 I reckon that I had more than a dozen vultures circling menacingly, and they were getting impatient for a feed. A sacked coach is a huge story and it rarely comes out of nowhere. There's usually a harrowing and protracted build-up.

In among that frenzy, I felt nobody from Melbourne was prepared to take a defiant stance, to stand up to the criticism and defend me. I definitely knew I was in trouble.

I was hearing third hand about meetings behind the scenes to discuss the club's future and whether I had a role in it. Whenever I broached the subject internally, the club's response was always, 'Oh, no, no, that's not right.' One evening I phoned Paul Gardner, the chairman of the Melbourne board, to ask what was going on and he assured me there was nothing to worry about. But there were a lot of shenanigans going on behind the scenes, a lot of manoeuvring. The team wasn't winning games, the club was under a lot of pressure from sponsors, supporters and the media, and the possibility of moving the coach on is a delicate political exercise.

We had what we used to refer to as the three-legged stool at Melbourne – chairman Paul Gardner, the CEO, Steve Harris, and the coach – all working together. The three legs shared the load and kept things stable. If one of the legs became wonky, the whole thing was in danger of tumbling over. I was sensing that the old three-legged stool had become very, very wonky.

When Gardner told the media that I would have to reapply for the coaching position when I came out of contract at season's end, all of the trust was gone. Both parties were sensing the relationship was over; we could see it, feel it and smell it.

I know that losing trust is a two-way street. My trust in the club had been slowly eroding from as far back as 2002, waiting for the hierarchy to come up with a vision and strategy that would allow the club to thrive. So in mid-2007, it was no surprise that they were losing trust in me. I had told the board I thought the playing group had one more year in them, and I got it wrong.

Gardner was also trying to save face with the sponsors and supporters. Part of Melbourne's dilemma was that the club was broke, so they didn't want to sack me and have to pay me out.

I understood my role as coach – as leader – meant that I put the club before the individual, that I formed opinions and made the tough calls. The underperforming team was *my* responsibility. I had no problem with that. But I couldn't defend the charade of the Melbourne hierarchy's process. I was disappointed that they didn't respect me enough to have a plainspoken and respectful dialogue. If they had said, 'Look Neale, we think the club needs a change of direction and it's time for us to part ways',

I would have accepted their decision and thanked them for their honesty. After nine-and-a-half seasons, I thought I had earned the right to expect candour and transparency from the club.

Then came round 12, in which we lost to Richmond by 49 points. The following Wednesday, I had an off-site meeting with Gardner and Harris, and they reiterated their position: I would need to reapply for my job in 2008. So I decided enough was enough and called them out. I told them my time as coach of Melbourne Football Club was over. They had a couple of hours to let the sponsors know.

I headed back to Junction Oval to tell the players and then the media. I wanted to control the information that went out; I simply couldn't trust the club to deliver the news in the way I intended.

Perhaps my sudden departure caught the club on the hop – maybe it was too late in the week – but they asked me whether I could stay on for one more match. So it was that two days later, I was coaching Melbourne for a game for the 223rd and final time, and coincidentally for a game against an Essendon team coached by Kevin Sheedy.

A few of the injured Melbourne players found a way to push themselves up for selection – including our skipper, David Neitz, who was virtually playing on one leg. That Friday night, the Demons played their hearts out. We were in front in the dying moments until a ball spilled over the back of a pack and Scott Lucas kicked a goal to put the Bombers up by two points with six seconds left on the clock. It would have been nice to finish with a win against my old mentor, but it was not to be.

In the rooms after the match, we cracked open a few beers and I made sure that I spoke about every player and staff member, recognising their contribution during my coaching stint and thanking them for their support. The situation was terribly difficult for assistant coach Mark 'Bomber' Riley, a really good mate of mine who the club had tagged to see out the season as caretaker coach. But Bomber was part of a big crew that made its way back to our house that night and we kicked on into the early hours of Saturday morning.

Later, Sheeds would say that I should be proud of what I had achieved with Melbourne. 'Sometimes it's not the coach during the era, it's the club during your era,' he said. It was his way of being generous. And I *am* proud of what the team achieved during my time as coach, more for the spirit and realised potential than the win–loss record.

With hindsight, I have become even more convinced that to win premierships, clubs need to have all sections of their operation aligned from top to bottom, as well as a pinch of luck. In my time at Melbourne, I don't feel we ever managed to get our act together as an entire club.

★

It wasn't until a few days after that final match, when Jan and I took the opportunity to get away to Queensland for a short break, that I realised how emotionally drained and dog-tired I was from a decade of coaching Melbourne.

Rejection is a sharp and difficult emotion to process and I was in a dark and less trusting place after the way it ended at

Melbourne. That kind of experience can taint your view of trust – once your fingers are burnt, you tend to be more careful around the flame.

But testing times can also reveal the strength of all kinds of relationships. It meant a lot to me that a bunch of half-fit players who had been such a big part of my life at Melbourne dragged themselves over the line for my last game. I was grateful for the love of my family and a steadfast group of friends who didn't assess me in terms of a win–loss record – they just saw me as Neale or Dad.

But most of all, the whole experience made me appreciate the real value of knowing someone loves you unconditionally and has your back, without question. What a great support Jan was to me during that time. We have always maintained absolute trust in each other, but we well and truly gave our relationship the Bunsen burner test during my coaching tenure at Melbourne. I know that our kind of trust is worth its weight in gold.

In time I would come to appreciate what an incredible ride it had been at Melbourne and how much I'd learnt from the wild ups and downs of coaching. I'm glad I didn't choose the merry-go-round. That just goes around. I like the rollercoaster. You get more out of it.

21
Don't let the bastards win both ways

When the wounds of feeling wronged are fresh, it's hard to find the strength to forgive.

When I left the Demons, I was angry and disappointed. Misery loves company, and I found a ready-made friend in Mr Negative. 'Neale,' he whispered, 'you're doomed, mate. Your coaching career is done.'

Even though it's a big ask, we need to choose acceptance and forgiveness because it frees us to move forward; if we don't, we run the risk of staying trapped in the past. We become the victim of our circumstances, clinging to our entitlement to feel aggrieved.

The key to forgiveness is understanding that it's not the same as forgetting and it's different from reconciling. Reconciliation is about two parties coming together and having empathy for each other's position and finding common ground. Forgiveness is not about that: it's about acknowledging where the other person was coming from at that particular time, taking responsibility for your role in the situation and making a decision to move on. It's about changing your attitude, instead of plotting ways to exact revenge.

We can also be unforgiving of ourselves. But forgiving yourself means nothing unless you make a strong commitment to change your behaviour, and that's hard too. Seeking to understand why you acted in a particular way, and learning from it, is far more productive than beating yourself up about it.

It's unlikely that anything positive will come of holding onto a grudge – if you don't forgive, you might as well hand over the key to the prison cell of the past and remain hostage to your wrongdoer's will. It's an open invitation to bitterness.

Finding the capacity for forgiveness doesn't mean allowing yourself to be walked over. Standing up for something you believe in is positive; putting another brick in your prison cell wall is negative. Similarly, if you are the victim of injustice, the courage to forgive doesn't negate the pursuit of justice – otherwise the bastards keep on winning.

When we forgive, we create room for positive emotions to flourish. Think about it this way: you're not condoning anyone's behaviour. You're doing this for yourself. You're letting go of the hurt, and walking away from self-pity.

★

After the sticky circumstances of my departure as Melbourne coach midway through 2007, I felt a bit like the garbage that had been turfed out the back door. Mind you, my exit afforded me more dignity than many other sacked coaches have been.

I wasn't in a particularly forgiving mood towards the club chairman and CEO. The situation had led me to resign, and the club flagged that it didn't intend to pay out my contract for the rest of 2007 because it was cash-strapped. I didn't think this was right; I thought I'd done the right thing by the club, but I shouldn't have to pay the price of their financial problems just because, technically, I wasn't sacked. Instead of stewing over it, I acted swiftly.

The league was bankrolling the club, so I rang AFL boss Andrew Demetriou and asked him his thoughts on the scenario. When he agreed that I deserved compensation, I asked whether he could help me out. Demetriou contacted the club, and rather than using threats to lean on them, he said, 'Look, the guy has been under your roof for the past decade, he's the third-longest serving coach in your club's history and he helped guide you through some tough times. Do the right thing.'

Every coach, administrator and player who is shown the door by an AFL club would feel some sense of injustice, but from the club's perspective it might prove to be the right call. It's in the eye of the beholder. You might think someone has betrayed you, and yet they had honourable intentions. I'm sure there would have been a few Melbourne players and former players lining up to say, 'It's time for him to go.' Is that betrayal? At the time I probably thought so, and I know that Jan certainly felt that way.

Regardless of the ill feeling towards the Melbourne hierarchy, I didn't see the point in holding a grudge. It was a tough caper, but I was a big boy. By nature, I'm not a vindictive person. I've never held grudges or had any interest in looking to square up. I wished it had all been handled better, but there was nothing to be gained by obsessing over what-ifs and whys. Intuitively, I knew it was time to move on.

As time passed, I could think, *Well, from Melbourne's point of view, it probably did look like the right time for me to go.* In the years that followed, while I conceded that it might have been a bit awkward when I crossed paths with Melbourne chairman Paul Gardner, I didn't actually have anything against him. He had a job to do. I'd also been in the unenviable position of making decisions that were career-ending for other people.

My attitude towards moving on is in keeping with a line from an American author and psychiatrist Gordon Livingston, who wrote that, 'the most secure prisons are the ones we construct for ourselves'. When we don't forgive, there are all sorts of issues from the past that can create a secure prison cell if we allow ourselves to dwell there.

There will always be injustices and *perceived* injustices, depending on the point of view. You'll come across people who don't rate you, people who dent your ego, people whose evaluation you might want to prove wrong. If you dwell on the injustice for too long, you're likely to fool yourself into thinking there's something to be gained from clutching that bitterness close to your chest.

And here's the thing. Unwittingly, we add to our own injury because we allow someone else's opinion or thoughts to impact on our lives. Whereas if we can leave it behind and think, *Well, that's just someone else's view of things, why should it burn away at me?*, it allows us to let go of the perceived injustice. It also helps us if we know within ourselves that we acted according to our values and behaved with integrity, and I was comfortable with that aspect of my departure from Melbourne. Letting go is the crucial part of forgiveness; it allows us to be the dove flying out of the prison yard.

I'm not a turn-the-other-cheek guy, advocating that we just let other people walk all over us. Remember, I was raised to believe that our dealings with other people should be 'tough but fair'. It's more about doing the best we can to deal with the situation in the moment and then finding a way to cope if mistakes are made or feelings are hurt.

It's a lot easier when the other person is apologetic, but you have to be prepared to forgive even if the other person doesn't apologise. Remember that forgiveness is about controlling your attitude to what has happened, rather than allowing others to control your life, locking you up somewhere that you do not want to be.

Forgiveness is something for after the event, it's not the first card to reach for in the moment.

Some people might say, 'Fine, it's easy for you to let go and move on after being shuffled on as an AFL coach; you still had your health, a beautiful family, a nice house and good prospects. Realistically, the blow you sustained was one that put a dent in your ego.' And they would be spot on.

So what about forgiveness when somebody more grievously wrongs us? I'm not talking about the stress caused by a blue with the neighbour over an overhanging branch or the rubbish bins, I'm talking about serious misdeeds. Well, the same principle applies: don't let the offender's actions eat you up inside.

There is a big difference between forgiveness and seeking justice when the wrongdoing is at the extreme and complicated end of the scale. When people assault us, steal from us or do some sort of harm to our kids, forgiveness doesn't mean absolving them of responsibility for their actions nor does it mean giving up the expectation that justice will be served to them. How can anyone be expected to forgive monsters who kill or rape? Particularly if they avoid conviction and we feel that justice has not been served.

I've never been in that extreme situation and can only imagine that for victims and their families, it must be horrendously distressing. It would feel impossible to put the incident behind you. All I can offer is that you need to be wary of allowing these awful people to get you both ways. First, the fiend who has committed the crime has hurt you so very deeply, and second, the mongrel now has a grip on your life.

Don't let the bastards win both ways. You might find you can never truly let it go, so even if you can't bring yourself to forgive them, don't let the bad guy take your life from you by trapping you in malice. It might be a long and difficult process that requires professional help, but forgiveness brings some solace and is preferable to a lifetime of harboured resentment.

★

In the months after leaving Melbourne, I was hypersensitive to criticism. Commentators are less inclined to hold back once the boom has come down, and after the event, everybody wanted to point out where it all went wrong. Coaches are most touchy if when the new regime comes in, they take shots at the previous one. Thankfully, I was spared that indignity.

After the 2007 season, Melbourne appointed Dean Bailey as senior coach, and former Fremantle coach Chris Connolly came on board as football manager. It would have been an easy hit for them to look at the sorry state of the club and blame the previous coach, but I felt they had a bit of empathy for what I'd been through and were very respectful. Jan and I really appreciated that gesture. That was important in helping us move on.

There were four senior coaching changes at AFL clubs that season: there was my departure, Chris Connolly moving from Fremantle to Melbourne, the sacking of Denis Pagan by Carlton and over at Windy Hill, Essendon made the momentous decision to not renew Kevin Sheedy's contract after 27 years at the helm. Inevitably, my name ended up on a short list of candidates to take over from Sheeds. In hindsight, I'm not sure I had the energy to take on another AFL senior coaching role so soon, but I loved my former club and thought it was too good an opportunity to pass up. I went through two rounds of interviews and waited to hear from the selection panel as to whether I'd made it to the last round.

A few days later I was lying in bed, waking up to the 7 am news on the clock radio. The sports bulletin led off with an item: 'The race for the vacant Essendon coaching job is now down to two after the club yesterday ruled Neale Daniher out of the running.' I looked across at Jan and raised my eyebrows and she looked back, equally nonplussed. Without saying a word, we both shook our heads and thought, *Really? Did that just happen?*

Later that morning, when I rang my old mate Kevin Egan, an Essendon director, he was embarrassed. 'Hasn't anyone spoken to you?' he asked. In my heart, I hoped that it was a genuine oversight, because I didn't expect to be blindsided by a club I had such a strong relationship with. Terry reckons he rang the club and gave them a spray, and to this day Jan still tut-tuts when recalling the experience.

I wasn't surprised to miss out on the job and I also got the sense that the club was determined to head in a new direction, to get someone from outside the Essendon family who hadn't been tarred with the Sheedy brush. Another former Essendon player, then Hawthorn assistant coach Damien Hardwick, was the next candidate to be cut. Coaching novice and former Richmond captain Matthew Knights got the gig. I wasn't privy to the club's thinking, but I think they underestimated the challenge of filling the very big boots of a coaching legend.

It would have been easy for me to feel slighted at being rejected by the two clubs to which I'd devoted over 20 years of my life. It would have been easy to play the blame game. I'd been tempted down that path before – when my knee collapsed the second time, I wanted to blame the club's management or a doctor or a surgeon. Anyone really. I wanted to rage about why we hadn't waited for another month or tackled rehabilitation differently, but at the end of the day, I had to accept that blaming others was not going to change my reality.

Blame is all about momentarily making yourself feel better about your situation. You can sit there and say, 'My predicament has not been brought about by me and therefore I am not at fault.' You can tell yourself that the responsibility was beyond your control – you'll probably feel pretty comfortable thinking that. And you can dream up how wonderful that parallel universe would have been if only that sliding door hadn't slammed in your face.

Society more generally has moved in the direction of finding someone to blame. Who can we sue, who can we blame when little Johnny gets a poor grade, or when we don't get a promotion? Our ego demands that if anything fails or falters, it cannot possibly be our fault, and don't let any bugger tell us that it is. But that sort of rationale is just setting us up for a sucker punch. At some point, reality is going to hit, and hit hard.

Holding a grudge is part of the blame game. I'm sure there are numerous people who have wronged me in life, and if I held grudges then dozens of examples might spring to mind. People who do hold grudges can take us through their list, blow by blow, recounting in great detail that time forty years ago when they were going to steer their Year 10 cricket team to victory but that bloody umpire gave them out for an LBW when the ball was clearly going to miss leg stump.

We all know those people. And all we want to say to them is, 'Mate, let it go.'

★

It's fair to say we're generally better (and faster) at forgiving ourselves than we are at forgiving others. When we forgive others, we expect them to do better next time. But it's tempting to let ourselves off the hook without putting in the hard yards to accept responsibility and try to change.

When you forgive yourself, do so on the proviso that you learn from the experience. There has to be reflection and accountability. It can be unhealthy to forgive yourself all the time, particularly if you do it so often that you virtually never take responsibility for your actions.

Often we judge others on their actions and ourselves on our intentions. Sometimes you just need to acknowledge that you didn't like your own behaviour and use that understanding to grow and improve. There are times when I've looked back at the way I acted in a situation and thought, *I don't really like that guy,* but I've learnt from it rather than beating myself up over it. We all make mistakes, but we can't keep stuffing up, forgiving ourselves and not changing. Learning to forgive yourself should be a path to becoming a better person.

Forgiveness is liberating. Trust me, when you forgive, it's a weight off your shoulders.

Pass it on

Sometimes in life, things go wrong: remember, life doesn't promise to be fair. But when we take the chance to pause and reflect, hopefully we can also recognise that across the years there have been times when life has also been bloody good to us.

We've all had successes and special moments along the way, including some that we take pride in, feeling like we did it all on our own. In those moments, our ego wants to tell us that we are the hero, thanks to our own talent, hard work and determination. But with the development of the character trait of humility, we come to realise that other people have always played a major role in getting us there, even if we didn't appreciate it at the time or recognise the full worth of that help.

In reaching the better moments in life, we are fortunate to stand on the shoulders of others. How lucky are we that those people lifted us up, not necessarily because we deserved it, but simply because they could? These are the blessings we should count.

If you get the chance at the time, make sure you thank those people personally. But often we don't understand the significance of the help we've received and it's too late to thank in person. But there is another way of respecting what people did to help us, and it involves lifting others up onto our own shoulders when we can.

In passing it on, not only do we provide opportunities for others to have special moments, we are letting our actions do the talking and that's the most powerful statement of all.

★

My proudest cricket moment came when I scored 157 for Assumption College. Afterwards, I thought it was a pretty special effort and that I was a bit of a star. But I was only there because my father had poured a concrete cricket pitch in our backyard and my brothers had bowled to me for hours. I was only there because the school had been organising cricket matches for decades, someone had lovingly prepared a pitch to play on, a batsman was at the other end, there was an opposition, there were two coaches and umpires to run the game as well as people to record the score in a book.

During my time as Melbourne coach, the summer months offered the rare chance to have a few weekends away from the all-consuming stresses of AFL football and to spend time with our kids. On Saturday mornings we would head down to Stradbroke Park where they all competed in Kew Little Athletics meetings. Some parents helped run the program, some – like me – sat back and watched while others dropped their kids off before disappearing to do a few chores. I used to lean back in the sunshine at the top the grassy slope with a cup of coffee, open the paper and look up from time to time to watch my kids compete in their events. I would think to myself, *How good is this? It's someone else's turn to take charge*, while reaching for a biscuit to dip into my coffee.

One Saturday in 1999, a loud official voice echoed over the crackling PA system: 'Hello parents, uncles, aunties, anyone really. We're looking for someone to give us a hand to officiate the long-jump competition. Unless we get some officials soon, we may have to cancel that event today . . . and no one wants that.'

I thought, *There aren't many people here, but surely someone will step up*, as I picked up the paper to read the latest footy news. A moment later, the bloke on the PA had another go: 'We're looking for someone to help,' he boomed. 'Up on the hill. Anywhere. Anyone prepared to help?'

I looked up from the newspaper and realised that I was actually the only parent on the hill.

'Ah, crap,' I muttered to myself before scrambling down the slope. That morning I stretched out a measuring tape and raked the sandpit for a couple of hours and found that I really enjoyed it.

The next Saturday morning, when the kids scattered to their age groups, I asked the bloke whether he was covered for parental assistance. 'We can always use help,' he replied, explaining that they needed people to either monitor individual events, or be responsible for taking an age group of kids from station to station. I chose the latter, thinking it would be fun to get to know the personalities of the kids in a group.

All the times when I'd sat on the sidelines for three hours, I'd be looking at my watch after I'd read the paper and still have a couple of hours to go. I'd do a bit of paperwork, still have an hour to fill, and think to myself, *Geez, this is taking forever.* But after I began helping out, I discovered I got a kick out of being involved and before I knew it, the hours would have slipped away and the meet would be winding up.

Unfortunately, the demands of my job meant that opportunities to be part of the kids' activities were limited, and much of the burden fell to Jan. At one stage during my time as Melbourne coach, Jan worked out that her typical week involved getting the four kids organised to attend 35 training sessions or sports matches – an average of five per day. That's a hell of a lot of hours spent looking up venues, organising carpools, scoring at matches and washing sports uniforms.

This commitment was so much more than the running around. Jan also instilled in them that you can never pull out or show up late because your teammates rely on you. Our kids understood that signing up to be a part of a team meant they had a responsibility to turn up, to never give up and to play their role to the best of their ability both at training and on game day. Whether it was a frosty morning for footy or at sunrise on a weekend for a triathlon or the end of a long school day for basketball training, Jan was marshalling the troops and cheering them on.

Jan set the parenting bar pretty high when it came to both pitching in and making sure the kids absorbed all the valuable lessons that come from taking part in sporting activities.

Our kids have taken those lessons into adulthood, just as we both did – Bruce and Marg McCorkell tirelessly supported Jan's passion for netball, while my parents knew that sport would not only keep us kids out of trouble, it would teach us to cooperate and compete.

It's only as an adult that you truly appreciate the sacrifices your parents – and others – made for you and start to get a sense of the satisfaction they must get from seeing the results of their efforts in the next generation. You feel indebted to them, knowing their efforts went far beyond dropping us off at a sports oval.

★

If you asked some younger football fans about the Daniher link to the AFL, they would tell you that Joe Daniher is a gun forward at Essendon. And that he originally played his junior football at Aberfeldie, an inner suburb of Melbourne. They might have heard something about Joe's father and his uncles playing football, too.

But very few would appreciate that were it not for Joe's grandfather, Jim, there might not even be a Daniher link to Australian Rules football.

The love of the game was in Dad's blood. His father, Jim Daniher Sr, was originally from Victoria, where he had played

Australian football, winning a best-and-fairest award for the Longwood Football Club and being a member of Euroa's 1913 premiership team. Not long after relocating to Ungarie, my grandfather had helped establish the football club, playing in the 1923 premiership and holding various positions including patron up to the time of his death in 1959.

His three sons – Jack, Jim Jr and Leo – wore the team's broad black and white horizontal stripes when playing resumed in 1946 after the war. On the farm, the brothers used to kick footballs made of a leather case stuffed with barley grass. If the Ungarie ground became too boggy to play on, due to a rising Humbug Creek, they would mark out a ground in one of the surrounding paddocks. Dad and Uncle Leo both won league best-and-fairest awards.

On Sundays after church, the farmers in the district would gather to put their aching bodies through a game of rugby league for Ungarie. Dad used to go all right in the 13-a-side game. Playing as an outside centre, he did well enough to be selected in the Riverina combined team and scored two tries in a match against the touring British team at the Wagga Wagga Showgrounds in 1954. Several Sydney-based clubs had sent letters inviting him to try out, but he knocked them back – he thought league was a bit of a basic game. The Australian code was his passion.

The first time my father ventured outside the district was as a 19-year-old in 1948 when Carlton Football Club invited him to try his hand in the VFL. Knowing that he had to organise his own work and accommodation, Dad was hoping to board in Melbourne with his uncle, a former police officer turned SP bookmaker, but upon arriving in the city he learned that Jack Daniher was in the middle of a trip to London. Fortunately, Dad was met at the Spencer Street railway station by a Carlton official, who bought him lunch at a city hotel – the first time my father ever saw anyone leave a tip.

For a few weeks, Dad caught the tram up Elizabeth Street to train with the Blues at Princes Park, bemused that the coach, Perc Bentley, used to conduct training from a chair in the middle of the oval. He was amazed at how many people would come along just to watch training – at one point, he took a nice mark and heard all of these fans start clapping. He was a bit dumbstruck, thinking, *It was just a solid grab, nothing special*, until he realised that the applause was because Bert Deacon – who had played in the previous year's premiership and won the Brownlow Medal – had just jogged onto the ground.

Dad played in a couple of scratch matches. He felt he could hold his own with Carlton's squad of players and could possibly have broken into the team, but he eventually decided league football wasn't for him and returned to the farm. He felt more comfortable in the bush. Back in Ungarie, he played in several Magpies premierships – including the 1959–61 treble – and captained the team for a decade. There was no coach.

But for all of his triumphs, some of the most enduring stories about my father's football career revolve around his ability to play through injuries. On one occasion, he was helping his brother Leo remove the wheel from a tractor when a heavy piece of machinery slipped and landed on his right foot, taking off the nail on his big toe. Come Saturday afternoon, he cut a hole in the top of his football boot to accommodate the mangled toe and kicked using his left foot.

'Except once, when I forgot. Did it hurt!' he lamented. 'Believe you me, I didn't kick with my right again.' Another time he broke a scaphoid bone, but took the plaster cast off to play and had it replaced after each game. 'I should never have let the umpires bluff me into taking it off,' he told me. 'I should have told them to go to buggery.'

Given his passion for football, it was inevitable that Jim Daniher would want his sons to play the game. The only problem was, there were no junior football teams in the district when Terry and I were young boys. Dad tackled the issue the best way he knew how: he got down to work and formed two teams – one for under-12s and the other for under-16s – before hitting the phone to farmers from the surrounding towns saying, 'Get yourselves a team together so that we have someone to play against.'

Dad said his motivation was for us boys and the other local kids to have a healthy activity that would keep us out of trouble. 'Otherwise, what else would you all have been doing? Mucking up,' he told me years later. 'There was not much else to do in town on the weekend – in my day, all the young blokes used to spend all day drinking and smoking and betting on the horses.'

Not only did he help organise the league and the games – and sometimes umpire them before playing in the men's team – he also used to select the Ungarie junior teams. Each week he would sit down at the kitchen table and scribble down the players' names in position on a piece of cardboard he'd cut out from the inside of a Corn Flakes box. Fortunately, with 11 children, our family used to go through plenty of Corn Flakes each week.

The nature of farming life meant that it didn't take much for a team to face a challenge in mustering enough players for a team. A town might find itself a few players short if a family was away one weekend, or it was shearing, sowing or cropping time, or if a worker moved out of a district. For away games, Dad often rounded up many of the boys on a Saturday morning and made sure they had transport to the game. Player numbers were fluid: matches might involve 14-a-side or 16 against 12. One weekend, when most of the Ungarie kids were away for a rugby league carnival, six Danihers and one of our mates took on 13 players from Lake Cargelligo. Somehow, we won.

I admire my father's commitment to junior football in the Northern Riverina – I have enormous respect for people who commit to a broader purpose than their own self-interest. Farming and football were important not only as his great loves, but in the context of having a meaningful life.

Ray Carroll was the same at Assumption College. He wasn't simply a devoted football and cricket coach, he was proud of the school's reputation for excellence with humility. Ray was a most decent person with solid values and a believer in the cause, which was the school and its ability to build character in young people. For all of his interest in their sporting prowess, he was equally interested in their welfare and personal development. A by-product of both of these men's devotion to their broader community was that what they built was strong, successful and enduring. In his 53 years at Assumption, Ray coached 70 football and cricket teams to premierships and helped guide 90 footballers towards VFL/AFL careers.

The countless hours that my father, his brothers and other men in the district contributed to junior football also made Ungarie a team to beat; the Magpies won nine consecutive under-16s premierships. The junior league also created a pathway for young footballers and stoked our enthusiasm for the game. As teenagers, my brothers and I always had an old scarred football in the back of the ute and whenever there was a gap in the farm work – and often even when there wasn't – we would grab the footy and have an impromptu kick. When the ball inevitably split at the seams we would beg, borrow or steal another one. Having the Ungarie juniors gave the four of us the chance to play interleague football, to represent New South Wales in the under-17 Teal Cup carnival (along with our cousin Pat) and set us up to achieve our dream of playing league football. The juniors also bolstered the senior team and helped the Magpies win several flags.

What would prove to be the only senior premiership of my playing career came with Ungarie in 1978. During Year 12, I managed to squeeze in a few games with the Magpies when I was back on the farm during school holidays. They were undefeated that season and made it through to the Northern Riverina grand final against Four Corners at Tullibigeal. I had enough games under my belt to qualify and the match fell during another school holidays break. Some locals were lobbying for me to line up, others thought I shouldn't because it would cost a regular his spot in the squad. I was content to go with whichever direction the club chose.

Eventually the club's executive had a vote and I was named in the team, with local shearer Clarence Ridley the unlucky one to be left out. Ungarie decided they wanted to show they could win without me and for three quarters I sat on the bench. When we trailed by 18 points at three-quarter time, the coach, Peter Bryant, sent me on at full-forward. With my cousin Pat (who was best on ground) dashing out of the centre and kicking the ball out in front of me, the poor bloke who'd already put in three quarters at fullback had no chance. John Ireland, a really good footballer who had played against my old man – that's probably why he didn't rough me up, out of respect for Dad – now had a fresh teenage jack-in-the-box running his tired legs around. I kicked three quick goals and we won by 10 points.

Even though I was too young to go to the pub, I could have joined in the raucous premiership celebrations, but I wasn't fussed. I was 17 and full of belief that I had bigger fish to fry.

Now I look back at that decision and realise that not only did I pass up my only chance to celebrate playing in a senior premiership, I didn't respect the work that so many Ungarie people had put into that season. It was only much later that I fully appreciated what that game meant to them.

I think that's why I've seized opportunities along the way to square the ledger and give back a little. I can't return to that time and take it all in, have a beer with those blokes, thank all those behind the scenes who did the hard yards over the decades. But I can pave the way for someone else, in their honour.

★

In 2008, when I was out of the AFL club system, a window opened that allowed me to take an active role in junior sport. By that stage my eldest son, Luke, was playing with Oakleigh Chargers in the under-18s TAC Cup, and my younger boy, Ben, and my nephew James were playing in a junior suburban league for the Kew Rovers. Heading into that season, their under-15s team didn't have a coach.

Whenever possible I had gone along to watch my children play, usually leaning up against a distant tree or staying beside the car with Jan and her father, Bruce, just wanting to enjoy seeing them run around, rather than mingling in the crowd and dealing with other parents' questions about how Melbourne was going or what I thought about the prospects of the team they barracked for.

I knew quite a few of the Kew Rovers parents through school and sport, and the coaching vacancy meant a few sets of eyes turned my way. I have to admit that I liked the idea of coaching my sons, just as my father had guided Terry, Anthony, Chris and myself, so I agreed to step up.

In reality, I was at a stage where I could take on the role without any ego, because judgement on whether I could coach was not going to be measured by where the those under-15s finished on the ladder. Too many junior coaches get sucked in to striving to prove themselves through their team's win–loss statistics. We've all seen examples of the ugly coach of a junior team who gets too worked up. Sometimes I've felt like wandering down to the boundary and saying, 'Mate, I'm probably the last one who should be saying this, but just relax.'

I saw coaching this team as an opportunity to create an environment where there was some real team spirit, where a bunch of 14-year-old boys could enjoy being part of something and feeling valued. The success of the season would not be measured on games won, but on whether the boys liked the experience enough to want to play again the next season. I channelled one of my father's guiding principles: 'Just let the kids play.'

The Rovers were in division two and the team was made up of players with a wide range of football talent. Some were physically well developed, while others – like Ben – were relatively small for their age. About a third of the kids could really excel in that division, a third were average and a third struggled with the standard.

There were three non-negotiable principles I set out going into the role: don't be driven by wins and losses, make football fun for the players and share the coaching responsibility with other parents. Two of the dads, Greg Skene and Peter Lane, joined in as fantastic assistant coaches and another father, Andrew 'the Prof' Grigg, did all the backroom organising. The Prof reckoned he was the architect, the Graeme Richmond-like powerbroker behind the scenes. Together as parents we kept it pretty light and it was a lot of fun.

At training we tried to have the football in the boys' hands as much as possible and we liked to have competitive little games that improved specific aspects such as contested marking, goal-kicking or two-on-one contests. The coaches would never keep score, but the boys somehow always seemed to know the score anyway. We tried to let the boys be boys, but there were certain character rules to ensure that they knew the expected behaviours. Anyone who spat the dummy in a game would have to come off the ground. And there was to be equal game time for all players.

Coaching your own boy can be tricky. You can't be seen to favour him but you can't overcorrect and be too tough on him and deny him opportunity either. If anything I probably leaned to the latter, but Pete and Greg would keep an eye on that for me. Every now and then during a game, we'd put a kid – not a prime mover, usually one of the little forward pockets – one-out against his opponent in the goalsquare and tell the other forwards, 'Righto, the rest of you need to push up out of his space.' Well, that kid would light up, love it and feel super important. Ben took his turn, and I could see how it helped his confidence grow – he even kicked a ripper of a goal.

As the season unfolded, what pleased me most was that I felt the boys were thriving. They got what we were about, and nobody dropped off. That didn't stop some adults viewing the scene through their own subjective lens. Occasionally I'd come up against an opposition coach who gave the impression that they wanted to win so that they could say they'd knocked off an AFL coach. In one game I took off my jumper during the third quarter and forgot to put my blue coach's bib back on over my T-shirt. After the match I went over to shake the opposing coach's hand and he said, 'What, are you too good to wear the bib are you, mate?'

At season's end, the team was playing well, managed to finish second and made it through to the grand final. We weren't expected to win against Prahran and some of the parents were starting to make noises that we should consider abandoning the equal game-time philosophy and favour our strongest players in the grand final at Heidelberg West. Some thought we should just play the minimum number allowed on the bench. But we were determined to play every one of the available 31 players and, more importantly, to give all of them their fair share of time on the ground.

As it happened, we won the match by about 10 goals and although the result wasn't the be-all and end-all to me, it was pleasing for the boys to experience the reward for working so well together. After the match, Terry – one of many Danihers in the crowd that day – wandered over, gave me a nudge and winked.

'Well done, old son,' he drawled. 'You've finally won one.'

That year made me realise I would love to have had more involvement in junior sport throughout the years. You might be reading this thinking, *I wish I'd helped out more, too*. Well, it's not too late. You'll be amazed how much meaning you will find from it. Get involved, there are plenty of ways to do it if you look. Clubs always need someone to cook the sausages, keep the score, help with the paperwork, manage a team or update the website. Sometimes they even need someone to rake the long-jump pit.

For me, that year was also a way of showing my appreciation for all the people who had lifted me up along the way.

★

One thing I admire about legendary coaches Ronald Dale Barassi Jr and Kevin Sheedy is that they have taken personal responsibility for the game for future generations. Over their lives, they have both really cared about the game itself.

Barassi was always looking to expand the game, especially north of Victoria, and Sheeds took the Bombers to every nook and cranny in Australia to promote the game. He's taken the game to the world and continues to spruik it at every available opportunity. He once said to me, 'Neale, coaches are paid to win but we need to look after this great game.' I took that to heart, adding that we also need to look after the great people who've given so much of their life to the game.

In 1998, my first year as coach, Melbourne knocked St Kilda out of the finals race on our way to a preliminary final. Soon after, St Kilda sacked their coach, Stan Alves. Alves had coached St Kilda to its second minor premiership and first grand final in 26 years in 1997, earning him the AFL Coach of the Year award.

Stan's sacking was just another reminder of how ruthless the industry was. Clubs would throw all their energy into welcoming a new coach through the front door, but who would greet the old coach as he left via the back door? I didn't think it was right that there was no formal support network for sacked coaches. Who was looking after the sacked coach on his way out? Who had been developing the next prospective coach-in-waiting? Frankly, I believed that these issues were not serving our game well, and I had been looking for opportunities to do something about it.

In late 2000, early 2001, I had conversations with former AFL Players' Association (AFLPA) administrator Peter Allen around the possibility of a coaches association founded along similar lines, to give the coaches a collective voice. We involved Sheeds and Hawthorn coach Peter Schwab in the initial conversations. In 2002, the AFL Coaches Association (AFLCA) was formed.

At the time we had no funding, and no backing from the AFL, the clubs or even the coaches. But you have to start somewhere. The game is hard, and we all know it, and we need to show some respect to people who have put their heart and soul into the game, some for decades.

From 2002 to 2007 the association slowly built momentum. Kevin Sheedy was one of the first to get on board, but many others were indifferent. Brisbane Lions coach Leigh Matthews took a typically pragmatic approach: 'Tell me exactly what is it that you want me to support. Give me clarity. Then I can tell you whether I'm in or not.'

We drew up a concise outline of the AFLCA's purpose, listing three main objectives.

The first objective was to help aspiring AFL coaches. How could they get a foot in the door of an AFL club, which could seem quite firmly closed from the outside? We wanted to give them a pathway, an accreditation course with the appropriate level of education and best practices that would help enhance their knowledge, skills and experiences to prepare for the elite level.

Second, once coaches had a foot in the door, we wanted to establish a way to provide ongoing support and development. If they wanted it, we wanted to provide people who could continue to mentor and advise them.

And third, when coaches were reaching the end of their tenure, we wanted to be able to continue to support them then.

Leigh's response was, 'That makes sense. I like that. If that's what you're about, I'm in.'

We met resistance from several of the coaches, the clubs and the league itself. Some suspected our ulterior motive was about unionising the coaches or angling for them to be paid more.

My departure as Melbourne coach in 2007 meant I had more time to devote to the AFLCA. The executive thought we needed to accelerate our momentum and I was offered the inaugural role of AFLCA CEO. I was determined to convince everyone in the industry that having an involvement with the association was a win–win proposition for our great game.

I sold the line that the coaches were the AFL's partners in growing the game, and that the senior coach was the most influential person at every football club in the land. I said we needed to nurture them, educate them, give them more guidelines and a clearer framework around integrity. The better our coaches were, the better the game would be.

I enjoyed the challenge of getting the AFLCA in solid shape, ready to hand over to another CEO. Within a decade, the

AFLCA had become a representative body for football coaches at all levels of the game. With two extra AFL clubs and the AFLW competition in the mix, it was advocating for about 250 coaches at the elite level. All three objectives – supporting coaches before, during and after their AFL stints – were being met. And by 2015, the AFL introduced a Level Four accreditation program, a two-year course to help highly rated assistant coaches prepare for the demands of a senior coaching role.

Towards the end of 2016, I was invited to speak to the nine men who were part of the first intake of a mentoring program. The gist of my talk was that, as coaches, sometimes when we get in a rut, it's worth paring it all back to what it is we love about the game.

Every coach in the AFL system is passionate about the game, and these guys were as engaged as any coach out there. But with all of the pressures, and the focus on structures and game styles, it was worth reminding them not to forget that we all took up football because we love the game. Winning and losing is what coaches live and die by, but why did we fall in love with football in the first place and what responsibility do we have to the game? Our passion for football is important, but the love of the game gives it context.

I asked them to remember how footy grabbed hold of them as kids. I showed them a photo of me at the age of six, flanked by my older brother, Terry, and my younger brother, Anthony, all three of us young boys standing proud in our full Ungarie junior football kit, jumpers tucked in, hair combed back, smiling at the camera.

From time to time I look at that photograph on the mantelpiece – it's just about the only football image to be seen anywhere at home – and it stirs within me the memory of an innocent time when we were just boys being boys. And Mum and Dad just let the boys play. They took care of the detail – scribbling on the Corn Flakes box, marking out the oval, working in the canteen – and so did many other selfless people along the way.

I stood on the shoulders of others to become the man I am today. We've all stood on the shoulders of others, in all aspects of life. You can show your gratitude by passing it on to the next generation and helping them to have a beautiful experience. In looking outside yourself, one day when you're raking the long-jump pit, you might even find your 'why'.

Success is never final, failure never fatal

When you're staring down The Beast, knowing there's no effective treatment and no cure, it's impossible not to reflect on life, to think about success and failure.

Have I made enough use of my time on earth? How do my achievements rate? What about my blunders? How will I be remembered? Did I succeed in my roles as father, son, brother and husband?

You could argue that considering these questions is pure vanity. In the big scheme of the history of the universe, our time here is a mere blip, soon to be forgotten. True, but I say our little blip does matter, because *you* matter. What you do – both good and bad – to yourself, your family, friends, society, our nation, the planet will play out through this generation and the next. And because of this, I'm sure we matter.

I am also sure that success and failure mean different things to each and every one of us. As a 58-year-old man, I care about how those dear to me, my family and close friends, evaluate my life. But I don't care how I stack up against someone else's measures.

My personal definition of success involves the internal virtues that exist at the core of my being. Am I honest, courageous, fair, trustworthy, loyal, kind, forgiving, responsible and resilient? Are my relationships strong and meaningful? No matter what cards I've been dealt, have I played them well? Have I served something greater than my own ego?

The late American basketball coach John Wooden defined success as 'peace of mind, which is a direct result of self-satisfaction in knowing you made the effort to do your best to become the best that you are capable of becoming'. That resonates with me.

If we measure ourselves against the resumé virtues of status, wealth, beauty, power and fame, we're probably going to come up short. That kind of success is never final – it's a never-ending quest for more. As for failure, if you haven't faced it at some stage, you've probably played it too safe, haven't stretched yourself or pushed to be the best version of yourself.

I believe that to live a good life, we need to manage both success and failure well. When you succeed, it feels good – enjoy it. Your hard work is validated and your self-identity is reassured but remember you have been lifted up on the shoulders of many that came before you. When you fail, especially when you've put your heart and soul into the endeavour . . . well, to put it bluntly, it sucks. But learn from it, refuse to play the victim and play on.

Failure isn't fatal: it offers an opportunity to take responsibility, to clean up your mess, to change course. It's your glorious opportunity for redemption, a chance to make things right.

Don't waste your brief time on earth judging yourself according to other people's standards. Decide what is most important to you and find your own way to measure your progress.

After all, it's your life. Make it matter.

★

I remember getting off the school bus at home one day when I would have been eight or nine and looking out across a windswept paddock and thinking, *I wish I were a sheep.* To my young mind, sheep had such a carefree existence, not a care in the world. All they had to do was wander around, pick off the odd shoot of grass and have a sip of water whenever they were thirsty.

It's probably a reflection of me as a person that even at that young age I felt the burden of living a conscious life. But it didn't occur to me that a sheep can get taken by foxes or that they might have their throat cut so they could end up on someone's dinner plate! The point is that that little boy standing beside the dirt road in Ungarie was imagining how wonderful it would be to lead a less complicated existence.

As we reach middle age we sometimes fall for reminiscence; we look back through rose-coloured glasses at how carefree we were as teenagers or in our twenties. We forget that back then we had the stresses of that age group: worrying about appearance, or fashion trends, whether we fitted in socially, where our next dollar was coming from, whether we'd get a game in our sporting team that weekend. We had a whole raft of issues that might not seem so substantial looking back, but they were everything at the time.

It's easy to ignore the context of past concerns and compare them to the pressures of having four kids and a mortgage, but I challenge the nostalgic view that our lives used to be carefree when we were younger. The more telling difference is that when you're young, you have the precious commodities of hope and time in seemingly endless supply. Even if you spend a few years faffing around, you can still think, *OK, I've stuffed it up, but I'm only 24. Who cares? I've got an eternity ahead of me. Right, let's go out and party.*

As a young person, there's satisfaction in the milestone successes, such as finishing high school or university, getting your driver's licence or landing your first job and there's still the promise of better times ahead. But sometimes people get to 45 and start to feel like time is slipping away from them. They ask themselves, *What have I actually done?*

And that's when some people start to mourn the loss of their youth. We worry that society is going to park us to one side, and we yearn for our younger days when we felt invincible. It's a little grief cycle that we have to go through: facing our mortality. It is important to come to grips with that reality and contemplate what we've learnt along the way, but often we don't go there. When we're young, why would we?

We resist such serious contemplation because there are so many unanswerable questions. We become like a baseball batter who strikes out and keeps coming out swinging, but the longer the game goes on, the more he must be thinking, *Hang on, I haven't got many swings left here.* Do we stop trying to hit a home run and start worrying about just getting bat to ball?

In some spheres, particularly those that rely on physical prowess, we do peak in our youth. It can be the same with creative and intellectual pursuits, where we are no longer as sharp when we get older. But there are ways to adapt: older golfers don't hit their drives as far as they used to, so they devote more effort to placement and get smarter about other ways to card a good round. They work on their short game, become better at putting.

As we grow older, our reservations and doubts all stem from our ego trying to reinforce that narrow definition of success and accomplishments, trying to make it all about self-glorification. Rather than reminiscing and driving everyone to distraction with stories from 'back in my day', we need to embrace the idea that we are not going to last forever and consider what we want to do in that last third or quarter of our lives. What can we do that feels worthwhile and meaningful?

There are thousands of things we can do, but it's hard to think outside the box because some of the concepts are so foreign to us. There are opportunities to get involved in the community, to mentor, volunteer, support and serve and there is a lot of fulfilment to be found in that.

As Carl Jung put it: 'The least of things with a meaning is worth more in life than the greatest of things without it.'

It comes down to attitude, and that's the one aspect of our life we can always control. Embrace life for what it is. Grasp the opportunities. In the film *Dead Poets Society*, Robin Williams plays the role of English teacher John Keating, and in a famous scene he asks his students to consider the 17th century poem by English poet Robert Herrick, who wrote the line, 'Gather ye rosebuds while ye may'. Keating explains that the Latin term for that sentiment is *carpe diem* or 'seize the day', and the message is for the boys to take advantage of life while they are in the prime of their youth.

'Seize the day' is just as relevant later in life. Maybe with a tweak – don't mourn yesterday or fret about tomorrow, just seize today.

★

Often when we are speaking at a function together, I love to have a bit of fun at Terry's expense. I'll talk up my football ability and downplay his career. I always tell people that Terry played 300-odd ordinary games, while I played 82 of the best games you could imagine. Sure, he was a two-time premiership skipper, but he only got the captaincy because I coughed it up. Our two other brothers, Anthony and Chris, are my backups, my cohorts.

Terry takes it all with good humour, but I'm sure some people must think I'm full of myself. It's just part of our little comedy routine and we all get a laugh out of it. It's partly my way of deflecting from the embarrassment I feel, knowing that I was just a minor player in the whole orchestra that was Essendon in the 1980s. But the one upside of my playing career being cut short by injury is that people will forever romanticise what might have been with my career, and there's no way to disprove it!

In reality, I see myself as a kid who had the footy world at his feet at 21. And then there's a full stop. Nobody will ever know what the next sentences would have been if I'd been able to continue providing material for that story. What I do know is that I got married and had four kids, whereas if I had continued to be a self-centred footballer for another eight years, my life might not have turned out as well as it did.

In 2018, I was inducted into Essendon's Hall of Fame and in my acceptance speech, I thanked the selection committee but joked, 'If I was on the committee, I wouldn't have picked me.' Even though my induction undoubtedly had a lot to do with the story and the mythology, I feel extremely honoured.

I'm a fairly harsh judge of my football voyage. I think my playing career and coaching career both fell short – there was another level they could have gone to. But with both, there is an element of knowing that I couldn't have done much better given the circumstances: knee reconstructions with playing, six finals series in nine seasons as a coach with a playing list and a club set-up that both had certain limitations. But people don't care about excuses. And why go there anyway?

Successes are more testing of our ego. When we succeed our ego can easily come out of the cage and bring some repressed flaws with it, such as arrogance, pride, self-importance, opportunism and inconsideration.

Failure, on the other hand, is more a test of our character. Sure, our pride might take a bit of a battering, but it's more about an acceptance of where we're at, pinpointing what we can learn from the experience and searching for the opportunity to move forward. We need to take the lesson from the setback, the mishap or the train wreck and try to get ourselves going again with a positive outlook.

The great inventor Thomas Edison said: 'Failure is a learning opportunity.' It took him a thousand failures before he came up with a practical electric light bulb. His premise is sound although, granted, in some fields we don't get the chance to deliver a thousand failures before we conjure up a success. But in the medical research world – looking for a way to cure MND, for example – there is definitely a process of trying and failing in the quest for success. Even though certain trials and drugs fail, the hope is that the knowledge becomes universal and helps make sure that some other poor bugger in Sweden doesn't have to devote months or years going down the same path to discover the same information. In cases like these, it's better to fail quickly so that we can get to the success sooner.

All we can do is look at today and work out how we can next contribute, not worry about what someone will inscribe on our tombstone. What I have found is that many of us get to a point in life where we feel we have peaked, and we start to wonder whether our whole life is a success or a failure. But we have to take life's lessons and understand that there will always be greater and lesser people than us and accept that we just need to focus on how we can improve by our own measure.

★

In June 2008, West Coast CEO Trevor Nisbett organised to meet me for lunch in Melbourne. Over a sandwich, he mentioned that the Eagles' general manager of football, Steve Woodhouse, was going through a few health issues and was stepping back slightly to take a role in the club's list management area.

West Coast was looking for a strong football person who could help facilitate a change of culture and uphold their core values, as well as act as a sounding board for coach John Worsfold.

Two months before its 2006 premiership, West Coast had put a process in place to address a disturbing culture that had emerged within its playing group. In the weeks after the grand final, solid evidence had emerged of social drug use by half a dozen players, prompting the Eagles to flag to the AFL their concern that the problem had the potential to spread among the rest of the group, and to ask for assistance and extra drug testing for their players. Instead, the AFL chose to open an investigation into whether the club had brought the game into disrepute. The club's leaders and five senior players fronted the AFL Commission.

Nisbett spoke to me about how several of the senior players had believed that as long as they were playing great football, what they did off-field was irrelevant. He told me that some other players had followed suit, and that there was an influential core who didn't care what people thought of them or the club. The club's board, led by chairman Dalton Gooding, demanded an overhaul, regardless of whether the team would be weakened. The Eagles had been forced to let many players go and had committed to cultural change. Outside experts were brought in and an internal 'Core Values Committee' was formed, heavily weighted towards focusing on the playing group. There were biannual reviews of the football department and regular player interviews and surveys.

The Eagles had been premiers in 2006 and finalists in 2007. As Trevor and I chatted, the team was second last on the ladder midway through 2008 with just two wins on the board.

At the heart of the matter was an understanding of how to subjectively judge whether an organisation is succeeding or failing. A casual glance would suggest that the Eagles had succeeded in 2007, winning 15 games and reaching the semi-finals. Another perception would be that had they had failed, with former captain Ben Cousins entering a drug rehab program and later being delisted, with the club being investigated by the league and its reputation in tatters. Meanwhile, inside the club, there was some reason to believe they had at least succeeded in recognising their issues and committing to a course that would rewire their culture.

As a governing body, the AFL takes the holistic view that the success of the game is dependent on influencing attitudes and behaviours, and creating an environment that values qualities such as respect, inclusiveness and responsibility. Many other organisations do too, but we still see companies that strive for a big profit and juicy dividend for shareholders, while tolerating a culture of bullying and harassment among staff or underpaying workers.

Building a good football club, or any organisation, can't only be about an obsession with having more wins than losses. Success can't just be measured by the numbers written in the columns of a spreadsheet. The measure of success needs to take into account the quality of the people, the program, what you stand for and what you value. I admired the fact that West Coast had won a premiership and then made a brave call that fixing their culture was more important than getting the four points for a win the next Saturday.

Taking on the role as the general manager of football operations for the Eagles appealed to me. I felt my work at the AFLCA was almost done and, while I was keen to return to a club environment, I felt that the prospects of landing another senior coaching gig were limited. The prevailing school of thought at the time was to give coaching starts to younger, recently retired players, such as Matthew Knights, Mark Harvey and Brett Ratten, and it would trend towards an even younger next wave, which saw the likes of Michael Voss, Chris and Brad Scott, Matthew Primus, James Hird and Nathan Buckley get the nod. I felt my coaching card had been stamped.

My suspicion that Jan would relish the prospect of a return to Perth was right on the mark. The difference this time was that we would not be relocating a young family. Lauren and Luke were still living at home but were now adults and we also had two teenagers at home, so our kids needed to have a greater say in whether their lives were uprooted. Jan – the captain of our team – said there needed to be a consensus and wouldn't entertain the idea of the move unless at least three of the four kids agreed to it. The boys were up for the move, while Lauren opted to stay in Melbourne to pursue her nursing career. Bec, who was 18, decided to come too, only to change her mind at the last minute. By that stage we were on our way back across the Nullarbor.

★

As a football coach I always believed that success is never final, failure is never fatal. Whatever the situation, it's never as good or as bad as the picture some others might paint. It's a good thing to keep in mind.

In the end, it's really important that we don't make life all about vanity and ego. If ego is in control, we can be tempted to sit around and ponder whether long-passed phases of our lives were successes or failures. But what's the point? What has happened has happened, it can't be changed. You are far better off moving on and looking through the windscreen not the rear-view mirror.

One person could write the story of my life and say that it was full of successes and my ego would tick that off, but another might write that it was full of failures and I'd say fair enough and tick that one off, too. In writing my own story of my life, there's only one thing I'm sure of when it comes to success and failure. Whether we win or lose – whatever words we choose to rate our progress in life – we need to keep both in perspective.

I'll leave you with another piece of dunny-door wisdom that I've come to appreciate, from Rudyard Kipling's 'If—', a poem he wrote for his son:

> If you can meet with Triumph and Disaster
> And treat those two impostors just the same

24

Play on

We have all had junctures in our lives where we feel the need to make a change, and the seminal moment comes when we choose to open our minds to looking for opportunities to effect that change.

Sometimes we don't open the door to opportunity because we're safe and comfortable with the status quo, or because we're afraid to fail or look vulnerable, but that frame of mind can keep us chained to tedium or mediocrity.

At other times we don't open the door to opportunity because we are mired in grief or despondency, and our anguish blinkers us to the slivers of light that can bring us to hope. When your life is clouded by sadness and doubts, challenges and adversity, it can be difficult to reframe your perspective and eventually ask yourself, 'Where is the opportunity?' You might dread the possibility of more heartache. But we have the choice of being motivated towards something or away from something. I prefer to direct my energy *towards* a purpose (what I'm trying to get to), rather than *away* from what I'm trying to avoid.

Our time on this planet is limited, so we need to use it to search for what gives us fulfilment and meaning, and then give it a go. And then we have to deal with what comes from that, whether it be success or failure.

It's easy to talk the talk; the defining moments come when we are called to take up the opportunity to walk that talk. For me, the most defining moment came at the age of 52, and it arrived out of nowhere.

★

After more than a year on the outside, returning to an AFL club at the end of 2008 was energising. Joining West Coast brought back the stimulus and verve that comes from being part of a team at an elite level. The club was welcoming, professional and well resourced, with a hand-picked board and a CEO who had been in the role for a decade.

As a coach at Melbourne, I always sensed that survival-mode thinking permeated the corridors. As a player at Essendon, I felt the embrace of a strong community club with excellent leaders. Now as an administrator at the Eagles, I felt part of a formidable corporate entity that was well positioned to channel its energies into the quest to be thoroughly elite. To do so, however, the club first needed to deal with the substandard culture that had evolved among the playing group.

I was a fresh set of eyes, a cleanskin who had been brought in to help make sure the culture overhaul was working. I felt confident that West Coast's commitment was authentic and was having an impact. For the first six weeks in the job, all I did was talk to people – executives, staff inside and outside the football department, key individuals external to the club – always asking, 'What do you think of the situation?' They all recognised the problem and saw it as an opportunity to put in place sustainable guidelines that would cement West Coast's status as a best-practice club.

My role was to run West Coast's football department of about 30 staff and 80 volunteers, overseeing areas such as recruiting, list management, welfare, sport science, player development and staff performance reviews. If the department was humming along smoothly, that freed John Worsfold up to devote more time to coaching and improving the players and the team. Each week I would also sit in on match-committee meetings with John and his four assistant coaches, not so much for my views on selection as a conduit to the club's executive and to ensure the process was running well. If there was a tough selection call to be made, John might ask, 'What do you think, Neale?' and inevitably I would reply, 'John, at the end of the day there's only one selection voice that matters, the rest of us are just advisors. What do *you* want to do?'

In its quest to reconstruct the playing culture, West Coast moved on several senior footballers, effectively hastening the rebuild of a playing list that had delivered a premiership just a few dozen games earlier. Fullback Darren Glass, a heart-and-soul character, had taken over the captaincy at the end of 2007 after premiership skipper Chris Judd had requested a trade back to his home state of Victoria. Along with other team leaders, Darren helped drive the new standards and these were picked up and reinforced by emerging young leaders like Shannon Hurn, Matt Priddis and Josh Kennedy. Gone was the play-hard-party-hard culture that had led to erratic and unprofessional behaviour in the playing group.

John Worsfold believed that a player-led push to change standards would be more powerful than having the club's executive read the riot act. He did enforce some changes of his own, such as scrapping the end-of-season Mad Monday drinking session, telling his players they could have Mild Wednesday instead where they still had to uphold the agreed values.

Because the Eagles had finished second last on the ladder in 2008 – earning them two first-round draft picks in Nic Naitanui and Luke Shuey – our list management team was empowered to invest heavily in youth. Having such an inexperienced squad contributed to the team finishing eleventh in 2009 and last in 2010, but by then the change in culture had flushed through the playing group and over the next two seasons West Coast bounced back to play in the finals.

The great benefit of working for the Eagles was that they were organised and supportive. I enjoyed partnering with John Worsfold through the years of transition. The board was excellent, the CEO was very experienced and there was a shared vision for the club. The football department was talented, committed and well resourced.

In my time at West Coast, the best appointment I was involved in was that of Craig Vozzo. With Steve Woodhouse's failing health, we needed to find his replacement as list manager, in charge of recruitment and player contracts. We looked Australia-wide.

I knew very little about the partner of DMAW legal firm in Adelaide who had dabbled a little as a player manager. Trevor Nisbett and I interviewed Craig in August 2010 and even though he had no AFL club experience, he was very impressive. In many ways, he was similar to my mate Chris Fagan: he had integrity, was smart, very competent and friendly, but with some inner steel. He was a devoted family man. Craig accepted our offer and became an outstanding contributor to the team.

In the back of my mind, I thought that Craig would be my successor one day. I wasn't thinking about the timing of a handover at all, but as it turned out, life had its own plans.

★

Life was pretty good for the Perth branch of the Daniher clan. We had bought a house in Floreat, a few kilometres from the beach and a ten-minute drive from West Coast's Subiaco Oval base. Both our sons had settled back into their adopted city – Luke turning away from accountancy to set out on his own as a personal trainer, Ben studying at Hale School. Back in Melbourne, Lauren was established as an emergency department nurse, while Bec's rowing prowess had her involved in the national team set-up – her levers were not as long as some of the taller girls, but her heart and determination shone through and she could knock them off on the ergometer. And Jan had landed her dream job.

After decades of playing, coaching and taking on various voluntary netball management roles, in 2011 Jan was appointed team operations manager for national league team the West Coast Fever, and she was flourishing in the role.

Around late 2012 I started to contemplate what my next opportunity might be. I was probably ready for a change, and I presumed it would still be in the football realm. Playing football had been the most fun, being a coach was the next best option and administration was even further away. It was a little bit like having a ticket for the merry-go-round while your mates were on the rollercoaster.

Change came unexpectedly midway through 2013 when a neurologist told me to get my affairs in order because tests had confirmed that I had Motor Neurone Disease.

As I came to terms with having an incurable illness, the first position to think my way through was how to project optimism while letting people know that I had MND. When I spoke to Jan and the kids and the discussion unavoidably turned to the fact that the average life expectancy from diagnosis was 27 months, I assured them, 'Don't worry, I've got plenty more days in me yet.' The relationships I have with my wife and children are the most precious jewels in my world and I was acutely conscious of how living with MND would impact those bonds. Looking for optimism and humour has not only been important for my own wellbeing, it has also provided some sort of solace that it would ease the burden on my family.

After my diagnosis, I suspected that the story was likely to appear in the media and needed a way to first tell any family and friends I hadn't managed to speak to. I sent a group text message, concluding it with, 'Play on. Neale.' The footy phrase was a way of signing off on a positive note: we needed to get on with our days rather than dwell on what would come next with The Beast.

There were some awkwardly inconvenient practicalities to navigate: in discussing my role with West Coast, the club could not have been any more staunchly supportive. Because the symptoms of MND were not drastic at that stage and I felt physically fine, we mapped out a plan for me to stay on in 2014 as part of a handover of the football operations role to Craig Vozzo. He began to take on many of the responsibilities towards the end of 2013 and deserves a lot of credit for identifying Adam Simpson as the Eagles' primary target to take over as senior coach after John Worsfold resigned late in the season. Craig's proficiency allowed me to retain an overviewing role in 2014 and also meant I could focus on a specific project: muscling up an elite in-house coaching program to support Adam and the coaching, fitness and sport science teams.

★

Being diagnosed with MND unquestionably delivered a blunt reminder that time was limited and opportunities were running out, and I needed to sharpen my focus on fully appreciating them.

The relatively slow progression of my symptoms has helped our family come to terms with the idea of living with a terminal illness and has also afforded us some cherished time to grow even closer. I have treasured the experiences of walking two daughters down the aisle, being there for Luke's marriage and nestling his son, Cooper – my first grandchild – on my lap.

The knowledge that my remaining time would be measured in years, not decades, did not scare me. What plagued me the most was contemplating the hurt my passing would cause my loved ones. And what also preyed on my mind was the manner in which I would die. It was daunting to know that the journey always ended the same way for people with MND: unable to walk, to move, to speak, to swallow and, ultimately, to breathe. All this, while knowing that my mind would stay sharp to the end – I would be a helpless witness to my own demise. Wondering how I, let alone anyone else, would cope with that gradual and absolute physical deterioration was unnerving, intimidating.

To counter that fear, I needed to remind myself that I could not control what The Beast would take from me. The only thing it could not snatch, and that would always remain within my control, would be my attitude. It made me determined to go out with as much fight and courage and positivity as I could muster, otherwise it would feel like MND had stolen everything from me. I personally could not conquer The Beast, but I would rather get knocked out in the fifteenth round than not even enter the ring. Fear would rather have it that I didn't face up to The Beast, that I retreated to the corner and spent my time worrying about the future – paralysis, pain and suffering – or that I drifted into the nostalgia of the past. But I wanted to stay in the present and be drawn towards looking for the opportunity in my circumstances.

For some people with a terminal illness, that might involve making a bucket list and ticking off the items. That's fine, fair play to them, but I didn't want to devote my time to pursuits that centred around the bullseye of 'self', such as bungee jumping or visiting Niagara Falls. I wanted to be drawn towards a pursuit that would provide meaning and purpose.

I knew that many other people had endured far tougher lives than I had, and also had more reason to grieve – those who had been in wars, had lost a child or had been traumatically assaulted. What I believed, though, was that no matter how hideous the scenarios life delivered to us, if we stayed in the pit of grief and despair, it would do us no good.

There can be a temptation to play the victim when we are hit hard by adversity. We might want to blame others and may even think we are being very principled as we wallow in our persecution. We can rationalise it, but we're still playing the victim and it is unhealthy. It might serve us well for a little while, allowing us to feel sorry for ourselves – and there is some comfort in that – and might also allow other people to feel sorry for us and to want to nurture us. But in the long run, playing the victim is not helpful. Eleanor Roosevelt, the longest serving First Lady of the United States, said: 'A woman is like a tea bag, you can't tell how strong she is until you put her in hot water.' That applies to all of us.

In dire situations, the healthy attitude is to accept where we are at and look for the opportunity and, once we find it, that allows us to act. In the end, that's what really matters, for we are what we do. To be resilient in adversity, we need to understand that the situation might be pretty dire, but how can we think our way through it? Once we tell ourselves that we are not facing a catastrophe – or, alternatively, acknowledge that we are – we can then say to ourselves, *OK, this is the hardship, now where is the opportunity in this situation?*

The vast majority of setbacks are *not* terminal, although they might feel like it at the time, but usually if we can think our way through it, we realise that although our circumstances might be daunting, they are only temporary. Finding a way to cope in the darkest times is a skill that we all need to learn and develop over time, and an optimistic attitude and looking for the opportunity are the keys to moving forward.

For the life of me, though, I couldn't see that opportunity in the weeks after being told I had MND. Mr Negative would bounce around in my mind, telling me that there was no opportunity in this circumstance, that I was just going to die. Fortunately Mr Positive would pop up and counter that voice with a soothing: 'Don't listen to him. Keep looking for the opportunity and it will emerge. If you stop looking, don't expect the opportunity to come strolling along and find you.'

Two pivotal days set me on the path towards finding meaning and purpose in my situation. The first came shortly after my story became public in August 2014. I received a phone call from a Melbourne-based doctor, Ian Davis. Ian had been working as a haematologist at the Peter MacCallum Cancer Centre in 2011 when he was diagnosed with MND at age 33, and had since become a passionate campaigner for raising awareness of the disease.

'I hear you've joined the MND club,' he gently joked. Ian explained that he was in the process of putting together a television campaign to draw national attention to MND and wondered whether I could help given my AFL profile. Within days West Coast star Nic Naitanui and I were filmed in Perth delivering messages to help let the public know that 'MND is a killer'.

At that stage, I was not fully aware of the issues and challenges around MND, but the more I looked into it, the more dismayed I became at the appalling lack of funding into research and clinical trials. In 2014, $780 million was available for medical research in Australia (through the National Health and Medical Research Council) and a mere 0.37 per cent of that money was directly dedicated to MND. That's $2.9 million annually.

The Beast would just laugh at that: 'I'm going to keep killing people if that's the best you've got. Show me some respect.' Worse still, research scientists were moving away from neuroscience to more lucrative fields, such as cancer and cardiovascular disease. As Ian dryly noted, 'Scientists have to eat too.' It was no one's fault; it was just the existing landscape.

But it struck me that within that landscape there was an opportunity to hit back hard against The Beast. I hated the fact that every day two or three Australians received this diagnosis, one that effectively came with a death certificate. It ate away at me that each of those people would be plunged into the same helplessness I had experienced, knowing that there was no treatment and no cure. The disease was going to kill me, but surely we could find a way to change the outlook for the next generation and allow people to raise their heads with hope. When we set our minds and our will to it, humankind can achieve amazing feats and I realised that finding effective treatments and eventually a cure for MND was not beyond us. The opportunity was there to take a greater role in raising awareness of and funds for MND research, in the belief that it would be a life-changer those confronted with the same diagnosis in future.

The second pivotal day came in late November 2014. By that stage, Jan and I had decided to return to Melbourne, because we wanted to be surrounded by family. Our parents, daughters, sisters and brothers all lived east of Uluru. Ben decided to return with us to Victoria, while Luke plumped for remaining in Perth, where he had met the love of his life, Jess.

A Perth farewell was organised for a Sunday afternoon on 23 November 2014. One of my old Essendon teammates Tony Buhagiar agreed to host the function at The Stables Bar, which he owned in the city, and we decided to bill the event as an MND Charity Sunday Session: 'Come and join the sporting royalty of Perth, who are getting behind Neale Daniher to help find a cure for MND.' Along with friends and colleagues from AFL clubs West Coast and Fremantle, a few former Essendon teammates such as Bill Duckworth and Mark Harvey came along, and we managed to raise about $80,000 for the Motor Neurone Disease Association of Western Australia. If such an astonishing outcome was possible from one informal social gathering at an inner-city pub, what could be achieved if we set more people's minds and wills to the task?

There is always opportunity to be found, even when you're dying.

★

After our family returned to Melbourne, my initial instinct was to contact MND Victoria and ask, 'How can I help?' What seemed certain at that time was that there must be a way to tap into the good will of the vast AFL community to raise funds so that the best and brightest researchers could devote themselves to unearthing treatments for MND and eventually discover a cure.

I found it frustrating how much money was needed to help science move one inch; frustrating how much money was wasted within the health system and how much money was being flushed down the toilet in various national programs when it could be used better. Billions of dollars were devoted to schemes such as the national broadband network or building another submarine, yet it was a struggle to raise a fraction of that money for medical research. The waste bothered me. It was not a matter of arguing that the funding for one disease deserved more than the other. Rather than demanding that MND get a bigger slice of the pie, surely it was a case of the whole funding pie needing to be bigger.

Essentially there were two options to ramp up funding: advocate for more government assistance or go and raise the money ourselves. Given my belief that it's not what you say, it's what you do, I focused on the second option.

I had the genesis of a vague idea for a charity motor convoy through regional Victoria, with a working title Daniher's Drive, but was unclear about the logistical and financial backing needed to get such a project off the ground. The difficulty was that with MND Victoria's limited funding and resources being devoured by providing desperately needed care and support for those with the disease, it was difficult for them to catapult the Daniher's Drive concept into reality.

When I explained the various complications to Ian Davis, he revealed, 'I've been thinking that we should set up our own foundation with its core focus on finding treatments and finally a cure for MND.'

After barely a moment's thought, I replied, 'Let's do it.'

In that moment, CureMND was born.

Later we would rebrand as FightMND and our mission would be to build public awareness of the disease, and to help fund research, new drug development, clinical trials and assistance for Australians living with the disease.

Our third musketeer was a guy from AFL headquarters, Pat Cunningham, whose wife, Angie – a former leading tennis player and administrator – had been diagnosed with MND in 2012. Pat and Angie launched the Laugh To Cure MND campaign during the 2014 Australian Open, which had raised more than $100,000 during the fortnight of the grand slam tennis tournament.

Ian became the foundation's backroom boy, a super intelligent man and brilliant organiser. Pat is fantastic at generating ideas and handling promotion. That left the bloke with the roughest head to be the face of the organisation.

Also in 2014, the Ice Bucket Challenge – an American initiative to raise awareness and funds for ALS (Amyotrophic Lateral Sclerosis, their name for MND) – went viral on social media, with millions of people including Mark Zuckerberg, Bill Gates and Oprah Winfrey posting videos of themselves being soaked by a bucket of ice-filled water.

That August, Pat and Angie had helped organise a successful attempt to break the Ice Bucket Challenge world record at the AFL's Docklands Stadium, and Lauren and Bec had been among the hundreds who lined the boundary for a Mexican wave of upended buckets. We were looking for a way to seize the momentum of the American viral campaign, although the problem seemed to be that many people either didn't know what the hell the Ice Bucket Challenge was even all about, or took part in the challenge in a way that offered no real assistance to the cause.

The AFL community had already shown a willingness to throw its weight behind the MND cause, with many players, coaches and officials taking on the Ice Bucket Challenge. Given that support, there seemed to be a great opportunity to create a significant FightMND event, something special.

Pat suggested tweaking the concept of the Ice Bucket Challenge. 'How about we flip it?' he said. 'Instead of tipping icy water on people's heads, how about we tip people into icy water?'

That was the birth of the Big Freeze. Like many successful ideas, it was pretty simple. We had no idea whether it would be well received, but it was all about making a commitment to set out with no guarantee of success.

Pat and I and my old mate Bill Guest, the former Melbourne Football Club vice-president, sounded out Essendon and Melbourne – the two clubs where I had obvious connections – about staging the first Big Freeze at an AFL match in 2015. We were very mindful of stepping on the toes of the AFL clubs' revenue streams and weren't going to march in there and say, 'By the way, we want to use your club to make truckloads of money for our cause.' It was better to have the clubs making offers than us making demands. Essendon didn't have a suitable opening in its 2015 fixture but was open to working towards a date in the 2016 season. Melbourne, though, didn't have to tiptoe around as many other themed matches and offered in-principle support straight away.

'What do you have planned for the Queen's Birthday weekend match against Collingwood?' I asked the club's CEO, Peter Jackson.

'Nothing special,' he replied. 'Your concept might well slot in perfectly.'

We all became enthused by the idea of being able to stage the event at the MCG on the Monday of a long weekend.

'OK,' we agreed, 'sounds like we need to have a chat to Eddie.'

A few days later Collingwood president Eddie McGuire interrupted me when I began to explain that we were planning a pre-match event to help raise awareness about MND. 'Bugger that,' he snorted. 'Raising awareness is fine, but let's raise some serious coin. Now explain this concept to me.'

And just like that, the Big Freeze was a goer for 2015.

Sitting around the kitchen table with my family, we tossed around ideas about introducing merchandising. Perhaps selling T-shirts or maybe some of those silicon wristbands? How about bandanas? The next day Bec grabbed my arm. She and Lauren had come up with the perfect item for the middle of winter: beanies. Her partner, Drew, had even sketched a design.

Suddenly, the beanies were our signature apparel.

In that first year, we tentatively aimed to sell 5000 – we hit that target inside three days and people eventually snapped up 33,000 of them. Our family was up until 3 am some nights, sprawled across the living room floor packing beanies and hand-writing addresses on envelopes.

We hoped that first Big Freeze might raise $250,000 – we ended up fetching nearly $3 million. The Australian federal government came on board in the second year, which added momentum.

We've introduced several other fundraising events: Cycling Cares, the tennis-themed Smash MND, Sockit2MND and fun runs. Daniher's Drive not only got off the ground, it has become a rolling party through regional centres that has become a high-light of my year – a wonderful chance to spend quality time with family and friends and meet some unsung heroes who do amazing work in the fight against MND.

At the time of writing, FightMND has invested $40 million into care for MND sufferers and research into developing treatments and pursuing a cure. And we are really proud of the fact that we are accountable for our money and transparently show how it will be used to fight The Beast.

What moves me most about the FightMND foundation is the overwhelming support and energy that is channelled our way from every corner of Australian society. All of our fundraising events have become such a collective effort, whether it is kids scrounging loose change, local clubs and communities hosting events or sports stars and celebrities offering their time and help. There's a bit of battler appeal: it's all of us up against the injustice of how ordinary Australians are dealing with these dreadful deaths. It is heartwarming to know that so many of us agree that people should have the right to be drawn towards something – hope – rather than turning away from doing anything through fear, powerlessness and despair.

Campaigning for FightMND has made me a better person. It has required me to show vulnerability, basically to say to the world, 'Look, guys, I'm in trouble, will you do something to help me and help others? We *need* you to get on board.' I don't think I would have been prepared to show that sensitive underbelly to even some of my closest friends at the age of 30. It has taught me that not having all of the answers doesn't make you weak. Rather, it has shown that vulnerability resonates with the broader community. They think, *Look at that poor bastard, we need to do something about this*. So with my vulnerability has come humility.

My dream is that we will one day be able to scrap FightMND because it is no longer needed. That day will be when diagnosis no longer comes with a doctor offering open palms and a heartfelt apology, but instead allows that doctor to reach into the drawer for an answer. Worldwide, neurologists believe that if there is going to be a breakthrough in neurological diseases – whether it be MND, Parkinson's, multiple sclerosis or dementia – the breakthrough will begin with MND. They think they can crack the code if they can slay The Beast. If FightMND helps solve that puzzle after I've gone, you'll hear me from six feet under yelling, 'You beauty!'

That is what 'finding the opportunity' was all about. It was like that old Chinese proverb: 'A crisis is an opportunity riding the dangerous wind.'

When you're dying, everyone thinks you're a great bloke

After a doctor confirms that death is waiting just around the corner, it certainly paves the way for some deep thinking about mortality. Our thoughts about dying are like crates in the attic; we force ourselves to take a peek inside occasionally, but generally we're happy enough for them to sit up top gathering dust. We'll unpack them if we need to, but why go there if you don't have to? That would just cause more anxiety than necessary.

I don't think we should dwell on death and dying, even after being diagnosed with an incurable condition. After learning in 2013 that I had MND, people have inevitably wondered whether the diagnosis has brought a fear of dying into sharper focus for me. Personally, the concept of death doesn't scare me. It is something we will all face one day. If it wasn't MND, something else would eventually get me. When I was born, there was no contract to sign that offered me a maximum term.

345

Hopefully there is something beyond dying, but nobody knows. No one has ever managed to come back and say, 'Listen crew, there's nothing there.' Because we have no certainty about an afterlife, my focus has always stayed on living a good life while I'm here.

What goes on after the lights go out? Well, who knows? If I find out, I'll try to come back and write something on your wall, but in the meantime let's just focus on what we can do while we're in the here and now.

★

When you're dying, everyone thinks you're a great bloke. People want to make sense of who we all are, so they want to put everyone in boxes. When I was a footballer, they had me in the natural-born-leader box and then the unfulfilled-talent box; as a coach, they put me in the intense-bastard box, and now that I have a terminal illness, I'm in the such-an-inspiration box.

People would look at my public appearances after being diagnosed with MND and think it was no wonder I had an abrupt manner and used such unvarnished language. They'd be thinking, *Oh well, he doesn't have time to worry about niceties.* But I've always been the same. I care deeply about people, but I've never been too worried about what other people think of me. If anything, over the journey I've learned to temper my bluntness, have become more tolerant and better at biting my tongue. Emotional intelligence is an ongoing learning curve. But I know my personality has sometimes jarred with others over the years.

Some people are born diplomatic and tactful. They know how to keep people on board and always find ways to say the right thing. I'm not one of them. I'm impatient, I cut to the chase and I can be brusque and judgemental, and I've been fortunate to work mainly in environments that have allowed me to be that way. Jan's first instinct is to be nice to everyone and search for the goodness in them — that's why I love her — but that's not easy for me. Small talk is enjoyable with my family and friends, but I've always struggled to engage in facile chitchat with people I have just met. My impatience and sarcasm are never far below the surface.

There have been numerous times when I have spoken very frankly, even tersely, to get my point across. That's fairly well accepted within my family because they understand my nature, although it can still be unnerving for them when they see me being abrupt with others. Lauren used to have a go at me about my manner, saying I was too gruff and tetchy with people. She had a fair point, and I have learned to make an effort to pull myself up and hold back when tolerance doesn't come easily. But I'm sure that over the years, some people have interpreted my no-nonsense and forthright nature as rudeness. In the past few years, though, people have come to regard my direct approach as an admirable quality. I'm in the halo box now.

When you're dying and you crack a joke, people think you are laughing in the face of death. 'Isn't it great that he can still have a joke about it?' they say. But why wouldn't I? I like to think that, for all of my intensity, I've always enjoyed having a good laugh, often at my own expense and usually at my own jokes. It's true that since leaving the pressurised environment of the AFL bubble, I've become more relaxed and have learned to laugh off things that would have once annoyed me. And I also knew that after being diagnosed with MND, I had a choice to laugh or cry about it – and laughing is a lot more fun.

The fact that you're slowly dying is a fairly grim subject, so laughter brings a lot to the table and it also helps put family and friends at ease, helps people get beyond the awkwardness of the elephant in the room. When I can no longer trot out one-liners, I might have to hold up a card that says: 'It might not look like it, but I'm actually a really funny guy.' Being involved with FightMND has improved my life in that it's surrounded me with love and given me plenty of laughs and great times along the way. That can only be a good thing. So, laughing in the face of death? I'm sorry, that halo is showing again.

When you're dying, people think you acquire some profound perspective that gives you all of the answers in life. Sure, knowing that the finishing line is just ahead has probably helped to round out my perspective, but I still don't have a lot of answers. The truth is that nobody gets out alive and none of us will leave with all of the answers. What I can say with some certainty is that I am convinced that finding meaning and purpose helps everyone to lead more fulfilling lives than an existence centred around the hub of self. It's not just about being happy, life is about more than a mood. Even when we're on our way out the door, the choice is to curl our toes up and go gently into the good night or take responsibility for our situation and rage against the dying of the light.

When you're dying, people think that you gain clarity about spirituality. But I have been on the spirituality path for my whole life, initially through the Christian faith handed down to me by my parents. For as long as I can remember, I have believed that there is a deeper level to being fulfilled as a human being. I have always been inquisitive and always wanted to find a meaning in our existence.

In the Christian faith, there are 12 disciples and I reckon if somebody traced my genealogy, it would go all of the way back to one of those apostles, to doubting Thomas. That's because I believe the meaning of life is more complex than, 'Don't worry about this life, follow our denomination and our thou-shalt-not rules and your reward will come in the next life.' That may well be right, but I believe in making life count while we're here. I'll worry about what happens later on after I've signed off. We can't be all about doing the right thing just so that we get to heaven; we should be more motivated to just be good for goodness' sake.

When you're dying, people presume you become more philosophical about life. They're intrigued about whether you've gained any great insights. But being handed some medical test results didn't change my philosophy about life, although it did reinforce my views: life doesn't promise to be fair, it will deal us good hands and poor hands and it is up to us to take responsibility for how we then play those cards. Regardless of the situation, the one thing that remains in our control is the attitude we adopt, which can allow us to look for opportunities. There will be times in our lives when circumstances dictate that we can only channel our energy into what is immediately in front of us, but the challenge is always to try to create the space to step back, understand ourselves, look at the bigger picture and consider how we can find the meaning and purpose that leads to a more fulfilling life.

To me that spirit, that spirituality, is most likely found when we are in thriving and arriving mode. When we are thriving, our beliefs, values and attitude help us to seek out noble and worthy causes; to help others, be part of our community, just *doing* something that extends beyond self-interest. Because when all is said and done, more is said than done. Thriving is about what we actually do and on what basis we are doing it. And that helps us with arriving, which is the mode that allows us to really savour the marrow of life: those times when we are living in the present, not dwelling in the past – either too negatively, with regrets, or too fondly, by reminiscing – and are not sweating on the future – either too negatively, with anxiety, or too eagerly, concentrating on aspirations. If we can't get to that mode, we need to ask ourselves whether we are really living or just surviving.

Ego doesn't want us to arrive, because when we are 'arriving', it is banished to a little jar in a forgotten corner in the garage. But 'arrival' is not an easy point to reach, and it has often been a challenge for me throughout life, because my natural personality is to strive. In recent years, I've learnt the wisdom of not falling for that, of understanding that we can't control everything, and that, in turn, has helped me try to slow down, enjoy the rhythm of life and smell the roses.

Nothing has given me greater pleasure than sitting around the kitchen table yakking with the Daniher clan up at Ungarie; catching up with old mates for a coffee and a chat; the regular catch-ups with the old fellas in my street; enjoying a few glasses of red and some great music with friends and family. There have been sons-in-law, Mick and Drew, and a daughter-in-law, Jess, to welcome, ultrasounds to marvel at and FightMND events to organise with our crew, and I have cherished every moment of it.

Some of the most special moments have come in the middle of the MCG during the Big Freeze. Before that there must have been hundreds of times when I was in a football stadium – kicking the winning goal against Carlton, coaching Melbourne in a grand final – and I never took the opportunity to enjoy the moment. I was too busy striving. But living in the moment has never been an issue on a Queen's Birthday Monday at the people's ground. And after the celebrities have slid into the icy water, when Jan, Lauren, Luke, Bec, Ben and I have been blessed to walk across the turf, looking around the packed stands, surrounded by love and warmth and laughter and tears, it has really hit me. It is an understanding and appreciation of how wonderful life can be when we find meaning and purpose and can throw ourselves into a mission that helps others.

My belief is that we all get a crack at life and it is up to each of us to choose how fulfilling we want that experience to be. And that's regardless of how much we understand, because life happens anyway.

★

It's fair to say that 'arriving' has taken on another, more complex dimension for me over the past few years. In the context of dying, arriving will be getting to the point where I know I'm ready to die. That has been one of the upsides of having MND; getting to work out what's important and getting to say goodbye.

When I get to the stage where I'm totally stuffed, and The Beast has taken all of my movement and is trying to suffocate me, I hope I'm at a stage where I'm thinking, *OK, I'm ready to go.*

And when I do take my last breath and I cross to the other side, I reckon the man at the pearly gates will say, 'Welcome, Neale. You've finally arrived.'

Letter to my grandchildren

Dear grandkids,

I'm writing this letter while sitting on a fifth-floor balcony at Scarborough Beach, looking out to Rottnest Island where the glorious Indian Ocean meets the brilliant blue sky. Earlier this afternoon, in the little apartment behind me, your grandmother and I met our first grandchild, Cooper Anthony Daniher. He's only a week old and he's not sleeping all that well at night, but he's doing fine and so are his doting parents, Jess and Luke.

My hands are not strong enough to cradle Cooper in my arms, so when we met, I sat down on the couch and propped him between my legs, gently stroking his soft fuzz of hair and listening to him quietly gooh and gah.

It was one of those beautiful little snapshots where your Poppa could really enjoy the moment and think, *Life's pretty damn good.*

The sight and sound of Cooper – and that new-baby smell – opened the floodgates to happy memories of a time when your grandmother and I were young and unworldly and caring for our own children. Those babies have grown up to be your mothers or fathers.

Grandma and I used to gaze down on our newborn babies in just the same way that Jess and Luke are now watching Cooper. It's a giddy mixture of pride, responsibility, joy and apprehension, but most of all, with love in their eyes. We were like them: new parents realising that we're not kids anymore and thinking, *This is how life is meant to be.*

How I've loved watching those babies become the fine adults they are today. Lauren, the generous warmhearted giver, whose Irish jig always makes me break into laughter; Luke, my beautiful boy who is always on the go, willing to help; Bec, so determined with a loud laugh like her Dad's and Benny boy, so thoughtful and considerate, with a song list that rivals mine!

How I would have loved to be around to watch my grandchildren grow up, too. Not just your first smiles and your first words and your first steps. In my mind, I picture seeing you play your first game of netball, singing in your first concert and heading off for your first day of school. I would have loved to see you run in a race; to see how you reacted whether you won a ribbon or finished last. Little hints of what makes you the unique person that you are, your personality and character. And I will miss having little conspiracies: eating meat pies and chips down at the beach after school, even though your parents told me not to let you have any junk food, leaning in and whispering, 'Don't tell your mother.'

I don't expect to be around for all that good stuff, so I won't really get to know you. So I've written this book because I want you to understand a little bit about your Poppa, his upbringing and his life. And also to help you know something about where you have come from.

You will probably find it hard to imagine what my childhood was like, in much the same way that my mind struggles to imagine my own father's childhood. Picture your great-grandpa growing up on an outback farm, sleeping in a little wooden hut 100 metres from the farmhouse, still standing, in which I grew up. His older brother, Jack, had the single bed, so Dad shared a three-quarter-sized bed with his younger brother, Leo – and that bed only had three legs, meaning one corner had to be propped up by a four-gallon drum! When it was time to go to school, my father used to ride a horse an hour or so each way, sitting behind his sister, Mary, with a hessian bag for a saddle.

In many ways, life was harsh for my parents: just getting by, worrying about having enough drinking water and growing enough food for meals. They didn't have a lot of choices but were well served by a belief system that was laid out before them.

I know that you are unlikely to confront struggles like these, but you will come across plenty of challenges of your own. They'll be different and probably more complex: there will be issues that don't even exist as I write this letter. But no matter how different life is for you, there will be some big decisions that never change: where to live, what role or career to pursue, looking for a life partner and what moral code to choose to guide you in this life.

In all of this, you're probably going to have many more options in front of you than your Poppa or your parents ever did, maybe so many options that it might be confusing. Maybe even stressful at times.

The great advantage you will have is that you have been born in the best of times. In so many ways, this world keeps getting better for each new generation. You will have a higher standard of living, longer life expectancy, better technology, more gender equality and improved medicine. In my day, people died of Motor Neurone Disease, hopefully that won't be the case in your lifetime.

And you will have been raised in a wonderful place, with parents who have given you a foundation of some solid values and beliefs, which will have moulded your character and your attitude. I look at little Cooper and think about what a wonderful start he gets in life: he doesn't know it, but he's holding four aces.

It may be that your parents lay out a structured belief system that will help you navigate your journey, but along the way you'll still have to nut out what works best for you. Just remember that whatever you believe about life, if you haven't reflected on it, then ask yourself whether you're just being dragged along by the current of the river. Believe in something. Keep thinking about life, keep challenging. Be at the high end of sceptical, but the low end of cynical. Don't worry, you'll stuff up at times. We all do.

Life can be tough, you will have your hurdles and setbacks, you'll hit potholes and dead ends, you'll have to make detours.

That's all part of the journey. When those things happen, I don't want you to feel overwhelmed or to become a victim, I want you to learn a bit of grit, a bit of resilience, because life is no bed of roses. So my wish for you is that you can conduct yourself in the right way, in the face of those difficulties.

But what's the right way? The right way is simple, but sometimes hard to do. (You'll have to read the book!)

My wish for you is that you will find the courage to take responsibility for your own life. If you can do that, I'll rest in peace knowing that you won't shy away, won't pass the buck, won't procrastinate. You'll find that courage somewhere in the better side of your character, and it will emerge and help you respond, to prevail, to look for the opportunities that life gives you. That's the right way, but remember, do it your way.

I didn't write this book to tell you what to believe – I'm not that smart – but I wanted you to at least have the chance to know my story and understand what it was that I believed. I've walked my path through life, and you will walk your own, and I just wanted to leave a few signposts along your path. It's up to you whether you read them or find them of any use. Only you can choose which direction you want to walk. Nobody can ever take that decision away from you.

One more thing. Make sure you have some fun. As far as I know, there's no limit on the smiles and laughter you can share in life, so grab every opportunity to spread some joy.

The mark of any person is not necessarily what they feel, think or believe: ultimately, it's what they do. So get stuck into life! Go out and discover for yourself what it's all about.

I'm looking out across Scarborough Beach, thinking about little Cooper again, and I've got one last word for you all: don't believe a word your grandfather has told you. Put everything I've said to the Bunsen burner of your own life.

Play on.

Love,

Poppa

Songs of my life

Great music is magical to me – it can shift my mood from the very first chord. It lifts me up, calms me down, makes me melancholy but, most importantly, takes me away from the here-and-now issues of the day and into another realm. Into my conscious day-dreaming world. Whether I'm listening intently alone or there's music in the background when I'm with friends, whether it's in happy or sad times (and everything in between), life without music would seem incomplete.

Here's a playlist I've put together, selected songs that enhance the stories in this book.

'Fields Of Gold', Sting (1993)

Hillview days, harvest time, fields of golden barley and wheat.

'The Way It Is', Bruce Hornsby (1986)

Stephen Covey's habit number 2 is 'Start with the end in mind'. If Sister Teresita had played me this song when I was six I mightn't have quit piano lessons.

'Stairway To Heaven', Led Zeppelin (1971)

This song broke all radio rules. An 8-minute masterpiece from my early days at boarding school.

'Band On The Run', Paul McCartney and Wings (1973)

I wore out this cassette in Year 9.

'Living In The 70s', Skyhooks (1974)

ABC's *Countdown*, Shirl and Red . . . what legends.

'Old Man', Neil Young (1972)

Dad and I were different . . . but also the same.

'The Logical Song', Supertramp (1979)

Supertramp understood my life from age one to 17, from the innocence and wonder of childhood to the confusion of adolescence.

'The Chain', Fleetwood Mac (1977)

My number-one priority when driving the tractor: don't forget *Rumours* cassette.

'September', Earth, Wind & Fire (1978)

Footy trip with the boys, my first time overseas, Hawaii, 1979 . . . every nightspot was playing this classic song.

'Waiting On A Friend', The Rolling Stones (1981)

Mateship, still doing pub lunches four times a year with the Essendon lads.

'Bow River', Cold Chisel (1982)

Turning 21, so many great Aussie bands emerging in the 80s.

'Boys In Town', Divinyls (1982)

Cross Keys Hotel in Essendon, watching Chrissy Amphlett at her best. The room was edgy – this was gangland Moran territory.

'Don't Change', INXS (1982)

There was a time at Essendon when, as a young leader, I realised I had to change.

'The Green Fields Of France', The Fureys (1977)

Anti-war song. Willy McBride could easily be Willie Kidd, Jan's great-grandfather. Let those who come after see to it that his name be not forgotten.

'Have I Told You Lately', Van Morrison (1989)

A song for Jan.

'The End Of The Innocence', Don Henley (1989)

By the end of the 80s, I'd definitely grown up; I was married, had kids . . . the song title summed it up.

'Forgotten Years', Midnight Oil (1990)

How lucky were we to be just playing footy; not signing up to fight wars. Peter Garrett was a great frontman.

'Why', Annie Lennox (1992)

Beautiful song, relationships, hurt, apologies (and maybe a visit to the lighthouse – read Chapter 12).

'Long Train Running', The Doobie Brothers (full guitar mix, 1993)

Loved both versions of the band. The original track appeared in the 70s but this is the best version by far, one of my very favourites.

'Babylon', David Gray (1998)

It's great when your kids – in this case, Luke – start to introduce new music into your realm.

'Secret Garden', Bruce Springsteen (1995)

One of many songs I used for feel-good player highlight videos at Melbourne. Brought Mum's secret garden to mind.

'Everything', Lifehouse (2000)

When I was coaching and we lost, I'd skulk home, grab a bottle of red and go upstairs and disappear in mind and body for a while. This was one of my go-to songs.

'Mr Brightside', The Killers (Jacques Lu Cont's Thin White Duke mix, 2005)

This extended version is my family's anthem. We go off when this plays on the last night of FightMND's annual fundraiser, the Daniher's Drive.

'Pyro', Kings of Leon (2010)

'Don't play with matches.' Fires are part of life in the bush so this was drummed into us from an early age. But baby sister Fiona didn't listen. Next minute, Grandpa's old home went up in smoke. Gone.

'My Number', Foals (2012)

Ben's favourite band. We went to see them together in July 2019, special.

'I Won't Back Down', Tom Petty (1989)

I adopted this song since being diagnosed with MND in 2013.

'Afire Love', Ed Sheeran (2014)

The guy is a genius. I had to have one song on the list about a neurological disease (Alzheimer's) and death.

'When You Love Someone', James TW (2019)

This one reminds us all that life can get messy and kids are often caught in the middle.

'Someone You Loved', Lewis Capaldi (2018)

You will never hear me say, 'Music was better in my day.' Here's proof there is great music in all eras.

Feather Theme from *Forrest Gump*, The Intermezzo Orchestra

The closing scene of the 1994 movie – a feather floating in the breeze – is a good metaphor to close off on.

Reading list

'I believe in the discipline of mastering the best that other people have ever figured out. I don't believe in just sitting down and trying to dream it all up yourself. Nobody's that smart.'

—Charlie Munger, American businessman and philanthropist

Managing the Dream, Warren Bennis, Perseus Publishing, 2000

The Road to Character, David Brooks, Random House, 2015

The One Thing You Need to Know, Marcus Buckingham, Simon & Schuster UK, 2006

Man's Search for Meaning, Victor Frankl, Beacon Press, 1959

When All is Said and Done, Jack Gibson, Pan Macmillan, 1994

Stumbling on Happiness, Daniel Gilbert, Knopf, 2006

Ego is the Enemy, Ryan Holiday, Portfolio, 2016

Understanding Ourselves and Others: a reader friendly view of psychology, Dr Phil Jauncey, Designer Training, 1995

Who Moved My Cheese, Dr Spencer Johnson, G. P. Putnam's Sons, 1998

Thinking, Fast and Slow, Daniel Kahneman, Farrar, Straus and Giroux, 2011

The Wisdom of Teams, Jon Katzenbach and Douglas Smith, Harvard Business School Press, 1993

Too Soon Old, Too Late Smart, Gordon Livingston, Marlowe & Company, 2004

The Good Life, Hugh McKay, Pan Macmillan, 2013

12 Rules for Life, Jordan B Peterson, Allen Lane, 2018

The Blank Slate, Steven Pinker, Allen Lane, 2002

Flourish, Martin Seligman, Atria Books, 2012

Learned Optimism, Martin Seligman, Alfred A. Knopf, 1990

The Fifth Discipline, Peter Senge, Doubleday/Currency, 1990

The Black Swan, Nassim Nicholas Taleb, Random House, 2007

This is Water, David Foster Wallace, Little, Brown and Company, 2009

Acknowledgements

Over my lifetime, there are many people who have picked me up and dusted me off and carried me on their shoulders. I am forever thankful for how you have all helped me to become the person I am today.

Doing this book was a team effort. The idea first surfaced in late 2015 over coffee with publishing consultant Andrea McNamara. I would like to acknowledge Andrea's patience, persistence and wisdom in guiding me. Her suggestion of Warwick Green as co-writer was a masterstroke, both for his ability to capture my voice on the page, and his great company as we worked together to bring the story to life.

Andrea, Warwick and I started this project together knowing it would be a marathon not a sprint. I had visions of us running through the tape like Robert de Castella . . . in fact, it was an ultramarathon and we shuffled to the line like Cliffy Young.

Many thanks to Pan Macmillan, for having such faith in the book, and for respecting my wishes at every stage.

And lastly, a special thanks to the FightMND army who stand beside me in our fight against The Beast . . . without you, we won't find a cure. Fight on.

IT TAKES PEOPLE

To cure, to care, to make aware.

Founded in 2014, FightMND was established with the purpose of finding effective treatments and ultimately a cure for Motor Neurone Disease – 'The Beast'.

The foundation is the voice and the guiding star for Australians who want to fight The Beast. The horrible and debilitating disease gradually takes away the patient's use of their arms and legs, their ability to eat and swallow, their speech and their ability to breathe . . . all in an average timeframe of just 27 months.

FightMND is the largest independent funder of MND research in Australia, investing $40 million into research and care initiatives (as of September 2019).

DONATE

We couldn't do the vital work we do without your generous support. Every donation gets us one step closer to discovering better treatment methods and finding a cure.

fightmnd.org.au/donate/

Phone: 1800 344 486 (Monday to Friday, 8.30 am to 5 pm)